# Foundations of Modern Management:
# Organization Behaviour, 1890–1940

## Volume 7

Edited with a new Introduction by
Morgen Witzel

OVERSTONE

# Organization Behaviour, 1890–1940

Edited and Introduced by Morgen Witzel

Volume 1
*The Psychology of Management* (1914)
Lillian Gilbreth

Volume 2
*The Philosophy of Management* (1924)
Oliver Sheldon

Volume 3
*Creative Experience* (1924)
Mary Parker Follett

Volume 4
*Onward Industry! The Principles of Organization
and their Significance to Modern Industry* (1931)
James D. Mooney and Alan C. Reiley

Volume 5
*Leadership in a Free Society* (1936)
Thomas North Whitehead

Volume 6
*Principles of Industrial Organization* (1939)
Dexter S. Kimball and Dexter S. Kimball, Jr.

Volumes 7 and 8
*Collected Articles and Chapters*

Printed in England by Antony Rowe Ltd, Chippenham

# Collected Articles and Chapters

I

THOEMMES PRESS

This edition published in 2001 by

**THOEMMES PRESS**
11 Great George Street, Bristol BS1 5RR, United Kingdom

www.thoemmes.com

**ORGANIZATION BEHAVIOUR, 1890–1940**
8 volumes : ISBN 1 85506 632 7

PUBLISHER'S NOTE

The publisher has gone to great lengths to ensure the quality of this reprint but
points out that some imperfections in the original book may be apparent.
This book is printed on acid-free paper, sewn, and cased in a durable buckram cloth.

● Overstone is an imprint of Thoemmes Press.

# Contents

# Factory Life, American, Past, Present and Future[1]

## Lucy Larcom

The past has an interest of its own, but its chief value to us lies in its relation to the future. Progress being the natural order, every good thing makes us hope for a better. The history of American cotton manufactures has certainly been a record of external prosperity. Fortunes have been made, machinery has been improved, and employment has been given to vast numbers of people. Can progress also be traced in the condition and character of the toilers at factory labor? The material elements of civilization are not so important as the state of the human beings who make up a nationality. Persons are more than things. It is not impossible that much of our boasted advancement may be that of a railway train with its passengers left behind. If the painful pictures which have been given us of the tendencies observable in some of our large manufacturing cities are to be regarded as realities, another too familiar comparison suggests itself, that of the Juggernaut car. Mammon is an idol still worshipped; and he is as heedless now as in any former age, of the victims of whose souls he crushes. But there must be a brighter view for us, and better possibilities.

In comparing the past with the present, we may sum up what was best in the earlier life at Lowell, for so many years the representative manufacturing city of the United States. First, and last too, in importance, was the character of the toilers themselves. They were almost all New England women of an average much above mediocrity; intelligent, industrious, and conscientious. They were such young women as grow up everywhere around our country firesides, and in our village schools and academies. They were the daughters of the land, who have since become its mothers and teachers. Is there any large proportion of such women in our cotton mills now? And if not, why not?

[1] [*American Journal of Social Science*, vol. 16, 1882, pp. 141–6.]

The answer to these questions must follow a brief consideration of manufacturing life in its general traits, and in its earlier characteristics at Lowell.

A feature of the social life there, which must not be overlooked, was the great care for the morals of those employed, as shown by certain restrictions and regulations which grew, to a great extent, out of the moral sentiment of the community itself. All the previous associations of the Lowell mill-girl required a high standard of personal character among the people where she lived and worked. Employers and employed sympathized entirely in this matter. The same may be said of the churches. While their influence for good cannot be overstated, while it is true that the city was fortunate in her first ministers, it is also true that because these girls were what they were, the Christian idea as to purity and rightness of life was a controlling power among the people. The churches were not only filled, but often almost entirely supported by those who worked in the mills. However tinged with doctrinal peculiarities, the various Christian organizations were in harmony as to deeper spiritual principles, and practical rules of living; and they formed centres around which these young girls grouped themselves for companionship and for general helpfulness. Intellectual tastes formed also a common ground on which they met, so that, for many years, Lowell was looked upon much in this light of a school for mental and moral development. In this way the gathering of so many young strangers together was an advantage, rather than the injury which might have been feared.

They were nearly all, as we have seen, girls who had grown up under the wholesome strictness of New England family ties, who naturally kept fresh around them the spirit of the homes from which they were only temporarily absent. The comparatively small number then employed in the mills must also be considered as a favorable circumstance. True, there were thousands at work, but there are tens of thousands now, and these larger numbers complicate the question as to the civilizing influence of factory labor.

The congregating of very great numbers of people at any occupation cannot be considered as altogether favorable to personal development. Even the public school has its questionable aspect, although the purpose of the institution, and the surveillance of committees, and teachers are a protection. We instinctively feel that we were not made for a gregarious life; that something is lost by attrition with crowds. The necessity of mingling with a promiscuous throng was felt to be an evil, even in the days when one was sure of many pleasant companionships; an evil which was to be conquered, or turned into good by the resolute will of the individual. To hold faithfully to one's own distinct thought and purpose amid the confusions of a mixed multitude, is no easy thing. And self-respect by no means implies lack of sympathy; by the value we attach to our own separate personality, the worth of other lives may fairly be measured. Emerson bids us think of every human being as an island; and the island-nature of which we are all conscious in ourselves is to be respected. Men and women cannot regard other men and women, whatever their condition, merely as 'the masses,' without doing themselves also a great wrong.

In the old times the girl of studious tastes felt most keenly the impossibility of secluding herself among her books during the few hours she could call her own; but the difficulty was sometimes obviated by associating herself with girls of similar tastes. The chances were often against her being able to do this; yet if she found herself, as she not unfrequently did, one of three or four very dissimilar occupants of a room, she could, perhaps, manage to keep one little corner by the window sacred to her own chair and table and small pile of books; for room-mates were, in the main, considerate of one another's wishes. But, alas for her when the spirit of re-arrangement, which is one of woman's household weaknesses, took possession of her companions, and she came in, some evening, to find a revolution in the furniture of their common sleeping apartment, by which her one nook of refuge had been obliterated, and herself left to the condition of an ejected tenant on the highway without a shelter for what she held most precious!

A petty trouble this may seem, but it was no less a trouble for being a little ludicrous. If she could laugh her annoyance away, so much the better for her. Yet it is a somewhat serious matter when one cannot find seclusion for thought, or reading, or study, at any hour of any day. The Lowell mill-girl, in her boarding-house, and at her work, we know, did find ways of conquering circumstances, either by ignoring them, or accommodating herself to them; but to do so must always have required force of character. A little space around us, a door that we can sometimes shut between ourselves and the world, is what stronger and weaker alike require for self-development.

The necessity for close and indiscriminate contact must, perhaps, always be one of the unmanageable difficulties in the way of factory toilers. In other respects, things are certainly easier for them now than in earlier times. There is more leisure, ten hours a day instead of thirteen or fourteen; wages are higher than formerly; and we hear of libraries and reading-rooms established purposely for mill-people in some places. Judging the present by the past, and measuring improvement by opportunity, we should look for more cultivation among them, but the general report is that the reverse is true. And the evident reason of the change is in the different sort of persons employed at that kind of labor now. They are mostly foreigners, from the lower stratifications of European society, without the tastes and aspirations which have always characterized our New Englanders.

We go back to the question, how it was that this change earns about, and we find that it was inevitable. We do not like to say that it was inevitable from the very nature of factory labor, yet sometimes it seems so. A mill-girl among her spindles or shuttles, thirty or forty years ago, had not the slightest idea of always remaining there. When she went back to her country life and saw her daughters growing up around her in homes of their own, she did not expect them to go and toil in a mill as she had done. She had higher ambitions for them. She expected them to teach, or to take some other useful position in society; and she used the money she had earned in the factory to give them an education; or, if she was a woman of humbler desires, she laid it by for their dowry, against the time when they also should be mistress of their own households.

It would have been as unreasonable to think of New England women spending their whole lives at factory labor, as it would be to expect the students in a college to stay there always. Their work was not its own end; it was pursued for a purpose beyond itself; for an opening into freer life. It is true that some mill-girls have continued many years at Lowell, but usually those who have remained have taken some more responsible situation than that of daily labor; the care of a boarding-house, for instance. And it is also true that American girls still go to work in the mills, and are respectable and respected there; but the associations are far from agreeable, nod other employments are preferred. Most of the work in factories is too mechanical to be really enjoyed by an intelligent person. And the stolid nature is in danger of becoming more stolid in tending machinery which requires little thought, and of which the operator comes to be regarded, and to regard himself, merely as an adjunct. So employed, the toiler's only hope of elevation is in keeping his mind above his work.

As we have seen, the bright New England mill-girls of a former generation did not undertake their toil for its own sake, or with intention of continuing at it for any long time. It was for the interest of employers to introduce laborers who would be more permanent. In this way a distinct manufacturing population has appeared in our larger cities; and it is from what these are and will be, that the influence of factories is hereafter to be judged. We have now not so much our own people as the undeveloped populations of Europe to deal with. We cannot expect of them the intellect, the morals, and the Christianity that pervaded our first manufacturing towns, and that made the atmosphere there as pure and sweet as a summer day among the White Hills; it is the factory people of the Old World who now fill our mills; it is, in effect, Great Britain's unanswered labor problem that is handed over to us to be solved.

No better standard of civilization than that of our forefathers has yet been set up; namely, the intelligence, the morals and humanity of the people themselves, of whatsoever sex, station, or occupation. And it follows that our foreign mill-laborers must be educated up to the idea of American citizenship, must learn to hold themselves responsible members of the nation which has adopted them, or that our manufacturing cities will eventually become as great a disgrace to us as England's are to her. Until these laborers see this for themselves, those who invited them hither must largely be responsible for them. The more ignorant must be dealt with patiently and steadily, as if they were children; and every opportunity for mental and moral cultivation must be placed within reach of all. Never, for a moment, can we allow in ourselves a feeling of contempt for them, as 'the lower classes.' Whether we will or not, they are to control, to a vast extent, the destinies of our country; they are to stand beside us, equal members of a Republic we love. One indispensable element of true civilization is a common regard for the interests of every person composing the community. If factory labor makes a person less manly or less womanly, it is not a civilized occupation. But it has been proved not to have that effect, necessarily; and it may nobly be made a life-occupation when he who pursues it sees it to be his best way of supporting himself and those dependent on him.

With the introduction of foreign laborers a new phase of life in our manufacturing towns has appeared; the tendency is to the employment of whole families in the mills. Here may be an advantage for the future. Families must have homes; and if they are so cared for as to be true homes, those who grow up in them may find better opportunities for self-improvement than in boarding-houses. In its best days, the factory boarding-house was but a tent in the wilderness to the sojourning mill-girl, whence she looked with moist eyes to the home that awaited her in some rural Canaan beyond, her type of Heaven.

Whether in families or in boarding-houses, moral safeguards will always be necessary to the welfare of a floating population; and not least for the larger liberty of those who do not need them. Work, the mere use of the hands, as we all know, has in it no moral or progressive quality. Work is only great through the impulse that guides it, the motive in the worker's mind. The laborer must be greater than his occupation, or it will crush him. Work and money both find their only real value in lending power to manhood and womanhood, in strengthening the forces of humanity for good. The factory is a prison, if the toilers therein cannot find their way out of it, whenever that is their desire. Education is the laborer's right, and it is a key that opens many doors.

A modern writer has well said, with regard to liberal advantages of education for all: 'It is obvious that the more any man knows of a great subject, the less likelihood there is of his continuing in the position of a weaver or a carpenter. Intellectual vitality signifies social elevation; and though some may be disposed to ask the grave question, "How could society dispense with its weavers or carpenters?" yet our business relates primarily to the higher considerations, forasmuch as the man is of more importance than the weaver. When manhood rises, the industrial arts will feel the benefit of the elevation.' It is persons who make a people; and if we are a humanely civilized people we shall so guard the occupations we offer our citizens, that, if we cannot make them intrinsically elevating, they shall, at least, not be de-humanizing. If any form of labor needful for the general comfort becomes so, it must be through the selfishness or neglect of those who control affairs. And we have no better lesson for the future than that which the past grew to vigorous health in learning; that a free nation can grow up only through free opportunities of self-development for its individual members; that high personal character only can ennoble labor; but that character can and does elevate labor of any kind; and that it is not so much by industries and products, as by the men and women who make their work honorable, that we are to estimate the value of our American civilization, and find our true place among the nations.

# The Nature of Corporations[1]

## John P. Davis

The most important and conspicuous feature of the development of society on its formal side during the past half-century is the growth of corporations, and especially of industrial corporations.[2] They have shared to such an extent the rapidity and complexity of general social growth that social theorists have failed as yet to attain a full understanding of their relations to modern life, even if it be conceded that

[1]  [*Political Science Quarterly*, vol. 12, 1897, pp. 273–94.]

[2]  'The facility with which corporations can now be formed has also increased [the supreme court's] business far beyond what it was in the early part of the story. Nearly all the enterprises requiring for their successful prosecution of investments of capital are conducted by corporations. They, in fact, embrace every branch of industry, and the wealth that they hold in the United States equals in value four-fifths of the entire property of the country. They carry on slums with the citizens of every state, as well us with foreign nations, and the litigation arising out of their transactions is enormous, giving rise to every possible question to which the jurisdiction of the federal courts extends.' – Address of Justice Field at the centennial celebration of the organization of the federal judiciary, New York, Feb. 4, 1890, 134 U. S. Rep. 742.

'Before 1850 we had [in Michigan] about forty-five mining corporations, seven or more railroad corporations, a few banking corporations, several plank-road corporations, and a few of a miscellaneous character; all, of course, under special charters [with the exception of religious corporations]. General laws to the number of one hundred and fifty-six have been passed from time to time since 1850, for incorporating almost every kind of lawful business and association, and the result has been that we now have about eight thousand corporations which are organized under those general laws, divided as follows, manufacturing and mercantile, twenty-five hundred; mining, thirteen hundred and twenty-eight; railroad, seventy-nine; street railway, one hundred and thirty-two; transportation, one hundred and twenty-three; state banking, one hundred and fifty-nine; charitable, two hundred and forty-eight; improvement, seventy-seven; miscellaneous, twenty-eight hundred and eighty-two. To this great number of domestic corporations must be added one hundred national banking corporations, and a large and not ascertainable number of foreign corporations…which do business in this state by its express permission.' – Address of President Alfred Russell at Jackson, Michigan, March, 1894, on 'Corporations in Michigan,' Publications of Michigan Political Science Association, No. 2, p. 97.

'Not far from one quarter of the wealth of the United States is held by trading corporations. It is not improbable that half the permanent business investment at the country is owned in this way.' – Arthur T. Hadley, Railroad Transportation (1885), pp. 42, 43.

serious efforts have been made to that end.[3] Like all other criticism of immature social institutions, the criticism of corporations has been largely negative and destructive, without recognition of their permanent and enduring elements. An effort must be made, however, to obtain a broader view of them – a view that, on the one hand, will reveal their necessary and permanent relations to society and social progress, and, on the other hand will exclude such relations as are purely accidental or temporary. No little difficulty is caused by the failure to separate the 'corporation question' from questions allied to it; it must be constantly borne in mind that this is primarily a question of social form, and only secondarily one of social content or function. Human energy is the content; the corporation is one of the forms through or within which the human energy becomes human activity. For example, the corporation question is often carelessly confused with that of the consolidated control of capital, or 'trusts'; but the latter comes within the scope of the former only through an inquiry as to what extent the corporation, by virtue of providing a fit or usual form for the activity of trusts, affects such activity by restricting, expanding or otherwise influencing it.

An exceptional degree of independence and self-reliance must be exercised in a study of corporations, because the historical and statistical material for the work is so scanty and unreliable, and the work of inter-pretation already done is of so little service. Less enlightenment on the nature of corporations than one would be inclined to expect is given by jurists either in legal treatises, in opinions or in judicial decisions though the jurists alone, with the exception of recent sociologists, have pretended to offer a systematic treatment of the subject. When new social forces make their appearance and begin to be expressed in new social relations the jurist endeavors to explain and control them by the application of legal principles already established in analogous social relations rather than by the application of principles that would be discovered through scientific study of the workings of new forces.[4] For most practical

---

[3]   Cf. Arthur T. Hadley, *Railroad Transportation*, p. 43.

[4]   When sleeping-cars first came into extensive use, the first efforts of the courts were to construe the liabilities of the companies operating them as those of either common carriers or innkeepers, but it was found later that the legal rules relating to those who classes of persons were inapplicable to sleeping-car companies. Now, 'according to the weight of authority, the liability of the sleeping-car company is neither that of a common carrier nor of an innkeeper.' – American English Encyclopaedia of Law, *sub verbo* 'sleeping-cars.'

It is believed that the chief difficulty in the legislative and judicial control of corpo-rations at present is due to the effort to apply them to legal principles elaborated in a

purposes, the lawyer must assume that society is not subject to historical development, though such an attitude, while it conduces to the stability and conservation of social institutions, imposes on the student of institutions the necessity of exercising extreme caution in the use of technical legal material. Yet, without pretending to discard the established legal principles, legislatures and courts have made so many modifications of the law of corporations that the principles formulated by Coke and Blackstone have become in modern times quite inadequate for it.[5] Consequently, the later writers who have treated of private corporations have struck at the very root of the older law by discarding, in whole or in part, the cardinal theory of 'artificial personality,'[6] though for very good reasons they have not been followed by writers on public corporations.

Writers of political history, it must be admitted, cast little light on the subject of corporations. Constitutional history, as written, may be relied on for a knowledge of the form or framework of the state, and popular history, for a knowledge of national activity. Corporations, however, have constituted for the most part the framework of society, subordinate to that of the state, and have been overlooked or ignored by both classes of historians.[7] The results achieved by recent sociologists are more serviceable. In recognizing that all men and all combinations of men have their peculiar and appropriate social functions exercised in relations and sets of relations subject to constant change and development, they have been led to a comprehensive view of the formal or institutional side of society, and have avoided the narrowness of both jurists and historians. But in their efforts to classify and systematize social forms and functions,

---

system of law founded on individual social units instead of modifying the existing system so as to make its principles applicable to aggregate social units; the theory of 'artificial personality,' though harmless when applied with due limitations, has been the source of much confusion in legislation and legal decisions relating to corporations.

[5] Cf. Justice Miller in Liverpool and London Insurance Company vs. Massachusetts, 10 Wallace, 566.

[6] Morawetz on Private Corporations, § 1 (2nd ed.); Taylor on Private Corporations, § 22. W. W. Cook, in his work on Stock and Stockholders (§ 1), seems to adhere to the conception with modifications; as does also J. L. Lowell in his work on Transfers of Stock. See article on 'The Legal Idea of a Corporation,' in American Law Review, XIX, 114–116.

[7] Even Stubbs, in his monumental Constitutional History of England, views the English municipalities at the end of the Middle Ages almost solely as a part of the central administrative machinery of the state. Mrs. J. R. Green, in *Town Life In the Fifteenth Century*, has given an adequate treatment of one phase of corporate life. Gross's Gild Merchant is the only complete study of any one class of corporations.

they seem not infrequently to have chosen objectionable bases of classification and to have somewhat arbitrarily exaggerated or disparaged
particular at tributes of institutions. To such tendencies more extended
historical and statistical study of particular institutions must act as a
corrective.

All human activity has its social as well as its individual aspect. Man
is so essentially a 'social animal' that his every act, however insignificant,
has its effect, directly or indirectly, on his fellows. All men sustain social
relations to all other men. The effect of the social relations – growth,
stagnation or decay – is a product of two factors, the content (function)
of the human activity and the organization (form) within which it is
exerted. The existence of each factor implies the existence of the other.
Social functions are exercised only through the machinery of social
forms; yet the forms are continually suffering modification to meet the
demands of new or altered functions. In general function and form
depend on and react upon each other; growth, stagnation and decay in
each are reflected in some degree in the condition of the other. The
corporation is a group of natural persons embodied in one of the many
forms of organization within or through which certain classes of social
functions are exercised. The limitations of form and function will appear
in the following review of the several generic attributes of the corporation.

### 1. Associate activity.

The corporate form is one within whose limits associate, as distinguished
from individual, activity is exercised, and comprehends both the inter-
relations of the associated members and their relations with other organs
of society. The early distinction of corporations as aggregate or sole is
manifestly illogical and has been almost entirely abandoned in practice.[8]
There are probably no corporations sole in the United States, with the
possible exception of church parsons in Massachusetts;[9] if there are any,

---

[8]   'The idea of a corporation sole has been claimed as peculiar to English law, but the
novelty consists only in the name; and it has been justly remarked that as so little of the
law of corporations to general applies to corporations sole, it might have been better to
have given them some other denomination.' – Dr. Wooddeson, *Vinerian Lectures*, I, pp.
471, 472.
    'There are very few points of corporation law applicable to a corporation sole.' – Kent,
Commentaries, II, p. 273.

[9]   'It is possible that the statutes of some stales vesting the property of the Roman Catholic
church in the bishop and his successors may have the effect to make him a corporation
sole; and some public officers have corporate powers for the purposes of holding
property and of suing and being sued.' – Blackstone, Commentaries, bk. i, p. 468, note
of editor (Cooley).

their powers and duties may be fully interpreted by the laws of trust and trusteeship. It is significant that the later text-books on corporations give no space to the subject of the corporation sole. The inclusion of certain individuals in a classification of corporations was undoubtedly considered necessary on account of the presence in some public officers (or offices) of attributes common to them and to corporations, such as the legal limitation of activity (found in all public offices) or the limitation of control over property held for public purposes. From another point of view, the extended use of the term is explained by a particular application of the theory of artificial personality – a legal exaltation of the purpose for which property is held or power exercised above the personality of the person or persons holding the one or exercising the other.[10] Again, while the functions of corporations aggregate and corporations sole may be the same, the latter lack the continuity of existence that is so prominent a characteristic of the former. When it is said that the king never dies, and that he thus resembles a corporation, the actual continuous group life of the latter is confused with the continuity of existence of the public office not possessed by its successive incumbents.[11] Groups, but not individuals, may have continuous existence; social functions of both groups and individuals may endure continuously. Holding property for particular public purposes, with incapacity to use it for other purposes or to alienate it, does not alone make the holder a corporation, though it is one of the attributes of a corporation that its use of its property is limited by the terms of the charter to which it owes its creation. So-called corporations sole differ from true corporations, not in function, but in form; the former lack the internal social structure of latter.[12]

## 2. Creation by the state.

The corporate form, or sum of peculiar relations subsisting between the members of the corporate group and between them and other members

---

[10] This idea is elaborated fully by Pollock and Maitland, *History of English Law*, I, pp. 469–95.

[11] 'The law has wisely ordained that the parson, quatenus parson, shall never die, any more than the king, by making him and his successors a corporation. By this means all the original rights of the parsonage are preserved entire to the successor; for the present incumbent and his predecessor who lived seven centuries ago are in law one and the same person; and what was given to the one was given to the other also.'– Blackstone, Commentaries, bk i, cap, 18. This is verbal jugglery. See also the case of Overseers vs. Sears, infra, p. 285, note.

[12] See discussion of functions of corporations, infra, pp. 290–4.

of society, is created by the state; or, after spontaneous origin and maintenance by force of custom, is approved with the same legal, effect as if
originally created by it. Neither the group nor its functions, but only the
internal and external personal and group relations under or within which
the group exercises its functions, are created by the state. The progress
of civilization demands the increasing exercise of associate activity, but
not necessarily in the corporate form. As compared with the state, a
primary sovereign group, the corporation is a secondary, derivative,
subordinate group. Likewise, ecclesiastical corporations, under the
earlier conception of the church as society primarily organized on its
religious side (whether or not coextensive with the state), were subgroups
of the church, deriving from it their internal and external social relations.
To be sure, all social activity, whether of individuals or of groups, is
limited and conditioned by the system of law under which it is exercised;
for the state is itself, like the corporation, a group (though superior to all
others) acting through or within certain self-imposed forms; but the
corporate form brings to the members of a group internal and external
relations different from the usual and regular social relations imposed on
individuals by the existing system of law.[13]   Not only is the corporate
form artificial and exceptional, but the field of group functional activity
is narrowed or widened, or otherwise artificially and exceptionally created

---

[13] Whether given legal relations are regular or exceptional depends, of course, on the nature
of the system of law under which the relations are recognized or created and enforced.
Some systems, such as that of early Rome, have been based on a composite unit, as the
family or some other group; others – such as the Imperial Roman law and the English
(and American) law since the destruction of feudalism – have been based on the simple
unit, the individual. The members of a corporation act not as units, but as parts of a
composite unit, and their social relations are to that extent exceptional as compared with
the regular social relations of individuals regarded as social unit.

It is sometimes prophesied with a considerable degree of assurance (as in the quotation
in the note on page 292, infra) that society is in attain in the near future a stage of development in which the social unit will be aggregate or composite instead of individual,
as at present; and that the corporation is the institution through which socialism, in a
more or less modified form, is to be made effective. Unfortunately for such views, the
historical development of corporations has not as yet afforded them much support. If
the corporate form were always used, as one might expect, from a consideration of its
adaptability, it might serve as a stepping-stone to socialism; but as a form of social
activity, it has been perverted to highly individualistic uses, and has actually produced
more exaggerated individualism. The use of corporations has tended to result, not in
cooperative commonwealths, but in trusts. There is much more reason to expect that,
if socialism comes at all, it will derive its organization from above, not from below – from
the subdivisions of the state and not from the corporation; in other words, it is more
likely to be state socialism than cooperative socialism.

or modified, by the act of the state. Nor need the corporate relations owe their existence to a direct and special act of the state; they may be created through any subordinate agency of the state that it may see fit to select, or by virtue of 'general incorporation' laws, which cause the peculiar legal relations to arise upon the performance of certain preliminary acts by incorporators.[14] Some fields of social activity, such as the construction and operation of railways[15] and the formation and management of banks, may by modern law be occupied only by groups of persons organized in the corporate form. Whatever may be the purpose of granting special-group forms, or of contracting or expanding the field of group activity, the act is always that of the supreme social group organized as the state or the church. This attribute of corporations has always been fully recognized by courts of law, and the enforcement of the rule of strict construction of corporate powers and acts has been consistent with such recognition.[16]

### 3. Voluntary inception; compulsory endurance.

The assumption by a group of the corporate form and the acceptance by individuals of membership in the group are voluntary, as distinguished from the compulsory political status of citizens in the state and its subdivisions. To this distinction it may objected that the consent of the citizens of a municipality is not necessary to its incorporation, and that acceptance by them of a municipal charter is not necessary to make its provisions operative. Though that is now the well-settled rule with relation to public corporations, it is so generally regarded as repulsive to the spirit of English and American political institutions that some preliminary act in the nature of consent or acceptance on the part of the

---

[14] Blackstone, Commentaries, bk. i, pp. 473, 474.

[15] This is a broad statement of the fact as to railways. The exercise of the right of eminent domain is delegated to corporations alone. Some exceptional circumstances might enable individuals to construct and operate railways, but, speaking in general terms, the function is restricted to corporations. When railroads are sold at forced sale under decrees of foreclosure or on executions, it is held that an individual may purchase and operate the property, but that he may not succeed to the corporate franchise. Opinions in some cases seem to contemplate only a temporary operation of the property by the individual purchaser. At all events, individual ownership and operation of railways are regarded as justifiable only under ordinary circumstances and when absolutely necessary to the attainment of justice.

[16] Beach on Public Corporations, I, p. 92, and cases cited; Dillon on Municipal Corporations, I, § 91; Sedgwick on Construction of Statutory and Constitutional Law, 338; American and English Encyclopedia of Law, sub verbo 'corporation.'

prospective citizens of the municipality is required before the law of incorporation is permitted to take effect.  But, as a matter of fact, municipalities have exhibited a strong and increasing tendency to lose the character of corporations and to become more truly subgovernmental administrative bodies.  This tendency has been expressed in the enactment of general incorporation laws, the more particular classification of municipalities, the increased interference by legislatures in the government of municipalities and the modification of the doctrine of consent to be incorporated.  Municipal self-government is being rapidly transformed into a mere power of determining within narrower limits the means of executing laws imposed by state governments.  The decadence of city government in England in the seventeenth and eighteenth centuries was evidenced by the multiplication of local commissions acting under the supervision of the central government American cities seem to be passing at present through a similar phase of development, which indicates, so far as the present study is concerned, a decadence of corporate municipal life.[17]  But to say that the inception of the corporate form is voluntary, is not equivalent to saying that non-members may be voluntarily exempt from the external effects of the organization and activity of corporate groups.  One must be a citizen of some state; and whether or not a member of any corporation, his conduct must conform to the conditions imposed by the organized activity of the state, its subordinate institutions and the autonomous corporations created by it.

[17] It is not out of place to note at this point the general rule that the prevalence of corporations has always been characteristic of periods of social expansion as distinguished from those of social organization, or, if the expression be better, of extensive rather than intensive growth.  New forces rapidly developing have had their growth in the form of corporations; when the movements of the new forces have reached the maturity of their effects, they have been digested subjected to organization within the political framework of the state and their corporate form has decayed.  The new forces of post-feudal life in England were organized in corporations, and within them the new element of English personal liberty had its chief development and expansion; when the movement reached its maximum in the sixteenth century, the organization of the new social forces was accomplished through a stronger central government and improved administrative machinery – national poor-laws, responsible parliaments, etc., – while the municipal corporations decayed.  Likewise, the movement of the national expansion of England that followed 1550 was characterized by the use of great trading and colonist corporations; but when the maturity of the movement was reached, the corporations were replaced by a more efficient home government, new colonial governments and independent (American) states.  It ought to be expected, then, that the expanding social forces of American city life will be absorbed by the state governments as soon as their movements have reached the stage of maturity but that will mean that the corporate character, to a certain extent, has departed from city life.

There is a particular sense in which even the state organization may be described as voluntary; even if imposed by external force, it may be said to depend for its continued existence on the consent of the subjects upon whom it is imposed. But some kind of a political organization a society must have; and once organized, the state may coercively organize subgroups of its citizens for the exercise in detail of the functions of government. Such coercively organized groups are not, however, true corporations, though the name is often applied to them; legal writers have well described them as quasi-corporations, because they have many of the attributes of corporations, though lacking the essential elements of voluntary inception and autonomy.

After the corporate form has been assumed by a group, it is compulsory, from the side of the state, upon all its members, until forfeited for misuser or nonuser or regularly put aside in the manner provided by the state. From the side of the corporation, however, the corporate form may not be assumed or retained against the sovereign will of the state. The doctrine that 'a charter is a contract' is vicious; the conception of a bargain between a state and a group of its citizens is illogical; the only final guaranty for the protection of rights and for the performance of duties is a sound social sentiment.

The prevalence of corporations is, therefore, characteristic of a state of society in which individual and not state initiative is relied on, and in which individual responsibility is expected to serve as a steadying force. In rapidly developing communities, the individual initiative has often been unduly encouraged by making the maintenance of corporate relations (once assumed) less compulsory. Perpetual-lived corporations are usually born in epochs of social expansion; under settled social conditions, corporations are usually assigned a limited term of life.

### 4. *Autonomy, self-sufficiency, self-renovation.*

The group of members within the corporation is (a) autonomous, (b) self-sufficient and (c) self-renewing.

(a) Within the limits of the particular corporate form and function imposed or granted by the state, the corporate group controls the conditions (as to both form and function) of its own activity, without direction, interference or revision by other persons or groups of persons, including the state itself.[18] In this respect the true corporation is distinguished from purely ministrative or subgovernmental bodies, which possess and

---

[18] It is not necessary to assume that the state has made a contract with a corporation, the terms of which are expressed in the charter granted, in order to insure autonomy or

exercise only enough discretion to execute properly duties for the most part directed, controlled or revised by superior social groups. Thus the autonomy (and thereby the corporate character) of American municipalities is greatly limited by the interference of state governments in local affairs through frequent modifications of their charters, the creation of state commissions for local purposes, and the almost excessive use of the writs of injunction and mandamus by the courts. Though the courts theoretically recognize the element of autonomy by refusing to compel by mandamus the performance of other than purely ministerial acts, or to prevent by injunction a reasonable exercise of a corporation's powers within the terms of its charter the present tendency of legislation and judicial interpretation is to widen the category of ministerial acts and to Interpret the 'reasonable' more strictly. The limits of municipal activity are being narrowed, though the actual volume of activity within the narrower limits may be increasing. From the standpoint of historical social development, this characteristic of corporate relations has been most important; it is a proposition not difficult to establish that the earlier stages of nearly all the movements in the direction of what is comprehended in 'personal liberty' have been organized in the corporate form.[19]

(b) During the period of existence granted to a corporation by its charter, its general powers must be sufficient to assure it existence and maintenance, and to give the ability to exercise effectively the particular powers granted to it and to perform the duties imposed upon it, independently of external social agents, except in so far as all members of society are dependent upon their social environment. Such powers, if not expressly granted, are uniformly held by the courts to have been granted

stability of corporate life. It is entirely a question of public sentiment. In no other country could corporate powers and duties be so easily modified or destroyed by law as in England, for Parliament is supreme; but the social testament in favor of 'vested interest' is so strong that English corporations have always enjoyed an exceptional degree of independence. Rarely have corporations been deprived by Parliament of their powers even after long-continued misuse or abuse of them, without being provided with a liberal pecuniary compensation for them; yet no contract relations between England and the corporations could be considered to have existed.

[19] For the part played in the movement by mediaeval towns in England, see Mrs. J. R. Green's *Town Life in the Fifteenth Century*, II, pp. 437–48. For the connection between the organic structure of the English trading and colonist companies and the national and state constitutions of the United States, see *The Genesis of a Written Constitution*, by William C. Morey, in the Annals of the American Academy of Political and Social Science, April, 1891, I, p. 529 et seq.

by implication, some being considered as of the essence of the corporate organization itself, and others as necessary to the exercise of the particular activity of the corporation described in its charter. For example, if a corporation could elect necessary officers only when directed by some external agent so to do, it would not be self-sufficient; it might actually cease to exercise its functions for want of the official organs through which to act. Such a body would be merely an abortive, not a true corporation. In 1684, Charles II, by threatening to use the writ of quo warranto, compelled the London livery companies to surrender their old charters and accept new ones. In the latter it was provided that no one should be elected warden or clerk until his name should have been approved by the king; that the king should have the power of removing any warden, assistant or clerk; and that the wardens and commonalty were to be subject to the lord mayor and court of aldermen of the city of London (themselves to be appointed by the crown), who were to approve of all persons admitted to the clothing or livery.[20] The exaction of these concessions by Charles II and the attempt to enforce them by James II were readily recognized as tyrannous and had much to do with the expulsion of the Stewarts and the Revolution of 1688.

(c) A corporate group without power to renew its membership during the term of existence granted to it in its charter might cease to exist, and thus fail of its purposes for want of members. The existence of a group at all implies the necessity (real or assumed) of a plurality of persons for the due performance of some social function; if there were no such necessity, there would be no group. If, by the grace of the state, the group become a corporation through the assumption of a peculiar form, its character as a group does not cease to be necessary for the exercise of its social functions. The diminution of a very large number by the loss of even a single member might, in an extreme case, so impair the group as to make it inefficient for its work. The purpose of conferring the corporate form, however, is not to destroy the character of the group as such, but to make it more efficient by providing it with a form appropriate for its peculiar activity. Failure to provide adequate means for the renewal of a corporation's membership, therefore, would be inconsistent with the original purpose of conferring the corporate form. If at the same time the necessity of autonomy and self-sufficiency be given due weight, the means of renewal must be within the group itself – it must be self-

---

[20] Herbert, *History of the Twelve Great Livery Companies of London*, I, p. 218.

renewal.[21] Thus it is an established principle that the loss by a corporation of an 'integral part,' in the absence of power to supply it, works its dissolution. It has also been held that when no provision is made in a charter for the filling of vacancies that may occur, the power to do so by cooptation is implied.

The three attributes here considered under one head (because each involves and implies the, others) are in some cases very difficult to identify. They are all, however, found developed in some degree in every corporation, as well as in many bodies not usually regarded as corporations. When they are not highly developed, the corporation proper is not easily distinguished from the purely administrative body; indeed, it must be admitted that a critical analysis of most so-called quasi-corporations would reveal in them the presence of the three attributes. The question is one of degree of development: the corporation is in distinct, effective and clearly perceptible possession of them; in the purely administrative body they are indistinct, rudimentary and almost imperceptible, and accordingly such a body ordinarily depends on the state for supplementary activity to enable it to exercise its functions. The necessity of autonomy and self-sufficiency is the basis of the doctrine enforced by the courts (as an exception to the general rule of strict construction of corporate grants and powers) that corporate powers and duties shall be so construed as to permit the accomplishment by the corporation of the original purpose of its creation.[22]

### 5. Compulsory unity.

The creation of a corporation contemplates that, in all its relations with other organs of society, it shall act and be acted upon as a unit. Accordingly, it is provided by its charter (supplemented by its by-laws) with means of determining the group will of its members, with agencies

---

[21] In the Oversees of the Poor of the City of Boston vs. David Sears et ux (22 Pickering, 122), it was contended by counsel that 'the corporation thus created is more analogous to a sole than to an aggregate corporation. The two kinds run into each other, and the demandants (Overseers, etc.) are to be regarded as a sole corporation, with some of the incidents of an aggregate corporation. It is a necessary and inseparable incident of an aggregate corporation that it have the power of perpetuating itself by the choice of its members. Here the corporations have no such power, but they are chosen by the inhabitants of Boston; and they have a civil death annually, as the sole corporation dies a natural death.' See pp. 277, 278 supra.

[22] Beach on Public Corporations, I, p. 93, and cases cited; Dillon on Munich Corporations, I, § 87, and cases cited; Field on Private Corporations, pp. 66, 67; Taylor on Private Corporations, § 121.

through which the group will shall be executed, and with agencies through which other social organs shall maintain their relations with it. In the element of compulsory unity, corporations are distinguished from most other associate bodies, and resemble most nearly the state itself. Blackstone very aptly called them 'little republics,' though he would have been more faithful to history if he had called republics 'big corporations.'

The conception of compulsory unity is one of the sources[23] of the theory of artificial personality the corporation is said to have a common name, and to be, 'for certain purposes, considered as a natural person,'[24] 'vested by the policy of the law with the capacity of acting in several respects as an individual.'[25] There is nothing harmful in the recognition by the state of such a capacity in a subgroup of its citizens if the fact that it is still a group be not lost to view. Though unified in action, the corporation is none the less a group: indeed, its unity of action preserves it as a group; if each member persisted in following his own will in preference to finding a common ground on which a group will might stand, the group would be inactive, and lawyers would readily determine it liable to forfeit its charter for nonuser. The fact that the common will of the group may not coincide completely with the will of any one member ought not to exempt the members from responsibility for the effects of its execution. It is purely a legal fiction that a corporation is an 'artificial person', a conception which if it amounts to anything is but a stumbling block in the advance of corporation law towards the discrimination of the real rights of actual men and women.[26] It must be admitted however, that the theory of artificial personality has been discredited in practice, by the rejection or modification of many of the principles founded on it. One of these, the principle of limited liability, has been the source of an unusual amount of confusion. It is a logical deduction from the theory of artificial personality, that, as individuals, the members of a corporation have no ownership of debts due to it, and are not liable for debts owing by it: 'si quid universitati debetur, singulis non debetur; nec, quod debet universitas, singuli debent.' The principle has been so extensively

---

[23] The other source of the theory is found in the nature of the functional activity of the corporation, which will be considered below. – *Infra*, p. 290.

[24] Angell and Ames on corporations, p. 1.

[25] Kyd on corporations, p. 13.

[26] Taylor on Private corporations, § 51.

applied that the corporate form has come to be used more to secure the advantage of limited liability than for any other purpose.[27]

It may be conceded that some social functions are so public in character as to justify setting a limit to the pecuniary risk of those who perform them. But such limitation is independent of the social form (whether corporate or not) in which the persons acting are organized. There is nothing in the corporate form itself to justify the exaggerated application of limited liability. This pernicious movement has decreased the personal responsibility on which the integrity of democratic institutions depends, and has introduced into both investments and social services a dangerous element of insecurity. Limited liability of members was not a feature of early corporate life in England, and its prevalence in this century has been due to an overestimation of the importance of national internal development.[28] More settled economic conditions have already resulted in some improvement; and the element of personal responsibility is gradually pushing its way back into the management of corporations so far that limited liability, instead of being an advantage, is often regarded by promoters and investors as a positive detriment

*6. Motive in private interest.*

A corporation is composed of persons having a private or particular (or local), not merely a public or general, interest in the subject-matter of the group activity, whether it be political, social (in the narrower sense), religious or economic. This is partly deducible from the voluntary inception of corporate relations; for only those will desire to assume such relations who have the satisfaction of a private interest as their motive. A distinction in this respect is traceable between the quasi-corporation and the corporation proper. What the citizens of a county do as such they do as members of the inclusive society of the state: their acts are limited (theoretically, at least) to such as it is necessary for them to do

---

[27] 'The distinctive feature of the modern trading corporation is the limited liability of its members.' A. T. Hadley, Railroad Transportation, p. 43.

[28] The sentiment is fairly expressed to the following words: 'It is a well-known fact that many of the enterprises which have greatly developed the resources o the country, and which have been of great benefit to society, would never have been undertaken without corporate organizations. No new enterprise is a cinch [sic]; it is more or less uncertain and speculative, and where it involves large expenditures of capital, unless the men who undertake it can know the limit of their liability, it will remain undeveloped.' Suggestions for Amendment of the Laws Governing Corporations of the State of Michigan, by Jay P. Lee, in *Publications of Michigan Political Science Association*, No. 3, pp. 74, 75.

as members of the general society of the state, and do not include such as they have merely a particular, private local interest in doing. The same may be said of the citizens of a municipality; but here there is a field of activity in which they are considered to be actuated by a particular, private or local interest, not shared by society in general. Lower in the scale, members of a so-called private corporation, such as one for purposes of trade, are actuated almost entirely by private interest. In some cases, however, associations upon which a compulsory organization has been imposed by the rate have become corporations by perverting the machinery of the imposed organization to uses dictated by the private interests of the the associated persons; such was the origin of the old English corporation of the Merchants of the Staple, or Staplers.

Public and private, however, are relative terms: what is a public and what is a private interest are determined only by the of development that has been attained by a particular society. In a rapidly growing community, a body of citizens so influenced by patriotic sentiment as to establish a business enterprise largely for the purpose of 'booming' their country may be said to be actuated by something more than mere private interest; while a similar venture under mature and settled social conditions would have little of the public element in it. Public and private, social and individual, interests are always found in combination, and sometimes so blended and confused that it is extremely difficult to determine which is predominant. Legislatures and courts of law have often been driven in the application of the principle to assume apparently inconsistent attitudes toward very similar facts, though the correctness of the principle has not been denied. The principle must be adhered to, even if in many cases so hard to apply. In the corporation proper the private and particular interest is permitted to seek its own satisfaction and public and general interest is consulted, if at all, from the side of the corporation, only incidentally, collaterally or secondarily, as set forth in the paragraph following.

*7. Functions public and appropriate for associate activity.*
The social functions performed by corporations have had two enduring qualities. They have been (a) such as were regarded, under successive sets of social conditions, as conducive to the welfare of the public and of society in general, rather than to the particular welfare of the persons performing them; and (b) such as were more advantageously performed by associate than by individual activity. The first has reference to the relations of the activity of the corporate group to the society of which it

is a part; the second, to the relations of the group to the conditions under which its activity must be exercised.

(a) What now appears at first blush too narrow a view of corporate functions would probably have been accepted as sufficiently comprehensive before the beginning of the nineteenth century. The unprecedented growth of private corporations since 1830 seems to discredit the statement that their functions have always been regarded as having a public end; but it is believed that even private corporations find justification for their existence in the general opinion that public welfare is materially promoted by the more facile exercise in corporate form of social functions whose exercise is prompted by the pursuit of private interest.[29] Nor is the limitation inconsistent with the statement made in paragraph 6 above. The form has always been intended and used to promote public welfare through private interest, by affording to the latter a social mechanism through which adequately and effectually to express itself. The almost insuperable difficulty in the use of the corporate form has been to reconcile the private motive and the public purpose of the activity exercised within it. But the difficulty is due not so much to the corporate form itself a to the character of the activity; indeed, it is urged with much force that the use of the corporate form has a tendency to ameliorate the unfortunate social conditions incidental to some kinds of social activity. The class of social evils usually included in discussions of the 'railway problem' are evils due more to methods of transportation under modem social conditions than to the peculiar legal form in which the men engaged in transportation are organized. Ownership and operation of railways by individuals would entail greater evils than their ownership and operation by corporations.[30]

The public end of corporate functions is another source of the pernicious legal theory of 'artificial personality.'[31] The function is personified, and the aggregate of rights and duties involved in the performance of the function is separated in thought and law from the succession of natural

---

[29] See note on p. 280, supra. 'The purpose in making all corporations is the accomplishment of some public good. Hence the division into public sod private has a tendency to confuse and lead to error in investigation; for unless the public are to be benefited, it is no more lawful to confer exclusive rights and privilege upon an artificial body than upon a private citizen.' – Mills vs. Williams, II Iredell (N.C.), p. 558.

[30] Cf. A. T. Hadley, Railroad Transportation, p. 4; and R. T. Ely, The Future of Corporations, *Harper's Magazine*, LXXV, pp. 260, 261 (July, 1887).

[31] See p. 275, supra.

persons or groups of persons in whom they are reposed. Then the persons or groups are known to the law as corporations to the extent of their connection with the social functions in view. Hence the division of corporations into aggregate and sole. The early English parson was the persona ecclesiae; the church was personified in him; the land of which he had a limited use was the property of the church, or the property of society devoted to particular religious services performed by the parson.[32]

The private corporation pure and simple is a product of nineteenth-century social, political and industrial conditions, of which democracy and individualism are the foundations. The belief in the equality of men, combined with the tendency to restrict the area of state activity at the end of the eighteenth century, checked the creation of corporations involving class privileges, inequality and the limitation of individual activity. The state, it was held, must not delegate to corporations powers that it could not itself safely exercise. On the other hand, so far as functions dangerous to the liberty of the individual absolutely required associational activity, the nearer the associations were to the individual the less dangerous they seemed to be; accordingly corporations became more numerous in the early part of the present century. But again, no class distinctions could be tolerated; the assumption of the corporate form and the exercise of corporate powers must be free to all. General incorporation laws were therefore justified by social theories. The distinction between public and private functions is never easy to determine, and the problem is not made easier by democratic theories of society and the state; all functions have tended to reach the same level, and 'incorporation for any lawful purpose' has been freely permitted to all. A false definition of public and private functions has been the cause of the confusion. The 'private corporation' is a contradiction in terms, and has no place in a sound organization of society. The present tendency in the business world (as well as in the courts) is to distinguish more clearly between the various purposes for which corporations are organized, and to estimate the responsibility of the organized persons accordingly.

(b) The importance of associate activity as a means to social ends has been only gradually developed and appreciated in the progress of society. Before the present century even partnerships were unusual, and when they existed were usually composed of members of the same family. The object of pre-nineteenth century corporations was primarily to

---

[32] See Potluck and Maitland, *History of English Law*, I, pp. 483–6.

provide and to limit the conditions of individual activity, and only secondarily to afford a means of expression for unified associate activity. It is only in the nineteenth century that the latter attribute has been magnified (concurrently with a depreciation of the former) to such a degree as to menace seriously the stability and permanence of the individual as a social unit.[33]

The principle of association may make itself manifest in two degrees: first, in the imposition of conditions of activity by a group on its individual members; and second, in the absorption of the activity of its members by the group as a unit. The activity in the former case is so dearly appropriate for associated persons that it will not be discussed. As to the latter, whether absorption by a group of the activity represented by its membership is advantageous, depends upon the relation between the unit of greatest efficiency of the activity itself and the unit of ability to exercise the activity; in general, when the former exceeds the latter, association will be advantageous. The ratio of the two factors varies in successive stages of society, and the necessity of association varies accordingly. In some cases, both degrees of association have been manifested in the activity of the same corporation; in the fifteenth century fishing vessels were frequently owned by a borough and used by the burgesses in common, each conducting his business for himself, but according to the ordinances of the corporation, and using the corporation vessels in common with his fellows. The principle of joint-stock management of the entire activity of the corporation was first fully applied in the East India Company, and in that case it was a gradual evolution; originally an 'open' regulated company with several groups of investors and boards of directors, it later by degrees came to be a complete joint stock company with one body of investors under unified management.

---

[33] 'The modern form of corporation prevailed because it was found to be the best form of ownership for the large permanent investments under concentrated management which are required in modern industry.' – A. T. Hadley, Railroad Transportation, p. 46.

'As John Stuart Mill says, [the union of capitalists and laborers] must be brought about by the development of the partnership principle. No one...can tell exactly what form this will take, but some things seem already clear. Corporations will play an important part in this development, as they gradually become more democratic in their tendencies. Corporations and cooperative enterprises will become more and more nearly assimilated until they can scarcely be distinguished.' – Richard T. Ely, 'The Future of Corporations,' *Harper's Magazine*, LXXV, p. 260 (July, 2887). See comment on this view in the note on p. 279, supra.

The corporate function has both the attributes just considered. However fully developed either attribute may be, the function is not truly corporate if the other be wanting.[34]

After the foregoing somewhat extended discussion of the nature of the corporation, the following is offered as a definition: A corporation is a body of persons upon whom the state has conferred such voluntarily accepted but compulsorily maintained relations to one another and to all others that, as an autonomous, self-sufficient and self-renewing body, they may determine and enforce their common will; and in the pursuit of their private interest may exercise more efficiently social functions both specially conducive to public welfare and most appropriately exercised by associated persons.

[34] 'To render such an establishment [of a joint stock company] perfectly reasonable (a) with the circumstance of being reducible to strict rule and method, two ether circumstances ought to concur. First (b) it ought to appear with the clear evidence that the undertaking is of greater and more general utility than the greater part of common trades; and secondly (c), that it requires a greater capital than can easily be collected into a private co-partnery. If a moderate capital were sufficient, the great utility of the undertaking would not be a sufficient reason for establishing a joint stock company, because, in this case, the demand for what it was to produce would readily and easily be supplied by private adventurers. In the four trades [banking, fire, marine and capture insurance, canals and city water supply] both those circumstances concur.' – Adam Smith, Wealth of Nations, bk. v, cap 1.

# Business Men and Social Theorists[1]

## C. R. Henderson

Representatives of two very respectable classes of the community are apt to find themselves in hostile attitudes in the discussion of contemporary social questions – the scientific student of social phenomena and the 'captain of industry.' Has the student of sociology a right to discuss the central theme of his field of research? This is the matter in dispute. Professor Laughlin (Mill, *Political Economy*, p. 523) says: 'The laborer, if he would become something more than a receiver of wages, in the ordinary sense, must move himself up in the scale of laborers until he reaches the skill and power also to command manager's wages.... It leads directly to the means by which the lower classes may raise themselves to a higher position – the actual details of which, of course, are difficult, but, as they are not included in political economy, they must be left to sociology – and forms the essential basis of hope for any proper extension of productive cooperation.' This definition of the limits of economics and of the duty of sociology, made by a master, we accept; but find ourselves resolutely opposed at the very point where our discussion begins to have a real living human interest. What is urged against our discipline and our method?

It would be strange if the 'captain of industry' did not sometimes manifest a militant spirit, for he has risen from the ranks largely because he was a better fighter than most of us. Competitive commercial life is not a flowery bed of ease, but a battle field where the 'struggle for existence' is defining the industrially 'fittest to survive.'

In this country the great prizes are not found in Congress, in literature, in law, in medicine, but in industry. The successful man is praised and honored for his success. The social reward of business prosperity, in power praise and luxury, are so great as to entice men of the highest intellectual faculties. Men of splendid abilities find in the career of a manufacturer or merchant an opportunity for the most intense energy. The very perils of the situation have a fascination for adventurous and inventive

[1]  [*American Journal of Sociology*, vol. 1, 1898, pp. 385–97.]

spirits. In this fierce though voiceless contest a peculiar type of manhood is developed, characterized by vitality, energy, concentration, skill in combining numerous forces for an end, and great foresight into the consequences of social events. If the character is further analyzed we discover, along with some apparent heedlessness of pain and many compromises with con science, an integrity about contracts which makes it possible to build the business of the world on credit. Those who live in retirement and simplicity are apt to find the swift, brusque, imperious and impatient manners of the successful man somewhat severe and offensively dictatorial. But the ceremonial tediousness of the parlor would be out of place in the office of one who must think rapidly enough to keep thousands of telegraph operators, stenographers, clerks and other employees in occupation. Dainty speech and elaborate politeness under the conditions of life in a great commercial house would have all the effects of crime.

By extending this study of the psychical processes of typical business men we might be enabled to regard some social phenomena in a new and stronger light. Great business men, like some distinguished generals, let their deeds speak for them, they say, with some touch of contemptuous sarcasm and cynicism, they can hire talkers and buy books. So that to interpret their inner life we must seize the rare occasions when they venture upon speech. As the number of college men among merchants increases, the points of contact with academic men are likely to increase.

A few typical quotations may be taken as indicating the internal mental movements of representative business men.

A very common conviction of employers is expressed clearly and bluntly in the words of an able and upright manufacturer, recently deceased. 'The relation between capital and labor is one of the many questions in the comprehensive science of political economy, and as such is a purely business matter. Philanthropy has nothing to do with it, nor has religion or sentiment, any more than they have to do with astronomy or with the law of gravitation…. The essays of the humanitarian and the sermons of the preacher, however soundly based on the moralities and the ought-to-be, generally only confuse and obscure the real issues. However it may be in some ideal heaven, it is the fact that in this world it is not from motives of generosity or philanthropy that the master hires labor, and the laborer seeks service. And the sooner the whole matter is taken out of the realm of sentimental philosophy and placed on the bed rock of simple, practical business common sense the better.' He then proceeds to give an exposition of the determining factors in the settlement of the rate of wages; attacks all schemes of cooperation and profit-sharing as 'moonshine;' asserts that strikes cannot raise the real wages of labor; that increase comes from improvements in machinery and business methods; that laborers can secure higher income only by becoming more useful; that the only function of the state is to prevent violence. 'All that legislators and editors and preachers and philanthropists can do is to educate the people that they may be able finally...to pass out of these turbulent obscuring mists of ignorant and selfish struggle into the clear light of universal law and justice.'

In this concluding sentence the cultivated, generous, successful Christian business man opens .a wider door than his opening sentences promised; and it is a pleasure to add that his life was better than his inherited economic creed.

In a speech at St. Louis before the assembled representatives of the great commercial clubs of the country Mr. William Whitman, of Boston, voiced a certain feeling of his peers. Mr. C. D. Wright had suggested that in the future employers would be held responsible before the law and at the bar of public opinion for strikes; and that it would be held to be the duty of employers during prosperous times to set aside a fund for the payment of wages in times of adversity. Mr. Whitman declared both propositions to be monstrous, and asked of the gentlemen present: 'What do you think of them? Will they increase or diminish your burdens? Can you successfully prosecute your business under them? Do you think that this new philanthropo-ethico-economic management will attract the investment of capital?'

The particular propositions of Mr. Wright may be dropped out of this discussion. They are of interest here only because they drew the fire and showed the attitude of a typical business man toward theoretical students of society. Indeed the speaker himself turns from propositions to person-alities. 'Who are the men engaged in promulgating these so-called reforms, ostensibly for the benefit of workingmen? Are they not for the most part theorists with unbalanced minds, who have adopted unsound principles and are pushing them to the extreme? Are they not men without the knowledge and experience necessary to deal successfully with men or affairs? Why should men of affairs permit them, undisputed, unanswered, unchallenged, to arrogate to themselves the right to teach the world how we shall conduct our business?'

This speaker gives his reason for thinking that business men carry in their own bosoms and interests the guarantees of social welfare: 'The purposes of business, the sense of responsibility to others, the danger of personal loss and possible failure, and the hope of reward are the surest guarantees for the conduct of affairs in the mutual interests of employer and employed.'

It must be admitted that this rigorous protest against impertinent and ignorant intrusion of dilettanti upon the preserves of capitalist managers is not without justification. Social theorists need to be meek men, and should stand with head uncovered before the special gifts and services of the men of genius who are working the latter-day miracles of industry and commerce. Confessions of trespass on forbidden ground are in order, but these must be personal and auricular before any authority prepared to shrive.

It has been said that the laws of economics should be stated in the indicative and not in the imperative mode, and this is true of all purely scientific theory. The only person who can possibly decide in practical affairs is the responsible manager of the affairs concerned. When sincere fanatics vent their ravings under the titles of 'sociological science,' it is not to be wondered at that suspicion should extend to those who are really trying to 'mount to the summit round by round.' Orators with more heat than light are apt to be confounded with patient students of practicable reform.

And yet we are not ready to confess that the student of society is absolutely without a function, a mere useless parasite, or at best a phonographic reporter of the dead past. Mr. Lyman J. Gage, intimate friend of the seer, Professor Swing, said: 'To cherish false ideas concerning the motives of men who are sailing with us in the same ship of national destiny is to be raw and provincial. We are of the same blood, indissolubly united in our diversified interests…. By a clearer understanding of our mutual duties will we clamor less for what we consider our respective rights.' Mr. Gage would not browbeat into silence men who are intently studying the same phenomena which occupy business men, only from a different point of view.

It is the duty of the scholar to place and keep before the public the supreme criterion of social conduct, the common welfare. In a boiler factory, where the din and noise drown all sounds, the cry of a child cannot be heard. So men of affairs are apt to be deafened, by the uproar of those very affairs, to the neglected and forgotten members of our common humanity. A table of statistics, interpreted and illustrated by literary skill, may induce business men to enlarge the scope of their life plans. The scholar's duty is to aid in forming a judicial public opinion, as distinguished from the public opinion of a class and its special pleaders.

It is the duty of the scholar, if he is a living member of con temporary society and something beside an archaeologist, to secure a public recognition of all the elements of welfare. Such a scholar will give due place to what Carlyle calls the 'preliminary item,' bread, but he will help his fellows to see and realize that 'man cannot live by bread alone.' For this purpose is the scholar supported by society, in order that he may be its mentor and seer. It is true the idealist does not see intuitively how far or by what means these higher factors of good may be secured, but he can remind men by his own life and works that wealth is only a preliminary item, a means but not an end of life. And if a business man deserves the title of captain or king he will appreciate the social service which reminds him of the real dignity of his office.

It is the function and the duty of the social theorist to keep attractively before 'practical men' all the known and tried methods of obtaining the elements of human well-being. In performing this social duty the literary worker is not shut up to the meager resources of his own invention. If his suggestions of method are laughed out of court as the visionary schemes of a cloistered fanatic, his defense lies in a prosaic description of facts. When his plan of amelioration is pronounced impossible, he can bring to bear the resources of his knowledge of social experimentation. If inhuman greed, or routine habit, or vested interests oppose his suggestions on the ground that they are chimerical and millennial, he can set ingenious philanthropy over against obstructive avarice. And it is his social function as a scholar to make the great world act upon the mean world. It is only in such service that he can earn his salt.

It is not the function of the scholar to bury the dead past, nor to paint the future in pessimistic charcoal or optimistic vermilion, for the entertainment of the public. He is called to select the facts which will help generous and genial industrial leaders to promote the common welfare, and especially the welfare of those who are employed by them, and over whom their commanding position as leaders has given great power.

It is perfectly legitimate for the scholar to collect and use the testimony of great captains of industry to correct the unsupported assertions of other captains of industry. For example, in respect to the usefulness of trades unions, Mr. Dyer quotes the language of an employer: 'As an employer in one of the great staple trades, I have always held that we owe much of our prosperity in the manufacturing industries to trade combinations.' This citation of an individual judgment is followed by a clear summary of the actual achievements of the unions: the friendly and material help in hard times; the care of the sick; the agencies of education; the regulation of prices and production. 'The cupidity and selfishness of some would have made it difficult even for just and generous employers to do right.'[2]

---

[2]   *The Evolution of Industry*, pp. 110–1.

In arranging the programme for the 'Congress of Industrial Conciliation and Arbitration' it was difficult to secure the participation of employers. The responses to the Civic Federation indicated a profound skepticism in the United States as to the value of such methods. And yet men of affairs and experience were found who were willing to look for better methods of deciding disputes. Here again Mr. Lyman J. Gage, surely no visionary, said: 'In the business world of today, questions involving thou sands, nay, millions, are thus quietly and peacefully composed. Cannot methods so benign in their character, so healthful in their influences, find a place in the industrial relationships which now so intimately enter into the warp and woof of our modern life.'

In the same Congress Mr. William H. Sayward spoke for the National Association of Builders, and claimed that he represented an industry which 'comprehends an interest as large in amount as that of any other single industry.' He denied that his association was working for philanthropic ends, and yet contended that they were serving the public. So far from trusting merely competitive forces and the will of employers alone he reasoned that special organization of laborers and managers is necessary. 'It is essential to have organizations of employers, who together shall control and direct the general principles and policies governing the common interest, so that there may be no overreaching by selfish and reckless individuals on either side.' He accounts for the fact that many employers have refused to accept the plan by saying: 'The proverbial slowness of employers to know a good thing when they see it and their proneness to let matters drift until they get almost hopelessly entangled, in preference to taking a little trouble in advance,' is a sufficient explanation.

There are always business men who are not only sagacious managers, with a gift for amassing riches, but who are broad enough to go to the margin of ability in making experiments. The names of Robert Owen, Godin of Guise, Leclaire of Paris, Peabody of London and America, belong in this brilliant company. Every city furnishes examples of the same class and in increasing numbers.

Mr. O. D. Ashley in 'Railways and their Employees' is one of those who recognize the responsibility of employers to the public. 'If there is social unrest in the civilized world, a fact which will be hardly disputed, we are bound, not only as Christians but as parts of the human brotherhood, to give careful examination to all plans which contemplate man's improvement and elevation.'

We may discover in the very arguments by which the gentlemen of affairs warn ethical theorists out of the manufactory a need of theorists.

It is assumed by both gentlemen quoted in the beginning, that the class motives of employers and the laws of nature are the sufficient guaranty of social welfare. From this assumption of premises it follows that all discussion or intrusion from other members of society must be impertinent and vicious. But the state of mind disclosed in the quotations is itself a social defect. It is symptomatic of the unsocial temper. These quotations prove that many essential elements are ignored by very able and upright men. They imply that there is at least one class of the community who have no interest in the issue of social strifes, and no right to be heard on their own behalf. They imply that economic forces are automatic, natural and not human and ethical. The influences which fix the rate of wages are treated as if they belonged to the same category as the law of gravitation. Human intelligence, will and aspiration are excluded from consideration by such logic. Economics is put on the same level as biology, or even chemistry.

The corrective of this attitude of some practical men is not abuse but facts, just such facts as the studies of social history supply in abundance. It is the duty and function of the theorist to confront this automatic and fatalistic class theory of business with the history of factory legislation. There are few facts so pathetic as the opposition of John Bright, the pious manufacturer, to the movement by which ethical sentiment redeemed the laboring population of England from utter degradation.

It is the duty of the ethical theorist to show that the self-interest of the manufacturer and landlord do not secure the public welfare in any city of this country, and that it is precisely this self-interest, narrowly conceived, which prevents rational legislation against child-labor and sweat shops in Illinois. To show these phenomena, their causes and wide results is precisely the duty of the social scholar. 'Philanthropy has nothing to do with it...any more than with astronomy or with the law of gravitation.' 'The purposes of business, the sense of responsibility to others, the danger of personal loss and possible failure, and the hope of reward are the surest guarantees for the conduct of affairs in the mutual interests of employee and employed.' Compare with these assertions the evidence presented before the Poor Law Commissioners of England in 1834 and succeeding years; the black list of adulterations of food so familiar as to hardly excite comment; the pictures of degradation of laborers, the crippling of children, the demoralization of women due to unregulated 'free' competition, which are adduced by Professor Walker in his work on 'Wages,' and by Professor H. C. Adams in his essay on 'Relation of the State to Industrial Action.' Con the 'Hull House' Maps for Chicago facts; and then say whether there is no need of 'philanthropy' in the regulation of industry. It would be interesting to know what a factory would be worth in a community where 'sentiment' had died of asphyxia, and where the interest of one class was left to determine the terms on which industry should be conducted.

It is not denied that the sense of fairness and justice is strong in business men; but we do claim that without strong ethical feeling organized for common action, the meanest employer sets the pace for all those who really desire to be honorable and fair.

Take an example from the phenomena of women's wages. Here sentiment is a powerful factor in reducing wages. While the working girl is despised for kitchen labor; while the occupations open to women are overcrowded because the prejudices of both men and women close others; so long will women suffer from removable causes. So Professor Walker says: 'What is the remedy? Agitation and the diffusion of correct ideas. Let gifted women continue to appeal for public respect and sympathy for their sisters in work; let the schools teach that public opinion may powerfully affect wages, and that nothing which depends on human volition is inexorable! ... Efforts like these will not fail to strengthen and support woman in her resort to market.' There is one field of practice in which a social scholar as a citizen must enter, the field of local government. His activity may be limited, but here he fights for his altar and hearth. It is true that here again he meets the hostility or merry contempt of a certain class of 'practical' men. Now it is the turn of the scholar to find himself in company with the merchant, and both of them classed by politicians as 'laymen.' The local leaders of intrigue give both to understand that they are out of place and that they may as well let the machine alone, it is too complicated and mysterious for gentlemen to manage.

But it cannot really be impertinent for a scholar to deal with those practical affairs which touch every interest of his life as a citizen, a father, a patriot and an idealist. It may not be pleasant work to fight petty robbers in defense of his little property, the school of his children, the supply of light and protection, and the essential conditions of health. Nothing but intellectual impotence can excuse any citizen, least of all the social scholar, from a degree of direct effort on behalf of good local government. He is liable to make mistakes, but these will not be so fatal as the acts of men who sell or buy franchises under which the community is made to serve the clique. If anything can turn a quiet student into the noisy street, it is the conviction that the public thoroughfare is being taken from him without adequate recompense.

When the scholar enters the sphere of practice, he must prepare himself for the treatment given a man with a silk hat in the bull-and-bear pit on a board of trade holiday; he becomes the target for the wildest boys. If he says anything which by any chance tends to affect prices or nominations, he should not look for reverence. That is an obsolete virtue in American practical life. Nothing thinner than rhinoceros hide will do for an overcoat where conflicting interests are at stake, and arrows are flying in all directions.

And yet the scientific method is needed along with the practical method. The general interest can be served only by the union of science and art. The bronzed captain on the bridge can direct the ship in a storm or fog better than the author of 'Synthetic Philosophy' or 'Dynamic Sociology.' Rude sailors told the officious nobles to go below because they did 'assist the storm.' The best service of college professors when the wind blows worst is to stay in bed and set an example of quietness and confidence. And yet the educated captain knows that the mathematicians, astronomers, chemists, physicists and biologists have all contributed to his art. The more thoroughly he knows the history of navigation the more he respects the scholars who have made his craft possible.

The more college graduates we have in the counting rooms the more cordial and fruitful will be the relations between practical then and scholars. As 'scholarship' comes to mean social service, and is freed from mediaevalism and dialectics, it will be recognized and respected by the men who are driving the machinery of production. New and improved stocks come from cross-fertilization. 'Breeding in-and-in' causes deterioration. Study and counting room will be more vigorous, sane and serviceable for an alliance.

Science is itself conservative and judicial. The rich trustees of a university may well feel secure in keeping their hands off academic freedom. The professors of a science do not belong to a mutual admiration society. They are more nearly a swarm of critics, makers of honey but armed with stings. No criticism from the business world could be so persistent, pitiless and remorseless as that with which real scholars pursue the pretender and amateur. But aside from this cooperative chastisement the very discipline of modern scientific method begets caution. No man ever stated the difficulties in Darwinism more clearly than Darwin himself. There is no class of men who so fully realize the meaning of the oath to state 'the truth, .the whole truth and nothing but the truth.' The methods of science have much in common with the methods of business. Both are intolerant of gaps in the chain of causation. Both demand absolute continuity between end and means, Both are impatient of fog and speculation.

In this sense science is eminently 'practical,' because it measures by the most exact methods and instruments of investigation the available forces for attaining an end which seems desirable. The scientific ideal is an exact balance between the debits and credits, the causes and results of human action. There is an undetermined remainder, bad debts and losses, as in financial settlements, but the ideal is accuracy.

The social position of the 'social theorist' is an advantage. The nature of his studies compels him to come into touch with persons of all classes and interests. He hears and reads on all sides. His associations are with the refined, and his ideals of life are formed in the best company. But his professional pursuits compel him to weigh the claims of the entire community. The recent introduction of the 'laboratory method' in sociology is a guaranty that no department of human life will be neglected. Apart from the bitterness of competitive strife, interested in public welfare as others are but not directly interested in rich or poor alone, the student of social phenomena may be reasonably expected to bring to light and present for consideration elements of social well-being which hot contest ants for immediate and class advantage are sure to overlook.

It is of the essence of democracy that the interests of all should not be at the mercy of a few, but should be the care of representatives of the entire community. Kings by 'divine right,' and feudal lords by grace of birth, have assumed that they knew how to legislate for the 'lower classes' better than the chosen spokesmen of these classes. Nothing but rude blows of revolution and noisy Chartist petitions shook the ruling classes of Britain out of this delusion. Monopolies of social wisdom and virtue do not exist. The frank recognition of division of intellectual labor and of common social concern is all that is asked by the social theorist, and in an age when the pen is mightier than sword or hammer, his claim is not likely to be permanently ignored.

# The Directors and the Manager[1]

Joseph Slater Lewis

## I. THE DIRECTORS

1. The legal and other responsibilities devolving upon the Directors of Limited Liability Companies are of such an important and exacting nature, that every precaution should be taken to ascertain, from time to time, the precise condition of the business with which they are charged to deal. The details of the purely statutory formalities to be observed will, of course, receive attention at the hands of the Secretary, who must be acquainted with the general routine of company procedure. But leaving on one side for the present all questions of legal formalities, and considering mainly the duties of Directors in connection with the commercial work and organisation of an undertaking, it is to be observed that there are two classes of Directors (1) Working Directors, that is, those who devote the whole of their time to the interests of the company, and (2) Ordinary Directors, who do not devote the whole of their time to the company. It is desirable that the former should divide the duties in such a way that the particular abilities of each Director may be brought to bear upon that branch of work for which he is best fitted, whilst the latter should form themselves into small working committees, because it is obvious that the full Board would be quite unable to properly analyse and dissect all the minutiae incidental to a large establishment. Of course, the men most suited to the duties of each committee must be selected, and they should present a report of their proceedings to the Board from time to time. The value of these reports will entirely depend upon the form in which they are presented. Where possible, tabulated returns should be prepared, and it would lead to most beneficial results and prevent much waste of time if they were accompanied by diagrams or curves, showing the rise or fall of values, ratio of expenses, the increase or decrease of sales, wages, salaries, etc. (see Curves, Ch. XXV.).

---

[1] [From *The Commercial Organisation of Factories*, London, 1898, pp. 1–11.]

36

## 2. Calling Meetings.

It is for the Directors to decide whether their meetings shall be held at definite times and dates, or whether formal notices shall be issued for each. They will also decide what special meetings shall be convened, and how in all cases the agenda paper shall be prepared. The practice generally followed is for the working committees of the Board to meet on certain days without notice; and for Board meetings to be convened by circular, with all the proposed business clearly set forth therein. The practice of transacting business other than that specified in the circular is one which often leads to serious unpleasantness. Only under exceptionally urgent circumstances, and when the whole of the Directors are present and they are unanimously in favour of such a course being taken, should it be resorted to.

## 3. Attendance.

A Directors' Attendance Book should be provided both for Board and Committee meetings, and each Director should inscribe his name therein, thus preventing any subsequent dispute as to attendances. The book generally adopted is ruled and printed as on page 3.

## 4. Proceedings at Meetings.

The notice convening each meeting should be read, and duly entered in full on the minutes. The Secretary should provide the Chairman and himself with agenda note-books, in which they may make their own notes for future reference. Such books, in addition to the shorthand notes that he will of course take, will often be of service to the Secretary in drafting the minutes, and will also be of great assistance to the Chairman when the minutes come to be read at the next meeting. A chairman with any aptitude for business will recognise the necessity of having his own notes on which to make a stand in case of dispute.

The Heads of Departments, whose duties are to be reviewed by the Directors – whether at Committee or Board meetings – should, except when specially requested by the Directors to retire, be present when matters concerning them are being discussed. They are thus afforded a full opportunity of ascertaining the will of their superiors, and misunderstandings are thereby avoided. Directions sent to officers of the company through irregular channels, and which are frequently distorted and twisted into something never contemplated by the Board, are calculated to lead to rifts and internal dissensions which cannot be other than disastrous. Without perfect harmony between the Directors and the officers of the company, there can be no hope of an undertaking working successfully.  From this it follows that there must be the fullest possible confidence between the Directors and the Heads of Departments.  It is very mortifying to an honourable man, through whose hands, perhaps, thousands of pounds are passing, to be left under the impression that the Directors do not think he should be trusted with some business secret of probably a trivial nature.

## DIRECTORS' ATTENDANCE BOOK.

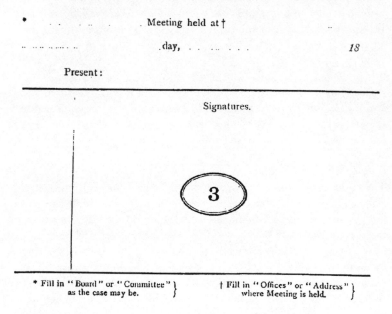

\* . . .. . . Meeting held at †  ..

.. .. ..... .. .day, . . .. . . .                                    *18*

Present :

Signatures.

3

\* Fill in " Board " or " Committee " } as the case may be. }        † Fill in " Offices " or " Address " } where Meeting is held. }

### 5. *Periodical Audit and Balance Sheet.*

The Heads of Departments should present to the Board at least once a month, returns showing the total value of purchases, sales, work in progress, value of finished stock, and the details of expenditure under the sundry heads of Establishment and Plant charges.  The Board should also be supplied with a detailed list of Debtors and Creditors (438) ; in fact they should have before them, once a month at least, a complete interim balance sheet, signed as correct by the Auditor, showing the financial position of the concern.  This should be accomplished within 21 days of the end of each month.  The Auditor would thus be enabled, at the end of any financial year, to promptly complete the accounts, since only that portion appertaining to the last month of the year would require verification. Such a method of auditing is beneficial in many ways. it largely prevents carelessness, misconduct and even serious loss; it also enables the Directors to present to the shareholders, within a month of the closing of the accounts of the financial year, a statement showing the position of the affairs of the company.

One of the most important detail duties devolving on the Directors is that of keeping an absolute check on the list of Debtors and Creditors. For this purpose it is desirable when paying accounts to send with each remittance a circular letter duly filled in, setting forth the amount remitted and the exact position of the account to date (38). This document should be actually compared with the ledger account and also with the 'suppliers monthly statement.' And, similarly, each monthly statement sent to the company's customers should be strictly compared with the ledger account, and the same initialled by a Director. A special feature should be made of asking the Debtors and Creditors to address all complaints *re* accounts to the Chairman or to the Auditor.

### 6. *The Chairman.*

The Chairman of the Board of Directors is of course the most important officer of the company, and he exercises a wide authority when there is no Managing Director. Where, however, there is a Managing Director, he generally controls the affairs of the company, subject, of course, to the supervision of the Board. It must be remembered, however, that the actual management of a company devolves upon the Directors as a body, and any neglect on their part to supervise the work of the Chairman or of the Managing Director might lead to serious personal consequences, especially in the event of liquidation. Where, therefore, extensive authority is vested in the Chairman and the Managing Director, they should be requested to furnish periodical reports of the most exhaustive description, otherwise the Board may lose that grip of the business which they, in self-protection, should hold.

### 7. *Powers of Directors.*

An individual Director has no personal authority as such. He can only act as one of the Board, therefore everything he does without the previous sanction of the Board should be subsequently ratified. Every Director is of course entitled to inspect the books, and to the fullest information as to the operations of the company. Directors should clearly understand that, when they exercise any authority beyond the powers of the company, they may be held personally responsible, and even when entering into contracts on behalf of the company and within its powers, it should be clearly set forth in such contracts that they are acting for and on behalf of the company. A Director is of course personally liable for anything in the nature of a breach of trust, whether by misapplying the funds of the company or by improperly pledging its credit. And when he becomes aware of any breach of trust by his colleagues he should at once take some active steps towards ventilating such misconduct, or he would be held personally responsible for any losses that the company might sustain in consequence of his silence or condonation. Directors cannot legally, except as shareholders, take any pecuniary or other benefit beyond their actual stipulated remuneration.

## II. THE MANAGER

8. There are certain statutory provisions which it is the duty of the Manager and Secretary to observe, such as keeping the registers and affording shareholders opportunities of inspecting the same; filing the annual returns, and plying with the provisions of the Factory and Local Acts. Besides these duties, it frequently happens that the articles of association specify certain duties to be performed by the Manager, but they are sometimes of such a nature that he cannot insist upon carrying them out as a matter of right. Apart, however, from his statutory and specially provided-for duties, the extent of the Manager's authority is limited to the ordinary control of the business of the company, under the direction of the Board. Not only in all the ordinary commercial transactions of the company, but in all other cases where the articles of association expressly provide for powers other than those relating to ordinary business, the signature of the Manager is binding on the company.

### 9. *Personal Qualifications.*
The duties of the Manager are, of course, of a most responsible nature, and special stress should be laid on the importance – the paramount importance – of his being a strict disciplinarian. He must be a practical man of the world, a good organiser, and, above all, must possess tact and judgment. He should be known as a man who means what he says, and who conveys the impression to one and all that he means to be obeyed. As regards the technical details of the business, he should be a thoroughly practical all round man. He need not necessarily have an intimate acquaintance with the mathematical or other minutiae of each branch

of the business, but must have a strong capacity for administrative work. He should have an instinctive knowledge of what his customers really require, and know the smartest and cheapest way of supplying their wants. He should be quite at home in modern office routine, in accounts kept by double entry, in the handling of large bodies of men, and in the application of modern machinery to all classes of engineering work. It will generally be found that those only can fill this position successfully who make completeness of work their chief and absorbing aim. The Manager should bear the reputation of being firm, and at the same time absolutely impartial to everybody under his charge, from his office boy upwards. He should always be ready to learn from any one, and, in whatever work he may have in hand, should adopt the latest processes and methods, and carry them out in the most efficient manner. If he has to erect a new factory, he should think out every detail before he commences operations, and not wait for developments during the progress of the work. If he has no experience of his own to guide him, he should promptly seek the advice of those who have. A badly arranged factory makes economical work an impossibility, and proves the Manager's incapacity. It is needless to remark in these days that every nook and corner of an engineering establishment should bear close inspection, because visitors, customers and inspecting officers are largely influenced by surroundings, and look upon a rough shop, badly laid out, where inattention and disorder are manifest, as the place where they would not expect to obtain good reliable work. And, similarly, neglect of correspondence, inattention to inquires, blunders in detail of construction, delivery, packing and invoicing, lead to a want of confidence and to the gradual decay of the business. People buy, nowadays, where they can be most promptly and well served, and therefore delays and excuses are fatal to business. The Manager, too, must know the best markets for purchasing materials, and be fully alive to all the tricks and dodges of each class of trader. He must unceremoniously show the door to any one who attempts anything in the nature of bribery to himself or his subordinates, and he should immediately close all dealings with any person, customer or otherwise, whom he finds guilty of underhand or dishonourable practices.

10. *Relations with Employees.*
Too much stress cannot be laid on the necessity for the cultivation by the Manager of a brisk and healthy tone amongst the employees. Bad time keeping, unsteadiness, smoking during working hours, and general 'larking,' all of which tend to destroy discipline and undermine organi-

sation, should be put down with a firm hand. Once any of these practices are winked at, they will spread with such rapidity that it will be difficult to regain lost ground.

### 11. *Routine Duties.*

The Manager should see all correspondence, and, in the event of his being away from business for a time, notwithstanding the fact that daily reports and extracts may be mailed to him, should on his return cast his eye over the Letter Register (44), and ask for any letter which appears to him to be of importance. He should also carefully read in the copy letter book, when he returns, all letters that have been written in his absence. The Letter Register should be examined at convenient intervals, with a view to ascertaining what letters remain unanswered or unattended to. Strictly speaking, he should sign all letters and documents except such as are specifically assigned to the Secretary. By these means he is kept fully posted on all matters which are the subject of correspondence.

It will be for him to decide which correspondence he will deal with himself and which he will pass on to be dealt with by others. His own time being valuable, he will have in a room adjoining his office his own stenographer and typist, who will thus be close at hand to take down letters from his dictation as occasion requires. His office should be placed in a central position, so that he can walk direct into the rooms of either the Accountant or the other leading officials, because when transacting business of a varied description it is often necessary to obtain direct information, sometimes of a private nature, there and then. Speaking tubes have many advantages, but it is not always convenient to carry on a conversation through them in the presence of a visitor.

The Manager should be furnished from time to time with all information touching the banking account, and other important financial matters. He should also direct his attention to the official monthly returns and accounts showing the current condition of the business.

### 12. *Curves of Expenditure, etc.*

As it is the Manager's duty to keep a sharp look out for extravagance, he should see that all expenses chargeable to revenue account are brought forward under their respective headings, and with this object it would be found of immense value to have each of them shown on a diagram for the purpose of rapid comparison (see Ch. XXV). Perhaps the most important of all is the commercial diagram, which shows on one sheet, by various coloured, dotted or waved lines or curves, the rise or fall of purchases, sales, work in progress, stock, stores, establishment charges and estimated profits. No more interesting and graphic method of indicating progress or decay can possibly be adopted. It enables those who do not possess the peculiar faculty of grasping the relative importance of figures to see at a glance how matters stand.

### 13. *Office Arrangements.*

It would obviously be absurd to expect the Manager to conduct the business satisfactorily when he is surrounded by piles of old letters, books and documents of every description. It is, therefore, suggested that he should have baskets for correspondence, clearly labelled at the end – one for letters to be filed, another for urgent communications, another for ordinary current correspondence, another for all documents awaiting his signature, and, finally, one for all documents signed and ready for mailing. Under no circumstances should any letters or documents be left lying about when they have been dealt with, and the subject to which they refer closed. Much time is lost in the majority of offices by men whose time is valuable, in consequence of their having to search for some document or other which, if properly filed, could he found almost instantly. It will be clear even to the most obtuse that the time of a smart boy engaged upon filing letters and other documents for only an hour or two each day is not to be compared with the time lost by a Manager who is in receipt of a large salary, and who has to neglect important duties whilst rummaging for something which, under almost any one of the modern systems of filing, could be turned up immediately. One of the most important duties, therefore, of the Manager is to see that all letters and documents of every description are promptly filed for ready reference at any time (67 to 70). Another and equally important duty is that of keeping the whole of the work in connection with correspondence and book-keeping absolutely up to date. It is the only way that business can be conducted successfully and without great worry and disorder. He should take care, too, that every office, together with all the drawers and cupboards therein, be kept tidy and free from all obsolete or useless forms, books and scraps of paper, since nothing confuses a clerk so much in his work, whether of the purely routine type or not, as being surrounded by odds and ends of this description. Practically speaking, neither the tables nor desks occupied by the clerks should be encumbered with any books or papers other than those that are being absolutely dealt with.

### 14. *Arrears of Work.*

Under no circumstance should a Manager permit clerical work to get the upper hand of the staff. There will, of course, be times of extra pressure, which a well organised staff will be able to cope with without difficulty; but once clerical work gets permanently in arrears, chaos and confusion will reign supreme. The Manager should possess the faculty of being able to select the best men for the various duties to be performed. This is a quality of paramount importance. Nothing will be more conducive to first-class results than bright, smart, civil officials, well versed in the latest and best methods of carrying out their respective duties.

# Private Corporations from the
# Point of View of Political Science[1]

## John W. Burgess

Any intelligent inquiry into the relations of private corporate life to the fundamental principles of political science requires at the outset some idea, however rude and tentative, of what a private corporation is, from that point of view. In the prejudice of the masses, it is some alien monster, that has nothing in common with the people and lives upon the sacrifices which it imposes upon them – some Juggernaut, that mercilessly crushes the people to earth under the wheels of his terrible chariot – some Moloch, in whose fiery embrace men, women and children are ruthlessly consumed. In the mind of the better educated, it is commonly conceived of as a fictitious being, without soul or heart or blood – a being of cold and crafty intellect, inordinate ambition and unlimited selfishness. But all such prejudices and notions are crude, superficial and harmful. A private business corporation is, from the point of view of political science, a group of human beings, usually belonging to the best class of citizens, associated for the prosecution of some great enterprise and endowed with certain privileges and obligations. This is, I contend, the view of common sense and of sound political philosophy as to the nature of private business corporations; and the law courts are beginning to manifest a tendency to make this conception the basis of their decisions – to make legal theory harmonize with political theory on this basis. They should have taken this position long ago, not only for the sake of consistency in their decisions, but because the fiction theory to which they have clung tends to create a false impression, both of the nature of the thing and of its relations in every direction.

The chief privileges which these corporate associations unusually enjoy are, continuity of existence despite changes in their individual membership, limited liability of the individual members, and the power to do business by majority act and majority representation.

[1] [*Political Science Quarterly*, vol. 13, 1898, pp. 201–12.]

With this rough and general concept of the nature and privileges of private corporations, we may, without inquiry at this point into the question of their obligations, proceed at once to consider their relations to the principles of a sound political science. Modern political science is a body of knowledge which is grouped about, and classified under, three fundamental doctrines: first, the theory and fact of sovereignty; second, the theory and fact of government; and, third, the theory and fact of liberty. Our question is, therefore, how the existence and activity of private corporations affect these theories and these facts.

In every modern political system there is, in theory, an original and ultimate power, which is the basis of all authority and of all liberty. It is called the sovereignty of the people, or of the nation, or of the state; but, in fact, this sovereignty is nowhere so fully, distinctly and independently organized as to exercise uniform and complete control over government. Almost everywhere sovereignty is legally organized either in the government, or in part of the government, or partly in the government, or makes use of the personnel or a part of the personnel of the government to construct a separate organization of its own. The people themselves are, in large states, unable to exercise their sovereignty over government directly, continuously and effectively. These facts may be easily established by a little study of the provisions and the practice as to amendment in the present political constitutions of the great states of the world. The tendency, in almost all of these states, is towards the assumption or acquirement of sovereignty by the government. The individual citizen or subject is, in his isolation, powerless successfully to obstruct this tendency. The fact is that the political science of the modern world is still engaged in the task of working out the distinctions between sovereignty and government, and that political practice is in the transition period between the sovereignty of the government and the sovereignty of the people behind the government.

In such an era and under such conditions, associations of individuals, both for social and for economic purposes, are absolutely necessary in order to prevent government from assuming sovereignty and lapsing into despotism. Among all of these associations the private business corporation is the most effective. Government is far more likely to assert unlimited power over property than over life or personal liberty. On account of its economic purpose the private corporation is as natural a defender of property against the encroachments of the government as is the individual man himself; and on account of its power, it is a far more effective defender than the individual man. Every lawyer knows that a very large part, if not the larger part, of the immunities of property, or rather the immunities of men in respect to property, against the powers of government, have been established through the resistance of private corporations to governmental encroachments.

On the other hand, it is not only conceivable that private corporations may become dangerous to sovereignty, but it is a fact that something like private corporations did much to produce the anarchy of the Middle Ages. If associations, whether corporate or not, prosecute their interests through political means, – that is, undertake to get possession of the government, for the purpose of exercising force in behalf of their several economic interests, – they are then certainly threatening the sovereignty of the people. Danger from this source, to become real, however, would require such a consolidation  or federalization of associations as would practically unite something like a majority of the political people in behalf of the economic interests of the combination – a situation which is practically impossible under modern conditions, unless produced, directly or indirectly, by government itself.  Again, if associations, whether corporate or not, combine to resist the powers of government and of sovereignty, and undertake to acquire, by physical resistance, immunities not accorded them by the constitution of the state, they certainly array themselves against the sovereignty of the people; but the success of any such movement is a possibility which may be practically disregarded under modern conditions, if the government only holds itself free from collusion.

On the whole, as things now stand in the modern states of the world, economic organizations, especially private corporations, are helpful in maintaining the sovereignty of the people against the almost inevitable tendencies of government to break over the limitations of the constitutions, placed upon government by the sovereign people in behalf of personal liberty and the security of property.  The day has altogether passed when such combinations may, of themselves, become a real danger to sovereignty.  The power of taxation, now firmly established over corporate property, is amply sufficient to overcome every hostile menace.  Modern political science, therefore, regards with disapproval the political party organization of society upon the basis of the economic groups and combinations into which society may be divided, as tending to make economic interests the sole purpose of sovereignty and to obscure the principles of justice and morality ; on the other hand, political science sees great advantage to popular sovereignty in the existence of such economic groups and combinations, so long as they confine themselves to their proper business pursuits, and offer, through regular constitutional means, those same obstructions to governmental encroachment upon the security of private property, which are the chief objects of constitutional limitations upon governmental power.

From the point of view of government, private corporations must be distinguished under two general classes. The one class comprehends every corporation engaged in a business, which, either wholly or in part, is naturally a governmental function, or is actually a governmental function according to the political system of the country in which the corporation exists. The other class comprehends corporations engaged in enterprises that are neither naturally nor actually governmental functions.

Considering this latter class first, we have only to say that, if government confers upon them any privilege above what is enjoyed by ordinary citizens in like pursuits, sound political science asserts the right and the duty of government to see that such privilege is not abused, to the injury of the public. Any failure to perform this duty will allow the power of the people for the support of the government to be diminished. For example, when the government confers upon a number of people, uniting themselves in corporate capacity, the privilege of limited liability, sound political science ascribes to the government the duty of seeing that the capital stock is all paid in and that it remains the corporate property. Again, when the government confers upon a number of persons, forming a corporate body, the power to do business by the will of a quorum and majority of them, sound political science requires the government to insure that the majority shall not so abuse this power as to deprive the individuals who happen to constitute the minority of any of their civil or political rights, as guaranteed to them by the constitution and laws of the country. Or, finally, when the government confers upon a corporate body the privilege of continued existence, regardless of change in personal membership, and thereby contributes towards making the body of shareholders a shifting body, the members of which will become largely unknown to each other and hence largely incapacitated from exercising any effective control over the officials of the corporate body, sound political science requires that government shall so control the relations between the officials and the rest of the shareholders as effectively to preserve and enforce the trust existing between them. If government does not exercise such powers and discharge such duties, it is easy to see how, through the device of the corporate organization, the few may despoil the many, and thus weaken the basis of popular government, if not of all forms of government.

But it is the corporations belonging to the other class that demand the more extended examination. These are the corporations whose pursuits are, either naturally or by the political system of the country in which they exist, governmental functions, either wholly or in part. Instead of exercising these functions through its own officials, government permits them to he exercised by private corporations. The reasons for such a policy are various and cogent. One of them, as distinctly stated by the Supreme Court of the United States in the noted Slaughter House cases, is that the interested vigilance of a private corporation is often more efficacious than the ordinary efforts of the officers of the law. Another reason is that through the employment of private corporations government may enlist private enterprise and private money, almost without limit, in the accomplishment of vast projects for the public good – projects which would be long delayed, if undertaken at all, should their accomplishment depend upon the means which government could command through taxation or loans. Another very cogent reason, from the point of view of political science, is that, through the management of private corporations engaged in such pursuits, most efficient education and experience in the science and practice of administration are acquired by a large number of private persons, from whose ranks the high officials of government may be taken. The country following such a policy is enabled to develop administrative talent and to hold it in readiness for official employment, thus escaping the necessity of recourse to bureaucratic discipline and the cultivation of the bureaucratic spirit.

Over this class of corporations sound political science demands, of course, a larger control by government than over the other class. In addition to those elements of supervision above mentioned, government must impose duties and restrictions corresponding to the additional powers and privileges bestowed. If government allows corporations to exercise the power of eminent domain, government must see to it that they take private property only for public purposes; that they pay a just compensation for it; and that all the machinery for condemnation, for ascertaining value and for securing the payment of the award shall be so constructed and employed as to preserve justice and the due process of law. If government allows them to engage in public business, i.e., business which government itself has a right to carry on according to the existing political system of the country concerned, then government must see to it that they serve the public without discrimination. If government permits them to fix their own tariffs of charges, government must see to it that opportunity for effective competition is maintained. And if government confers upon them severally the rights of monopoly that is, confers upon each of them the sole power to do a certain business within a given district and to prevent competition in that business within that district, then government must itself fix the maximum rate of charges.

So much, as to government's power, is clear from the point of view of political science; but the law of this country has already gone much beyond this. Not only does it sustain the widest governmental regulation of private corporations engaged in enterprises which, according to the political system of the country, government itself may carry on; but, according to the rule laid down in the noted case of Munn *vs.* Illinois by the Supreme Court of the United States, when any property is used in a manner to make it of public consequence, and to affect the community at large, it becomes clothed with a public interest, and must submit to control by the public for the common good. Upon this rule was based the decision that in this country the state legislatures have the power (1) to declare that any business which affects the community at large is clothed with a public interest, no matter whether or not government has put any money in it, or conferred any power on it; and (2) to regulate such business, even to the point of fixing finally and without appeal the maximum tariff of charges which those engaged in such business may demand.

It was realized within a few years, however, that this decision attributed to the state legislatures the power to confiscate the property of private corporations, especially such as were engaged in public or quasi-public pursuits, and that some of the legislatures were making good progress in that direction. In consequence of these experiences, the Supreme Court of the United States; by a series of decisions beginning with the case of the Chicago, Milwaukee & St. Paul R. R. Co. *vs.* Minnesota, so modified its earlier decision as to assert the power of the court to determine whether maximum rates fixed by a state legislature were reasonable or not, and to nullify them if, in its opinion, they were unreasonable.

From the point of view of the principles of political science, such complete control by government over private corporations is justifiable only on the principle that they are monopolies – that is, that they are furnished by government with powers to exclude competition. But in the recent Trans-Missouri Traffic Association case, it was decided by the Supreme Court that, while the state legislatures may deal with private corporations as monopolies and fix their maximum charges, Congress may, in all cases affecting interstate business, pass valid laws maintaining competition and forbidding any agreements between such corporations for the purpose of maintaining rates. Presumably the court would hold the same opinion in regard to the power of the state legislatures as to all internal business. It is now, therefore, the law of this country that government may not only fix the maximum tariff of charges for such corporations, but may also maintain competition between them, to any extreme it pleases.

In such a condition of the public law of the country, only the disposition on the part of the legislators is necessary in order to destroy the property of such corporations. It cannot be said that this disposition is wanting: apparently, it exists in great force. How much of it is feigned, and how much is real, it is impossible to know. But we do know that, in spite of our written constitutions and of all our judicial guaranties of property, the legislatures at last have their hands upon the throats of the corporations, and threaten the virtual confiscation of the vast properties in which hundreds of thousands of our best citizens are interested. We do know that behind the legislatures are the party organizations, under the control of the chairmen of national, state and county committees, who are virtually without responsibility to any one, and who must procure, in some way, the means to keep their machines in repair and in operation. And we all believe, if we do not know, that these politicians understand, far better than we do, just when and where to put on the screws with the best result. In such a situation of affairs the corruption of government and party management is simply inevitable. The cause of it is not so much the cupidity of the corporations, as the unlimited power of the legislatures to do what they will with corporate property, and the unlimited power of the politicians to make the corporations pay continuously for their very existence.

Such is the labyrinth of difficulties which we have created for ourselves by allowing the different branches of government, and sometimes the same branch, to work at cross purposes, in endeavoring to solve the problem of the relations of government to the corporations. It is not easy to see the way out. In general, three possible ways of escape may be suggested. We may treat these corporations as monopolies and, while government fixes their maximum tariffs of charges, may allow them to exclude competition, so far as they can, by extension, contracts and agreements ; or government may maintain the opportunity for effective competition and allow the corporations to fix their own tariffs of charges; or in some way liberal maximum may be guaranteed to them and reasonable agreements allowed for regulating rates thereunder. Unless we can bring the law of the land into line with one or the other of these courses, I expect, though no longer a young man, to live to see the day when at least every corporation engaged in the vast transportation interests of this country shall be bankrupt, every legislature in the land a body of venal hirelings, and every party management a gang of blackmailers; while the courts, to which we have been accustomed to look for protection against unconstitutional laws, will be bullied and intimidated until they yield in all important things to legislative encroachments. Then we shall all be found ready, willing and eager that government shall take these vast properties at its own price and operate them by its own officials. The era of the socialistic republic will have arrived. The much-ridiculed Populists understand the present drift of things far more clearly than is generally supposed; and, whenever they observe any effort to change this drift, they are always in evidence to paralyze it. In fact, there has lately been ground for the conviction that the Populists are the only party among us who know exactly what they want and how to attain it. If the present attitude of the legislatures and the courts towards corporations is not playing into their hands, it is hard to see how this could be done.

It is from the point of view of liberty, finally, that the word which modern political science has to say in reference to corporations is most important – especially in reference to those corporations which do the work that government would other wise be obliged to do. What we mean by liberty in political science is absence of government in a given sphere of individual or social action. We do not mean the rights of individuals as against each other – the great problem of private law; nor the freedom from sin and error involved in voluntary obedience to perfect law – the great problem of ethics we mean, simply, immunity from the power of government.

Keeping this meaning of liberty in our minds, it is easy to see how corporations are a great stay against paternalism in government. Except for railroad, steamship and telegraph corporations, government would be obliged to own and operate all the great means of transportation and intercourse. Except for banking corporations, government would be obliged to own and operate all the great means for mediating exchange. Except for educational corporations, government would be obliged to own and operate universities and colleges. Except for art corporations, government would be obliged to own and manage academies, museums and collections. Except for eleemosynary corporations, government would be obliged to furnish the means for and administer charities. And, except for ecclesiastical corporations, government would be obliged to have religious establishments. All of these things we must have, so long as we-are civilized and progressive men; and if we do not provide and manage them by private enterprise through the medium of corporations, government must and will occupy the ground.

Now, does modern political science favor this latter solution of this mighty problem? I do not think that it does: in fact, I feel very sure that it does not. If it did, it would not be distinguishable from the political systems of the period just preceding the revolutions of the seventeenth and eighteenth centuries. In other words, if it did, the principles of popular government would be indistinguishable from those of absolutism. Modern political science favors the greatest possible limitation of governmental power, consistent with the sovereignty of the state, the unity, independence and security of the country, the enforcement of the laws and the maintenance of justice. It favors keeping open to private enterprise the widest possible domain of business. And it absolutely demands that all institutions, through which new truth is discovered and the ideals of advancing civilization are brought to light and moulded into forms for application, shall be so far free from governmental action as to secure and preserve, at least, perfect freedom of scientific thought and expression. In a word, modern political science is very suspicious of state socialism, as it is called?[2] Political science requires, moreover, that when government assumes any business previously pursued through the means and methods of private enterprise, government shall be obliged to show, first, that it has the authority to do so under the existing political system, and, second, that the welfare of the people will be subserved in higher degree by governmental than by private management. In all such cases, modern political science throws the burden of proof upon government, and will not yield to the mere demand of government for the experiment, without conclusive evidence of the harmfulness of the existing conditions, and of the truth of the proposition that no other substitutes than the agencies of government can meet and rectify those conditions.

Of all forms of government, the federal republic is most hostile in principle to governmental socialism, and least likely to survive any extended development in that direction. The very essence of the federal republic is limitation of government, both as to the subject-matters upon which it may employ its powers, and as to the manner and degree in which it may exercise them. Any increase of such subjects and any removal of the limitations upon the manner and the degree of the exercise of powers arc to be regarded as a menace to the principle of the federal republic; and, consequently, any radical movement of this sort may, from the point of view of political science, be pronounced

---

[2] 'Governmental socialism' is the better term, and I recommend to the economist the adoption of the nomenclature. It would deliver then from a good deal of difficulty in their reasoning.

destructive both of civil liberty and of federal republicanism. Modern political science – especially the political science of the modern federal republic – would, therefore, view with grave concern the destruction of private corporations and the assumption by government of any considerable portion of the business which they transact. While a governmental control, corresponding naturally in each case with the governmental powers conferred on corporations, may be safely exercised with reason and justice, their destruction, either directly or indirectly, would lead to a catastrophe in liberty and government which federal republicanist would hardly survive.

# Evolution of Mercantile Business[1]

### John Wanamaker

My topic is one car of the long train made up by the general subject of the afternoon – 'Combination of Capital as a Factor of Industrial Progress.' This annual congress forms a kind of sounding-board for live questions for the entire country, and because of this I wish to contribute what I can to the general stock of information.

Evolution is that series of steps through which anything has passed in acquiring its present characteristics. The term 'mercantile' covers everything relating to trade and commerce. It was from a business point of view that this city, in which the American Academy of Political and Social Science to-day raises its sounding-board of live questions for the whole country, united some years ago its dozen or more separate districts and townships into one compact municipality, making possible an improved and economical city government.

Long since the slow movements of transportation by canal gave way to quick railroading. Naturally it was only a question of time for the sailing ship and slow freighter to be superseded upon the ocean by the fast steamship to expedite commercial transactions. The exigencies of changing markets, the factors of time, fashions, seasons, the value of capital locked up, compelled the initiation of the order of progression still going on throughout the mercantile world.

The first notable change in the conduct of commercial affairs was the partial withdrawal of agencies, commission houses and jobbing houses from Boston, New York and Philadelphia, and the establishment of offices and warehouses in the Western cities in the interest of lower freight rates and saving of time and expense to buyers coming from the West to the East.

As late as forty years ago, or before the war, the transaction of business in producing and distributing merchandise required many agencies: the

---

[1] [*Annals of the American Academy of Political and Social Science*, vol. 15 (sup.), 1900, pp. 123–35.]

manufacturer, importer, commission men, bankers, jobbers, commercial travelers, and retailers.

Until twenty years ago trade rules limited the sales of manufacturers to commission men, and those of commission houses to jobbers, so that the only market door open to retailers was the jobbers, whose goods were loaded, when they reached the retailer, with three or four unavoidable profits incident to passing the various fixed stages toward the consumer.

The conditions governing the placing of goods in the retailer's hands were not only heavily weighted with expense, but, in the main, the retail merchant was badly handicapped as a rule by

(a) Small capital, commonly borrowed by long credit for merchandise.
(b) Necessity of selling upon credit.
(c) Necessity for larger percentage of profit.
(d) Impossibility of utilizing to advantage store and people all seasons of the year.
(e) Non-accumulation of capital.

The consequence was, according to accepted statistics, that but four out of every hundred merchants succeeded in business. Getting a mere living forty years ago was generally secured in part by the occupancy of a part of the store premises as a residence. Naturally, an undercurrent of discontent with these conditions manifested itself, protesting against two or more prices for the same article, meagre assortments of goods, high prices and the custom that probably grew out of one rate to cash buyers and a different rate to buyers upon credit.

The Centennial Exposition of 1876 was, in my judgment, the moving cause of a departure toward general business by single ownership. The rising tide of popular desire to assemble under one roof articles used in every home and with freedom to purchase was a constant suggestion in 1876, not alone because of its convenience but because to some degree it would form a permanent and useful exhibition. This idea culminated in the formation of a Permanent Exhibition Company, which succeeded the Centennial. Being located in Fairmount Park and not in a business centre, and without skilled management, the scheme was abandoned in a short time.

Up to 1877, so far as now known, no extensive, well-systemized mercantile retail establishment upon a large scale existed in the United States. The nearest approach was the A. T. Stewart store in New York, which limited itself to dry goods of the higher class, until the death of Mr. A. T. Stewart, when it took on lower classes of goods, and a wider, but still limited scope.

That Centennial Exhibition in 1876 at Philadelphia, the principal manufacturing centre of the country, the first great exhibition in America, opened a new vision to the people of the United States. It was the cornerstone upon which manufacturers everywhere rebuilt their businesses to new fabrics, new fashions and more courageous undertakings by reason of the lessons taught them from the exhibits of the nations of the world. The continuing outgrowth of that exhibition has revolutionized the methods of almost every class of mercantile business in the United States.

The tendency of the age toward simplification of business systems and to remove unnecessary duplication of expenses, awakened throughout the United States a keen study of means to bring about a closer alliance with the producer and consumer. Almost simultaneously in a number of cities, long-established stores gradually enlarged and new stores sprang up to group at one point masses of merchandise in more or less variety, the movement everywhere arrested attention and provoked discussion because of the approval and practical support of the people at large.

Though there probably was never a time in any city that there were not bankruptcies of merchants and vacant stores, yet after the opening of the large stores, it everywhere became common with storekeepers and renters to charge all the causes of disaster to the large stores, then and now commonly called department stores, and an unsuccessful effort was made to decry them as monopolies.

For the time being, and even now, to some extent, prejudice and perhaps unconscious selfishness blinds a part of every community upon public questions. The inequality of talents and the unequal application of individuals must always carry some to the top and others to the lower places in all pursuits of life. The highest statesmanship thus far known has not been able anywhere in the world to maintain a permanent equilibrium for the slow, slovenly and misplaced workers with the thrifty, well-trained and properly fitted toilers, and criticism begins whenever and wherever one man and his family gathers a business that outgrows their own hands.

Whoever conquers a higher place than his neighbor is supposed to face a commanding position, that at least makes his business way more difficult with his fellow tradesmen. Doubtless there must be some disadvantages arising from large single businesses of every kind. The growth of our splendid free libraries will to a certain extent curtail the sale of books and affect other established libraries; the ever enlarging and wonderful facilities and inexpensiveness of the universities and colleges of learning will interfere to some degree with many private academies and schools. The trust companies that undertook insurance of real estate and titles and conveyancing, and who became banks of deposits, interfered with the lawyers and bankers. The trolley affected the business of the horse dealer. The large stores certainly affect a certain part of the small stores. Neither well dressed ignorance nor well-satisfied storekeeping ownership can argue down that fact.

In the olden times when any city was smaller the advent of even one more small store affected every other store in the block in which it located, mayhap in the entire city. The thing to be considered, and considered fairly from every point of view, is what the large single ownership businesses contribute to the well-being of the public to counterbalance any disadvantages arising from them.

First of all it must be remembered that society is not constituted for the benefit of any one particular class of the population. Economic questions cannot be voted on by any 10 per cent of the people; the other 90 per cent must have their say. Without sentiment or prejudice, the interests of all must be justly weighed and the greatest good of the greatest number must be gained.

I respectfully submit that the evolution in mercantile business during the last quarter of a century has been wrought not by combinations of capital, corporations or trusts, but by the natural growth of individual mercantile enterprises born of new conditions out of the experience, mistakes and losses of old-time trading; that the underlying basis of the new order of business and its principal claim for favor is that it distributes to the consumer in substance or cash compounded earnings hitherto wasted unnecessarily on middlemen; that thus far the enlarged retailing has practically superseded agents, commission houses, importers and large and small jobbers, thereby saving rentals, salaries and various expenses of handling; that the establishing of direct relations with mills and makers proves to be not only desirable for the saving of such costs as are dispensed with, but because less risks are incurred in preparing products and finding quick markets, thereby favoring lower prices; that the people must be taken into the equation when considering the right of certain businesses to a title of life, as they are responsible for the new conditions, highly value and heartily support them.

It is an old axiom that the water of a stream cannot rise beyond its level. Neither can any business rise or thrive except at the will of the people who are served by it.

I contend that the department store development would not be here but for its service to society; that it has done a public service in retiring middlemen; that its organization neither denies rights to others nor claims privileges of state franchises, or favoritism of national tariff laws; that if there is any suffering from it it is by the pressure of competition, and not from the pressure of monopoly; that so long as competition is not suppressed by law, monopolies cannot exist in storekeeping, and that the one quarter of the globe that cannot be captured by trusts is most assuredly that of the mercantile trading world.

I hold that the evolution in trade was inevitable, because it was water-logged by old customs that overtaxed purchasers; that there was at work for a long time a resistless force moving towards the highest good of humanity; that the profit therefrom to individuals who have risked their own capital, as any man may still do if he chooses, has been insignificant, compared to the people benefited both by the cheapening of the comforts of life and by the improved condition of persons employed.

Philadelphia is believed to be a buying centre for 3,000,000 people. If each of them in a year's purchase of personal needs and home necessities saves on an average ten cents a day, the saving is $10,095,000 in a year. Suppose it be but half that amount, there is still five millions to the good of the people to be put into their savings or their pleasures.

I may be asked how such a statement can be certified to. I reply, I am not offering this information as a statement of fact, because no statement can be made upon accurate statistics of the amount of merchandise purchased each year for individual consumption. I submit this as a fair estimate from an experience of twenty-five years and more of careful study, because I desire to be a witness for the truth, that it may be used for what It is worth in discussing economic and social questions.

I can, however, be more specific in pointing out the effect of modern retailing upon prices:

*First – Prices realized by the producer.*
As he sells in large lots to single firms, whose outlet he becomes familiar with as to quantities and qualities, the producer is able to count more surely upon steady employment of his work-people, and having but one risk instead of many, and smaller expenses in handling goods, can without sacrifice of his own profit, materially reduce the price of goods.

*Second – Prices paid by the consumer.*
The reductions of the producer, plus the lessened costs of concentrated distribution by the retailer, are turned over to the consumer. Further, the variety of goods upon sale by the large retail house, unlike the exclusive merchant having only a two-season business and sometimes only one at the holidays, does not require profits from two or three

months' sales to bear the year's rent, insurance and clerical force. An all year-round business, bringing a steady current of buyers, is the essential thing to use buildings and clerks to advantage and warrant small profits.

It is an easily proven fact that the operation of the American retail system has reduced the prices of many classes of goods one-half in twenty years. But for the length of this paper I would add items in books, bicycles, furniture, woolen dress goods, clothing, house furnishing goods and china. There are other causes of reductions operating in some instances, but a prominent cause is the bettered condition of retailing.

There are some who claim that the reduced cost of quinine was the removal of the tariff, but the fact is the Britons appointed a commission to learn the causes of its scarcity, and who, to reduce its price, sought the proper soil for the growing of abundance of trees, and thus increased the supply and lowered the price.

The evolution in American trading has planted trees that have borne good fruit for the people. General Grant, in proposing the health of Sir William Armstrong at a dinner, laid his hand upon a hundred-ton gun and said the inventor of it had produced the most powerful peace-compelling implement the world had ever seen.

I believe the new American system of storekeeping is the most powerful factor yet discovered to compel minimum prices. Perhaps someone will ask what relation reduced prices of merchandise have upon labor. It is a noticeable fact that lowered prices stimulate consumption and require additional labor in producing, transporting and distributing. The care of such large stocks, amounting in one single store upon an average at all times to between four and five millions of dollars, and the preparation of and handling from reserves to forward stocks, require large corps of men. Under old conditions of storekeeping a man and his wife or daughter did all the work between daylight and midnight. The new systems make shorter hours of duty and thus the number of employees is increased, while many entirely new avenues of employment for women are opened, as typewriters, stenographers, cashiers, check-clerks, inspectors, wrappers, mailing clerks and the like. The division of labor creates many places for talented and high-priced men, whose salaries range alongside of presidents of banks and trust companies and similar important positions. It is universally admitted that the sanitary conditions that surround the employees of the large stores are better than in the old-time smaller stores and that employees are considerably better paid.

Inventions and new processes do not destroy employment any more than the sewing machine or typewriter or Mergenthaler typesetting machine has done so. I grant that in these and many similar cases the lines of employment have changed, but the newspaper adds thousands to its circulation by being ready hours sooner for mails to carry it to distant points, and the sewing machine and typewriter-machine have, like the uses of electricity, telephone, etc., created work and employment that did not previously exist.

Taking the number of employees in the old-time smaller store at an average of five, it would require, when the full complement of employees are on the pay-roll of a representative large store, as many as 1,200 stores to furnish as much employment, while the total payments of salaries would be very much higher in the large store than under the small store system.

Some of the large stores are commercial universities, where the young people are in classes in the evenings under competent teachers, and engaged upon the practical work of the store during certain hours of the day. A part of the new business is the Mutual Benefit Association, which is managed wholly by a board of representative employees, through which, in cases of sickness, accident and death, benefits have been given from 1882 to 1899 amounting to two hundred and forty-six thousand two hundred and thirty-nine dollars and twenty-seven cents ($246,239.27), nearly a quarter of a million of dollars.

In addition to the usual salaries fully up to and believed to be above the level of salaries usually paid, one mercantile firm is known to have paid to its employees by various schemes of co-operation the sum of six hundred and ninety-seven thousand four hundred and twenty-eight dollars and twenty-three cents ($697,428.23), nearly three-quarters of a million of dollars, during a period of 1888 to December 31, 1899.

What is the effect of the modern retail store upon competition? Are its tendencies monopolistic in the control of merchandise or of trade? I counted yesterday the number of mercantile licenses of dealers, places and stores in Philadelphia in the year 1870. There were 16,560. Today I obtained the number of notices of mercantile licenses thus far sent out in Philadelphia representing the stores and places of business, and the figures given me are a minimum of 34,000, with an additional number yet to be issued.

The population in 1870 was 674,022, twenty years later it was 1,046,964, and is now variously estimated at from 1,250,000 to 1,300,000. The number of stores in 1870 (16,560) to the population of that date was 245 for every 10,000, while at the maximum estimate for 1900 the number of stores is 267 for every 10,000 persons. The increase in the number of business dealers has more than kept pace with the growth of the population.

Very few, possibly not more than 5 per cent of the retail stores of the United States are incorporated. They are as a rule under private individual ownership, and their business enterprise represents capacity and capital coupled with executive ability. It is not always the result of generalship; – oftener it is, that it is 'dogged that does it.' Of such incorporated stores there are in this city twelve that did not exist in 1870 upon their present plan which furnish employment, by careful and, I believe, accurate estimate of 15,270 persons, a number almost equal to all the stores existing in 1870.

Extensive retailing in this country is the product of competition in buying and selling for there does not exist in retail business any known combination for the control of unpatented and unpatentable merchandise, nor for the fixing of prices in the interests either of merchants or manufacturers. The, entire practical influence of the modern department store is powerfully against monopoly in any branch of manufacturing or selling. Retail merchants, in common with the public may be at times for brief periods subject to combinations of makers of goods to control prices and create profits, but they are not, and never have been, parties to such measures, at least so far as publicly known.

If all the storekeepers of any one city were to combine, such a combination would not stand twelve months because of the power of manufacturers to become retailers, and further, such a city of combinations would be overwhelmed with independent storekeepers from every other city, who would very properly expect and command the support of the people.

Public service is the sole basic condition of retail business growth. To give the best merchandise at the least cost is the modern retailer's ambition. He cannot control costs of production, but he can modify costs of distribution and his own profits. His principle is the minimum of profit for the creation of the maximum of business. The keen rivalry of retail trading is inimical to a combination between different and competing firms and companies. Such a combination would advance prices and diminish consumption and increase cost of production. The vast varieties of merchandise required by the modern retail store make combinations for the control of articles in process of, and possible of manufacture in every part of the world practically impossible. It is possible for retail merchants in several localities to combine purchases for the sake of economy, but such co-operation differs widely from the organizations commonly known as trusts. Neither would it affect retail prices save to reduce them.

Any control of the retail trade attainable rests entirely upon superior service and lesser prices, and must always be an unknown, or at least a changing quantity. It can never be vested permanently as a possession in any single hands, nor in any group of organizations. Popularity, founded upon distinct actual worthiness, is its only power to command. Success in some branches of mercantile life has its intense individuality, and is a matter of intense personality, much the same as in the journalistic and other learned professions. Only when personal ability and character can be translated into a franchise, can a retail business become a valuable entity. Until then merchandise, real estate and plant, such items as have commercial value, are its only assets.

I fully agree with the President of the United States in his last message, where he says: 'It is universally conceded that combinations which engross or control the market of any particular kind of merchandise or commodity necessary to the general community by suppressing natural and ordinary competition, whereby prices are unduly enhanced to the general consumer, are obnoxious not only to the common law, but also to the public welfare.'

The evolution in business which I have endeavored to discuss has not sought nor has it the power to limit production or stifle competition or raise prices. On the contrary, its chief objectors are those who claim that it makes prices too low. It affects articles of supply of every home and of so many thousands of kinds and ever changing character that no other restriction can obtain than the natural demand. The fact that it deals with distribution and affords intelligent and economic treatment of merchandise increases employment.

It has demonstrated advantages to the public hitherto not common, if at all possible, to former systems. In increasing values of real estate, wherever large businesses are located, smaller stores crowd around them, in some instances changing the values of an entire neighborhood. Statistics prove that it does not anywhere crowd out competent and useful merchants. It saves a multiplication of agencies to the benefit of the consumer in reduced prices.

It introduces into mercantile business a measurably good civil service and provides a systematic commercial education for beginners in business in many business places. It elevates the position of employees, the large number of persons required, affords self-respecting assistance to employees in misfortune, and for the losses arising from sickness and death. It offers opportunity to educated business people of advancement and earning power not possible otherwise. Its system of prices, guarantees and return of goods for refund, not as a favor but as a condition of the contract of sale, is a boon to the ignorant and hasty buyer and to the public generally, not known until introduced by the new order of business.

The alteration in business conditions in the last quarter of the century has not only removed oppressive burdens resting on the public and added to the safety of investments in manufacturing, but it must surely reduce the number of wrecks along the shores of mercantile life.

The elevation of the standards of trade and business transactions must raise the level of the mercantile calling. There will come again a new race of merchants like Amos Lawrence, of Boston; William E. Dodge, of New York; Samuel Budgett, the Morleys, father and sons, the Copestakes and George Moore, of London; William Ewart, of Belfast, and Madame Boucicaut, of Paris.

It rests with the people to commend and command what serves them best. It is only when the fuel ceases that the fires of good government or good business methods burn out. If the public chooses to permit unwarranted taxation or restrictions upon private business enterprise, large or small, that cheapens whatever enters into the daily wants of every home, it only adds to the expense of living. Whatever the fixed charges of business are, whether they come from wastefulness or ignorance of merchant or legislator, it is the consumer who in the last analysis foots the bill. The keys of every public question are in the hands of the people, and it is the people alone who, by neglect and discouragement, slow up and stop the wheels of progress.

# Works Management for Maximum Production[1]

## J. Slater Lewis

*Mr. Slater Lewis' concluding paper, which gathers together and fastens in one center the lines of argument in his preceding articles, has been delayed in its appearance by his much regretted ill health. Circumstances, however, give an unusual keenness of interest to the appearance of the paper at this moment. The United States have just felt the menace of a conflict like that which convulsed England's engineering industries in 1897. The lessons of Britain's experience are invaluable to those who are meeting the conditions through which she so lately passed. The outcome of the American situation is of the highest interest to European competitors. In view of the inevitable tendency toward apparently opposing organisations of employers and workmen, in both countries, it is indispensable to study the means by which such organisations may be brought into cooperation and harmony, instead of antagonism and discord. Trade unions, with all their defects and arrogance, are admitted to have wrought much that is intrinsically good. Employers' unions, directed with the broader view which is, or should be theirs, should be yet more beneficent and freer from mistakes of motive or abuses of power. This movement, which was primarily militant, should be eventually all efficient in putting an end to bitterness.*

It should be obvious that the advantages to be derived from the adoption of modern plant and organisation may be more than neutralized by the cost of labour or materials, by the action of trades-unions, municipalities, or governments, or by circumstances peculiar to local or national life in England and elsewhere. Perhaps in course of time many of these factors may have a universal standard of value, when all manufacturers will be on a fairly equal footing – except, perhaps, in regard to freights and packing charges, which will always remain in favour of those who can deliver their goods quickly without costly packing and at nominal transport rates. For the purpose of

[1] [*Engineering Magazine*, vol. 19, 1900, pp. 211–20.]

today, however, we must, in considering the profitable introduction of specialised machinery, reckon with things as they are, making reasonable allowances for future contingencies.

Some may ask: 'What have all these subjects to do with the profitable introduction of specialised machinery?' I would reply: 'Just as much as the theoretically correct disposition and arrangement of all the parts of a steam-engine or a dynamo have to do with the efficiency and economical manufacture of the finished article.' Let any one item be wrongly disposed towards another, and instead of a good machine you have a bad one. But some may say: 'Is it not then, altogether a question of technical education?' Well, technical education alone is not going to wipe out those engineers who have found the careful collaboration and dissection of commercial facts and probabilities the principal desiderata in locating, founding, organising, and controlling their works. Commercial traffic takes the line of least resistance, and neither technical education, specialised machinery, nor anything else will enable a man in India to make money by manufacturing snow-halls for Icelanders. A man may build a shoe factory in China, where labour is plentiful, and he may equip that factory with automatic machinery and every appliance calculated to cheapen production; still, if he had to buy his leather in America and find a market for his goods in France, where a hostile import tariff was in existence, he would find it hard work indeed to compete successfully with the Frenchman, who, although his works and plant and commercial organisation were not in accordance with modern thought and ideas, had leather in abundance at his door and a ready market for his shoes when he had made them.

Let us therefore analyse very briefly the main practical considerations lying around the subject before us.

*Trade Unions.*
These must be seriously reckoned with in the consideration of the subject, since the effect of their operations in various countries differentiates to a very important extent and consequently affects prices. As, therefore, trade unions have such an important bearing upon trade, it may lead to a better understanding if we trace briefly their origin.

We know that enterprising people prefer to lead and to carry others with them by the process of induction. We know also that others of less enterprising natures prefer to follow, and to be dragged along by the force of circumstances. Not many decades ago the bulk of the masters in Great Britain believed, unfortunately, in the short-sighted policy of regarding their men as so many machines, unworthy altogether of human consideration. Questions of hygiene, such as sanitation, light, and warmth, never concerned them, much less did questions of instruction. To lower wages and to keep their men in a state of subjection was the ideal principle of their profession. Any calculation with a view to proving the wisdom of providing for the comforts and the social and moral well-being of their men was beneath contempt. And what was the result? The best-skilled men, discouraged by that sort of thing, sought wider spheres, where their energies and intelligence not only met with due reward but have been the means of bringing home to us, and in very drastic form, the folly of attempting to stem the tide of progress. It is, therefore, to the principles of that ancient species that we are indebted for trade unions. Revolutions are brought about by oppression and the grindstone of tyranny – never by trusting the people, nor by making a cringing community into full-blown men. America has, comparatively speaking, had little trouble with trade unions, all because careful observation, enlightened management, and scientific enquiry have taught her that urbanity of motive and cosmopolitanism of thought produce in the long run the best results, financial and otherwise.

However, trade unions having established themselves in Great Britain, what happened? English employers not only affected to ignore their claims, but had a sublime disregard for any kind of defensive organisation. It was only after enormous mischief had frequently been done to trade by strikes, and when business became almost impossible, that they suddenly and simultaneously discovered they had too long ignored the fact that an organisation for the protection of employers was of vital importance. Trade unions took advantage of the position in many ways and were busily engaged in the operation of forcing the manufacturers' hands by sectional tactics, which individual masters were powerless to cope with. A combination of the engineering employers and a costly lock-out became inevitable. Everybody remembers it. But it has put the British engineering trades on a sounder footing and has enabled manufacturers to begin the process of measuring swords with their foreign competitors. And, further, it has led to a better understanding between master and man, and has removed much of the deadly friction which hitherto existed. Whether this happy result in any way accounts for the abnormal success of the country during the post two years I cannot say, but the imports and engineering exports have beaten all previous records, and the revenue of the country is millions of pounds in excess of any previous financial period. Whatever may be said to the contrary, there can be no doubt that masters' unions and men's unions are alike desirable and necessary for the regulation of the labour traffic, and those who think otherwise only deceive themselves.  But what the British manufacturer really requires is a levelling of wages the whole world over, and he should pray most earnestly for the success of the trade unions in those countries which do not at present enjoy the attentions of the representatives of those institutions.  However, what we have to ask ourselves at the moment is this: 'Is it possible under the present conditions of labour, or desirable under the prospective conditions attaching to trade unions, for Great Britain to attempt to manufacture goods profitably, by the introduction of specialised machinery, in competition with America and the Continent?'

*The Cost of Labour.*
Between the  nett cost of labour and the hours of work in America and England there is perhaps not much difference, but that there is a striking difference in the Continental practice no one will deny, inasmuch as the 'working-day' on the eastern side of the Channel is much longer, and the rate of pay much less than obtains in either of the other countries mentioned.  Perhaps some day our neighbours may be able to place a correct estimate upon their services, but for the moment their cheap labour and long hours tell heavily against English engineers.

Many arguments have been adduced by the workman's representatives with a view to proving that the British working man is, after all, no better off than his friends on the Continent – in other words, that the British manufacturer has nothing to grumble about.  It is, indeed, often contended that the ratio of wages earned to the actual net value of work performed is no greater in one case than time other.  My experience, however, satisfies me that the contrary is the fact, and as cheap labour affects all industries, it follows that coal, coke, iron, timber, and other commodities will he affected favourably for the manufacturer, and that in consequence our Continental friends can cut prices below the British remunerative limit and yet secure a large share of profit for themselves.

Englishmen used to meet that particular aspect of the subject by the 'made in Germany' excuse, but sarcasm soon ceases to have an effect when people's pockets are touched.  The phrase answered its purpose for awhile, but the superior class of goods now manufactured on the Continent has turned the tables completely and 'made in Germany' is now regarded as a valuable national trademark – one, in fact, in which Britishers would fain have never heard of!

*The Cost of Materials.*
The cost of raw materials is, more often than not, a matter of paramount importance to the manufacturer and cannot be ignored in the consider-

ation of the question before us. It will be obvious that the manufacturing engineer who uses large quantities of heavy materials should be within the shortest possible distance of the producer, and should have railway sidings and the best facilities and appliances for the efficient handling of the material when it arrives at the works. If only small quantities of light materials are required, that particular feature of the internal economy of the establishment may be disregarded in favour of more importance such as access to suitable labour, water power, and good markets.

### 'Protecting' Labour.

The British government and the British municipal and country authorities, not content with the many burdens which manufacturers have to bear, must, forsooth, impose labour and fair-wage clauses upon contractors, which, when reduced to first principles, will not bear scrutiny at the hands of even the most thick-headed philosopher. For instance: 'standard rates of wages' must be paid to all men employed upon a number of dynamos being made, say, for the British War Office. Now, if the whole of the raw materials used in the building of those dynamos were produced by the dynamo-maker himself, and were not purchased from outsiders, there would be some sense in the system of preventing 'sweating,' but no manufacturing engineer is independent of outside manufacturers. All have to buy something from the outsider, and here we often find the 'sweater' in his most heinous form. He stands little chance of being molested. It is not the contractor of first instance, he who is compelled to pay standard rates of wages and who produces the bulk of his finished materials from his own raw materials – the sort of man who brings real solid wealth to the people – who gains by these arbitrary clauses, but the contractor of first instance who produces little from the raw material, and who buys most of his materials, not, perhaps, from the person whom we may call the contractor of second instance, but from the contractor of the third or fourth instance – those men who are never troubled by public regulations of any kind, and who 'sweat' their men and women with callous brutality.

I am quite aware that, legally, permission has first to be obtained to employ the sub-contractor or contractor of second instance, but it is a rule more honored in the breach than in the observance. And what is the result? Why, the contractor of first instance, who buys the bulk of his material from the 'sweater,' can 'wipe out' the genuine contractor, who produces his own goods in the entirety, and who, as the contractor of the first instance, is compelled to pay standard wages to all classes of labour.

The rottenness of such a system of 'protection' becomes more pronounced when we ponder over the fact that any article of foreign manufacture will be accepted by these public bodies and paid for without any inconvenient questioning as to rate of wages or hours of labour. This phase of the question needs to be carefully considered in connection with the subject of Works Management for Maximum Production, since it is rapidly becoming a question not so much of 'What can we do' as 'What may we do?'

*Free Trade versus Reciprocity.*
I do not propose to say much regarding this question, but one thing is clear – that the Americans and all our Continental friends not only have large markets of their own, but a free and open door into the vast English markets. The combination of those two factors is of supreme importance in connection with the subject of 'mass production,' where quantity and the extent of the field of operations are the very soul and essence of success. The British manufacturer, go wherever he will, is opposed by tariffs not only prohibitive in magnitude but 'ad valorem' and hostile in spirit. When Great Britain was regarded as 'the workshop of the world' and other nations had no alternative to buying British goods, it was a case of 'Hobson's choice'; but now that half a dozen other countries have manufacturing pretensions and facilities at least equal, if not superior, to those of England, it must be obvious to the most obtuse that unless the one-sided conditions now existing are modified, our operations will be closely invested by the enemy; Britain's position as a manufacturing nation will be no longer in the ascendant, and mass production, from an English point of view, will be robbed of its principal charm.

*The Theoretical and Technical Aspect.*
This side of the question of mass production is of course a very important one – one which varies with circumstances, such as public requirements and tastes, the necessity for cheap workmanship combined with lightness and high efficiency, or – the reverse of that – the very highest possible class of workmanship in machinery of substantial proportions, where efficiency, as applied in the technical sense, is necessariiy and purposely disregarded.

Here we approach a phase of the subject so vast in extent that I must be excused making more than a few remarks anent the fashionable or prevailing idea that technical education alone is going to 'run the show' in future. The term technical education very often reminds me of the old saying – 'The theory of music is one thing – playing the instrument another!' A learned professor may enlarge for an hour or two upon the art of driving a nail, or driving a golf ball; but the student, and perhaps the professor himself, might find the first few attempts at driving either the one or the other to be associated with some, little surprise, if not with damage to person and property. It is the same in most things. The youth who 'works' his skates for the first time or two, will learn more in five minutes about 'contingencies' he will by studying the theory of skating for a life-time.

Technical education without practice will not enable a man to jump right into the arena of industrial warfare and fight all comers – nor will it give him initiative, 'grit,' rough-and-ready common sense, determination and energy, or the peculiar faculty of making hard bargains and finding the best market for his goods. Neither will technical education alone give a man an eye for the beautiful, the graceful, or the practical. All those qualities are in-born to a large extent in the most successful men. Very often young children have pronounced tendencies and striking individualities and ideas long before they even have made the acquaintance of the A. B. C. of their education.

It must not be assumed from the foregoing that I am a heretic in the religion of technical education. I am nothing of the kind. I regard technical education, to a certain extent, as being the only door to success. When, however, it attempts to make a man understand all things at all times it becomes a farce and a clog to progress and ruins the prospects of thousands of young men – men who have aimed too high for their real abilities or opportunities. Technical education, by which I mean technical education in one branch of trade or in one profession, is of vast importance to the youth who wishes to be, not a walking authority upon every conceivable subject, but thoroughly well versed in and fully equipped for the particular business or calling which he has chosen for his future career.

Take the man who wishes to become a leading gun maker. He must not only understand the theory of the gun, as well as of the explosive, but be a mechanic of the first water. If he wishes to make guns in large quantities, he must be fully acquainted with the most modern machine tools and be capable of taking full advantage of even the most minute improvements in the manufacturing processes. Greek, ancient history, and a perfect knowledge of all the classics would be of about as much value to such a man as a knowledge of dress-making. I had recently the opportunity and the gratification of being shown over a foreign gun factory, and I was assured that the cost of the labour and the material in connection with an extremely well-finished and handy little rook-shooting rifle was four shillings and two pence. The man who wishes to out-step the results in that establishment would have to begin very early in a morning, even if he carried a technical school about with him in his pocket.

Mass production has reduced the cost of labour in guns, bicycles, sewing machines, and many other similar goods, to a bed-rock condition of things, and nothing but an extensive experience in each branch of business, with a full and wide-awake knowledge of all the tips and tricks of the trade – both technical and practical – will enable a man to keep abreast of the times, much less to wipe out his opponents.

There is no royal road to success in the matter of the organisation and the working of factories where mass production and standardisation are the dominating features. It may not be altogether a question of the best machine-tools, nor of the design of the article to be manufactured, but one, perhaps, of commencing operations by efficient 'jigs,' careful checking of operations as they proceed, and many other considerations which can only be acquired by experience and by coming into contact with the best men and the best appliances.

Some people believe in making themselves into professional men first, and engineers afterwards. They bang away at every conceivable technical subject till they are bald and then emerge into the world in search of employment. If they have a fond parent with a long pocket, and are favoured by opportunity and possessed of patience, energy, and gumption, they may ultimately succeed in life; but with out those qualities and advantages they stand a poor chance indeed. Let me illustrate the meaning of all this by quoting a passage from a letter which I recently received from an old engineering friend in America. It is particularly pertinent to this subject, because we are here dealing with a matter which has called forth the best energies of the professorial element, in the endeavour to prove that the technical school is the only channel through which money-for that is what most people are striving for-is to be made.

'Hang any and every profession!' The average counter-jumper makes a better living than a professional man – and indeed, in nine cases out of ten, the commercial man is more valuable both to himself and humanity at large than the professional man.

'The insight which I get in the working of the greatest corporations on earth confirms this view to me, and I fully believe that the men who plotted out the time-tables and organised the Pennsylvania Railroad System are at least as capable and valuable as the engineers, bridge-builders, and others who built the line. I am, of course, an interested observer and may be wrong in my conclusions, but I see it clearer every day that the best engineer is the one who does most with the least means, and that success and reputation follow concentration of energy, applied to one particular field 'which can be developed.'

I engaged a man last week who is a thoroughly competent architect. He built villas abroad and can lay out a cathedral in a 'jiffy' – or a synagogue, which would deflect all the traffic if erected near any stock exchange – he has a wife and children, but no overcoat, and I let him make tracings and am not quite sure whether he will maintain himself on this work even!'

How sad! But it is only the case of many draughtsmen over again. I have known quite a number of young fellows who have been thoroughly well educated; who were splendid draughtsmen and who had had a technical training of the 'heavy' order – yet earned much less than fitters and turners in the shops, and had to keep up appearances. They were, however, short of commercial knowledge; knew nothing of handling men, nor of the great world of hard experience through which the successful mass-producer has to travel almost barefooted!

*Conclusion*

It will be seen from this and previous articles that establishing new works for the profitable introduction of specialised machinery in order to arrive at maximum production is a matter of great complexity, involving questions of the highest importance, which must vary in accordance with the surroundings of each particular trade.

For me, therefore, or any other man, to attempt to lay down a set of hard-and-fast rules for the profitable introduction of specialised machinery for any and all classes of work would be impossible; and would be only imposing upon the credulity of my readers. In my treatise upon the 'Commercial Organisation of Factories.' I have dealt with system and organisation as the cardinal principles underlying successful shop management – whether it be a shop where articles are manufactured in large quantities or in small. System and organisation studied and practised with keen and enthusiastic intelligence, will bring out most of the good qualities essential to 'Works Management for the Maximum of Production.'

In concluding this series of articles I cannot do better than quote the words of a well-known American engineer – Mr. Tregoning.

'It has been said that "system is the triumph of mind over matter," and there is no doubt about the truth herein contained; we only get suspicious of the fact when taking a measured survey of the inner workings of some large factories, and gaze sorrowfully at the triumph of matter over mind.

'To work systematically is to work successfully. Method is the essential element on which every solid and substantial concern is based; and that factory, institution, or establishment of any kind which ignores it, conveys to the observer an impression that nothing permanent or abiding is intended, whilst on the other hand a systematised manner of working stamps it at once with permanency – an establishment that means business and intends to carry it on for all time.

'I have heard it remarked that in business three things are necessary: knowledge, temper, and time; but I have seen all three prostrate and powerless for want of method in the management. Such is the evil of working in an unmethodical and slipshod manner, that it is not too much to say results have followed well-nigh ruinous to the concern.

'There is no doubt that the subject of factory organisation has been badly neglected in past years. That we have not advanced with the order of the times is the complaint I lodge against the doors of many managers. We are working on old systems which have served their day and generation-systems which "have had their day" but, unfortunately have not "ceased to be"; for a brief glance at many of them, both great and small, will prove that little or no method is used, and that the concern moves under conditions which are disgraceful; the wonder is how it moves at all. My observations have led me to conclude – and I say it after twenty years' experience – that the first and foremost want of many of our large factories is not work, but a thorough revision of the machinery that manages and directs the whole concern. It is not a want of brains, it is not the difficulty of working out a vast and complicated scheme, it is not a matter involving the company in a large outlay of money – it is simply a question of method – the application of a few simple rules, and a respect for the time-honoured principle that order is the first law of the universe, and the nearer our approach to it the more harmonious will our arrangements work.

'A perfect organisation I consider an essential and vital element in securing success, in whatever form of institution we may wish to carry on, whether political or religious, mechanical or social. I contend that it is not possible to found a lasting power upon a management in which systematic action is eliminated or ignored; a ramshackle condition of things is the ultimatum; and in many cases establishments have closed simply through a break-up from within of its managing machinery.'

# Business Enterprise[1]

## Thorstein Veblen

The motive of business is pecuniary gain, the method is essentially purchase and sale. The aim and usual outcome is an accumulation of wealth.[2] Men whose aim is not increase of possessions do not go into business, particularly not on an independent footing.

How these motives and methods of business work out in the traffic of commercial enterprise proper – in mercantile and banking business – does not concern the present inquiry, except so far as these branches of business affect the course of industrial business in the stricter sense of the term. Nor is it necessary here to describe the details of business routine, whether in the mercantile pursuits or in the conduct of an industrial concern. The point of the inquiry is that characteristically modern business that is coextensive with the machine process described above and is occupied with the large mechanical industry. The aim is a theory of such business enterprise in outline sufficiently full to show in what manner business methods and business principles, in conjunction with the mechanical industry, influence the modern cultural situation. To save space and tedium, therefore, features of business traffic that are not of a broad character and not peculiar to this modern situation are left on one side, as being already sufficiently familiar for the purpose in hand.

In early modern times, before the regime of the machine industry set in, business enterprise on any appreciable scale commonly took the form of commercial business – some form of merchandising or banking.

---

[1] [From *The Theory of Business Enterprise*, New York, Charles Scribner's Sons, 1904, pp. 20–65.]

[2] The ulterior ground of efforts directed to the accumulation of wealth is discussed at some length in the Theory of the Leisure Class, ch. II. and V., and the economic bearing of the business man's work is treated in a paper on 'Industrial and Pecuniary Employments,' in the Proceedings of the thirteenth annual meeting of the American Economic Association. Cf. also Marshall, Principles of Economics (3rd ed.), bk. I. ch. III., bk. IV. ch. XII., bk. V. ch. IV., bk. VII. ch. VII and VIII.; Bagehot, Economic Studies, especially pp. 63 et seq.; Walker, Wages Question, ch. XIV.; and more especially Sombart, Moderne Kapitalismus, vol. I ch. I, VIII., XIV., XV.; Marx, Kapital, bk. I ch. IV.; Schmoller, Grundriss, bk. II. ch. VII.

Shipping was the only considerable line of business which involved an investment in or management of extensive mechanical appliances and processes, comparable with the facts of the modern mechanical industry.[3] And shipping was commonly combined with merchandising. But even the shipping trade of earlier times had much of a fortuitous character, in this respect resembling agriculture or any other industry in which will and weather greatly affect the outcome. The fortunes of men in shipping were on a more precarious footing than today, and the successful outcome of their ventures was less a matter of shrewd foresight and daily pecuniary strategy than are the affairs of the modern large business concerns in transportation or the foreign trade. Under these circumstances the work of the business man was rather to take advantage of the conjunctures offered by the course of the seasons and the fluctuations of demand and supply than to adapt the course of affairs to his own ends. The large business man was more of a speculative buyer and seller and less of a financiering strategist than he has since become.

Since the advent of the machine age the situation has changed. The methods of business have, of course, not changed fundamentally, whatever may be true of the methods of industry; for they are, as they had been, conditioned by the facts of ownership. But instead of investing in the good as they pass between producer and consumer, as the merchant does, the business man now invests in the processes of industry; and instead of staking his values on the dimly foreseen conjunctures of the seasons and the act of God, he turns to the conjunctures arising from the interplay of the industrial processes, which are in great measure under the control of business men.

So long as the machine processes were but slightly developed, scattered, relatively isolated, and independent of one another industrially, and so long as they were carried on on a small scale for a relatively narrow market, so long the management of them was conditioned by circumstances in many respects similar to those which conditioned the English domestic industry of the eighteenth century. It was under the conditions of this inchoate phase of the machine age that the earlier generation of economists worked out their theory of the business man's part in

---

[3]   It is significant that joint-stock methods of organization and management – that is to say, impersonally capitalistic methods – are traceable, for their origin and early formulation, to companies of early modern times. Cf. K. Lehmann, Die geschichtliche Entwickelung des Aktienrechts bis zum Code de Commerce. The like view is spoken for by Ehrenberg, Zeitalter der Fugger; see vol. II, pp. 325 *et seq.*

industry. It was then still true, in great measure, that the undertaker was the owner of the industrial equipment, and that he kept an immediate oversight of the mechanical processes as well as of the pecuniary transactions in which his enterprise was engaged; and it was also true, with relatively infrequent exceptions, that an unsophisticated productive efficiency was the prime element of business success.[4] A further feature of that precapitalistic business situation is that business, whether handicraft or trade, was customarily managed with a view to earning a livelihood rather than with a view to profits on investment.[5]

In proportion as the machine industry gained ground, and as the modern concatenation of industrial processes and of markets developed, the conjunctures of business grew more varied and of larger scope at the same time that they became more amenable to shrewd manipulation. The pecuniary side of the enterprise came to require more unremitting attention, as the chances for gain or loss through business relations simply, aside from mere industrial efficiency, grew greater in number and magnitude. The same circumstances also provoked a spirit of business enterprise, and brought on a systematic investment for gain. With a fuller development of the modern close-knit and comprehensive industrial system, the point of chief attention for the business man has shifted from the old-fashioned surveillance and regulation of a given industrial process, with which his livelihood was once bound up, to an alert redistribution of investments from less to more gainful ventures,[6] and to a strategic control of the conjunctures of business through shrewd investments and coalitions with other business men.

As shown above, the modern industrial system is a concatenation of processes which has much of the character of a single, comprehensive, balanced mechanical process. A disturbance of the balance at any point

---

[4] Cf. Cantillon, *Essai sur le Commerce*, 1e partie, ch. III., VI., IX., XIV., XV.; *Wealth of Nations*, bk. I.; Bücher, *Enstehung der Volkswirtschaft* (3d ed.), ch. IV. and V.; Sombart, *Kapitalismus*, Vol. I bk. I

[5] Sombart, vol 1. ch. IV.–VIII; Ashley, *Economic History and Theory*, bk. II., ch. VI., especially pp. 389–397.

[6] Cf. Marshall, *Principles of Economics*, on the 'Law of Substitution,' e.g. bk. VI. ch. I. The law of substitution implies freedom investment and applies fully only in so far as the investor in quest is not permanently identified with a given industrial plant or even a given line of industry. It requires great facility in shifting from one to another point of investment. It is therefore only as the business situation has approached the modern form that the law of substitution has come to be of considerable importance to economic theory; for a theory of business, such as business was in mediaeval and early modern times, this law need scarcely have been formulated.

means a differential advantage (or disadvantage) to one or more of the owners of the sub-processes between which the disturbance falls; and it may also frequently mean gain or loss to many remoter members in the concatenation of processes, for the balance throughout the sequence is a delicate one, and the transmission of a disturbance often goes far. It may even take on a cumulative character, and may thereby seriously cripple or accelerate branches of industry that are out of direct touch with those members of the concatenation upon which the initial disturbance falls. Such is the case, for instance, in an industrial crisis, when an apparently slight initial disturbance may become the occasion of a widespread derangement. And such, on the other hand, is also the case when some favorable condition abruptly supervenes in a given industry; as, *e.g.*, when a sudden demand for war stores starts a wave of prosperity by force of a large and lucrative demand for the products of certain industries, and these in turn draw on their neighbors in the sequence, and so transmit a wave of business activity.

The keeping of the industrial balance, therefore, and adjusting the several industrial processes to one another's work and needs, is a matter of grave and far-reaching consequence in any modern community, as has already been shown. Now, the means by which this balance is kept is business transactions, and the men in whose keeping it lies are the business men. The channel by which disturbances are transmitted from member to member of the comprehensive industrial system is the business relations between the several members of the system; and, under the modern conditions of ownership, disturbances, favorable or unfavorable, in the field of industry are transmitted by nothing but these business relations. Hard times or prosperity spread through the system by means of business relations, and are in their primary expression phenomena of the business situation simply. It is only secondarily that the disturbances in question show themselves as alterations in the character or magnitude of the mechanical processes involved. Industry is carried on for the sake of business, and not conversely; and the progress and activity of industry are conditioned by the outlook of the market, which means the presumptive chance of business profits.

All this is a matter of course which it may seem simply tedious to recite.[7] But its consequences for the theory of business make it necessary to keep the nature of this connection between business and industry in mind. The adjustments of industry take place through the mediation of

---

[7]  See Sombart, Kapitalismus, vol. I. ch. VIII.

pecuniary transactions, and these transactions take place at the hands of the business men and are carried on by them for business ends, not for industrial ends in the narrower meaning of the phrase.

The economic welfare of the community at large is best served by a facile and uninterrupted interplay of the various processes which make up the industrial system at large; but the pecuniary interests of the business men in whose hands lies the discretion in the matter are not necessarily best served by an unbroken maintenance of the industrial balance. Especially is this true as regards those greater business men whose interests are very extensive. The pecuniary operations of these latter are of large scope, and their fortunes commonly are not permanently bound up with the smooth working of a given sub-process in the industrial system. Their fortunes are rather related to the larger conjunctures of the industrial system as a whole, the interstitial adjustments, or to conjunctures affecting large ramifications of the system. Nor is it at all uniformly to their interest to enhance the smooth working of the industrial system at large in so far as they are related to it. Gain may come to them from a given disturbance of the system whether the disturbance makes for heightened facility or for wide-spread hardship, very much as a speculator in grain futures may be either a bull or a bear. To the business man who aims at a differential gain arising out of interstitial adjustments or disturbances of the industrial system, it is not a material question whether his operations have an immediate, furthering or hindering effect upon the system at large. The end is pecuniary gain, the means is disturbance of the industrial system, – except so far as the gain is sought by the old-fashioned method of permanent investment in some one industrial or commercial plant, a case which is for the present left on one side as not bearing on the point immediately in hand.[8] The point immediately in question is the part which the business man plays in what are here called the interstitial adjustments of the industrial system; and so far as touches his transactions in this field it is, by and large, a matter of indifference to him whether his traffic affects the system advantageously or disastrously. His gains (or losses) are related to the magnitude of the disturbances that take place, rather than to their bearing upon the welfare of the community.

---

[8] It is chiefly the passive owner of stock and the like that holds permanently to a given enterprise, under the fully developed modern business conditions. The active business man of the larger sort is not in this way bound to the glebe of the given business concern.

The outcome of this management of industrial affairs through pecuniary transactions, therefore, has been to dissociate the interests of those men who exercise the discretion from the interests of the community. This is true in a peculiar degree and increasingly since the fuller development of the machine industry has brought about a close-knit and wide-reaching articulation of industrial processes, and has at the same time given rise to a class of pecuniary experts whose business is the strategic management of the interstitial relations of the system. Broadly, this class of business men, in so far as they have no ulterior strategic ends to serve, have an interest in making the disturbances of the system large and frequent, since it is in the conjunctures of change that their gain emerges. Qualifications of this proposition may be needed, and it will be necessary to return to this point presently.

It is, as a business proposition, a matter of indifference to the man of large affairs whether the disturbances which his transactions set up in, the industrial system help or hinder the system at large, except in so far as he has ulterior strategic ends to serve. But most of the modern captains of industry have such ulterior ends, and of the greater ones among them this is peculiarly true. Indeed, it is this work of far-reaching business strategy that gives them full title to the designation, 'Captains of Industry.' This large business strategy is the most admirable trait of the great business men who with force and insight swing the fortunes of civilized mankind. And due qualification is accordingly to be entered in the broad statement made above. The captain's strategy is commonly directed to gaining control of some large portion of the industrial system. When such control has been achieved, it may be to interest to make and maintain business conditions which shall facilitate the smooth and efficient working of what has come under his control, case he continues to hold a large interest in it an investor; for, other things equal, the gains from what has come under his hands permanently in the way of industrial plant are greater higher and more uninterrupted its industrial efficiency.

An appreciable portion of the larger transactions in railway and 'industrial' properties, *e.g.*, carried out with a view to the permanent ownership of the properties the business men whose hands they pass. But also in a large portion of these transactions the business men's endeavors are directed to a temporary control of the properties in order to close out at an advance or to gain some indirect advantage; that is to say, the transactions have a strategic purpose. The business man aims to gain control of a given block of industrial equipment – as, *e.g.*, given railway lines or iron mills that are strategically important – as a basis for further transactions out of which gain is expected. In such a case his efforts are directed, not to maintaining the permanent efficiency of the industrial equipment, but to influencing the tone of the market for the time being, the apprehensions of other large operators, or the transient faith of investors.[9] His interest in the particular block of industrial equipment is, then, altogether transient, and while it lasts it is of a factitious character.

The exigencies of this business of interstitial disturbance decide that in the common run of cases the proximate aim of the business man is to upset or block the industrial process at some one or more points. His strategy is commonly directed against other business interests and his ends, are commonly accomplished by the help of some form of pecuniary coercion. This is not uniformly true, but it seems to be true in appreciably more half of the transactions in question. In general, transactions which aim to bring a coalition of industrial plants or processes under the control of a given business man are directed to making it difficult for the plants or processes in question to be carried on in severalty by their previous owners or managers.[10] It is commonly a struggle between rival business men, and more often than not the outcome of the struggle depends on which side inflict or endure the greater pecuniary danger. And pecuniary damage in such a case not uncommonly involves a set-back to the industrial plants concerned and a derangement, more or less extensive, of the industrial system at large. The work of the greater modern business men, in so far as they have to do with the ordering the scheme of industrial life, is of this strategic character. The dispositions which they make are business transactions, 'deals,' as they are called in the business jargon borrowed from gaming slang. These do not always involve coercion of the opposing interests; it is not always necessary to

---

[9] Cf. testimony of J. B. Dill, *Report of the Industrial Commission*, vol. I. pp. 1078, 1080–5; 'Digest of Evidence,' p. 77; also testimony of various witnesses on stock speculation and corporate management, and particularly the special report to the Commission, on 'Securities of Industrial Combinations and Railroads,' vol. XIII., especially pp. 920–33.

[10] The history of the formation of any one of the great industry coalitions of modern times will show how great and indispensable a factor in the large business is the invention and organization of difficulties designed to force rival enterprises to come to terms. E.g. the manoeuvres preliminary to the formation of the United States Steel Corporation, particularly the movements of the Carnegie Company, show how this works on a large scale. Cf. E. S. Meade, Trust Finance, pp. 204–17; Report of the Industrial Commission, vol. XIII., 'Review of Evidence,' pp. v–vii, with the testimony relating this topic. The pressure which brings about a new adjustment (coalition) is commonly spoken of as 'excessive competition.'

'put a man in a hole' before he is willing to 'come in on' a 'deal.' It may often be that the several parties whose business interests touch one another will each see his interest in reaching an amicable and speedy arrangement; but the interval that elapses between the time when a given 'deal' is seen to be advantageous to one of the parties concerned and the time when the terms are finally arranged is commonly occupied with business manoeuvers on both or all sides, intended to 'bring the others to terms.' In so playing for position and endeavoring to secure the largest advantage possible, the manager of such a campaign of reorganization not infrequently aims to 'freeze out' a rival or to put a rival's industrial enterprise under suspicion of insolvency and 'unsound methods,' at the same time that he 'puts up a bluff' and manages his own concern with a view to a transient effect on the opinions of the business community. Where these endeavors occur, directed to a transient derangement of a rival's business or to a transient, perhaps specious, exhibition of industrial capacity and earning power on the part of one's own concern, they are commonly detrimental to the industrial system at large; they act temporarily to lower the aggregate serviceability of the comprehensive industrial process within which their effects run, and to make the livelihood and the peace of mind of those involved in these industries more precarious than they would be in the absence of such disturbances. If one is to believe any appreciable proportion of what passes current as information on this head, in print and by word of mouth, business men whose work is not simply routine constantly give some attention to manoeuvering of this kind and to the discovery of new opportunities for putting their competitors at a disadvantage. This seems to apply in a peculiar degree, if not chiefly, to those classes of business men whose operations have to do with railways and the class of securities called 'industrials.' Taking the industrial process as a whole, it is safe to say that at no time is it free from derangements of this character in any of the main branches of modern industry. This chronic state of perturbation is incident to the management of industry by business methods and is unavoidable under existing conditions. So soon as the machine industry had developed to large proportions, it became unavoidable, in the nature of the case, that the business men in whose hands lies the conduct of affairs should play at cross-purposes and endeavor to derange industry. But chronic perturbation is so much a matter of course and prevails with so rare interruptions, that, being the normal state of affairs, it does not attract particular notice.

In current discussion of business, indeed, ever since the relation of business men to the industrial system has seriously engaged the attention of economists, the point to which attention has chiefly been directed is the business man's work as an organizer of comprehensive industrial processes. During the later decades of the nineteenth century, particularly, has much interest centered, as there has been much provocation for its doing, on the formation of large industrial consolidations; and the evident good effects of this work in the way of heightened serviceability and economies of production are pointed to as the chief and characteristic end of this work of reorganization. So obvious are these good results and so well and widely has the matter been expounded, theoretically, that it is not only permissible, but it is a point of conscience, to shorten this tale by passing over these good effects as a matter of common notoriety. But there are other features of the case, less obtrusive and less attractive to the theoreticians, which need more detailed attention than they have commonly received.

The circumstances which condition the work of consolidation in industry and which decide whether a given move in the direction of a closer and wider organization of industrial processes will be practicable and will result in economies of production, – these circumstances are of a mechanical nature. They are facts of the comprehensive machine process. The conditions favorable to industrial consolidation on these grounds are not created by the business men. They are matters of 'the state of industrial arts,' and are the outcome of the work of those men who are engaged in the industrial employments rather than of those who are occupied with business affairs. The inventors, engineers, experts, or whatever name be applied to the comprehensive class that does the intellectual work involved in the modern machine industry, must prepare the way for the man of pecuniary affairs by making possible and putting in evidence the economies and other advantages that will follow from a prospective consolidation.

But it is not enough that the business man should see a chance to effect economies of production and to heighten the efficiency of industry by a new combination. Conditions favorable to consolidation on these grounds must be visible to him before he can make the decisive business arrangements; but these conditions, taken by themselves, do not move him. The motives of the business man are pecuniary motives, inducements in the way of pecuniary gain to him or to the business enterprise with which he is identified. The end of his endeavors is not simply to effect an industrially advantageous consolidation, but to effect it under such circumstances of ownership as will give him control of large business forces or bring him the largest possible gain. The ulterior end sought is an increase of ownership, not industrial serviceability. His aim is to contrive a consolidation in which he will be at an advantage, and to effect it on the terms most favorable to his own interest.

But it is not commonly evident at the outset what are the most favorable terms that he can get in his dealings with other businessmen whose interests are touched by the proposed consolidation, or who are ambitious to effect some similar consolidation of the same or of competing industrial elements for their own profit. It rarely happens that the interests of the business men whom the prospective consolidation touches all converge to a coalition on the same basis and under the same management. The consequence is negotiation and delay. It commonly also happens that some of the business men affected see their advantage in staving off the coalition until a time more propitious to their own interest, or until those who have the work of consolidation in hand can be brought to compound with them for the withdrawal of whatever obstruction they are able to offer.[11] Such a coalition involves a loss of independent standing, or even a loss of occupation, to many of the business men interested in the deal. If a prospective industrial consolidation is of such scope as to require the concurrence or consent of many business interests, among which no one is very decidedly preponderant in pecuniary strength or in strategic position, a long time will be consumed in the negotiations and strategy necessary to define the terms on which the several business interests will consent to come in and the degree of solidarity and central control to which they will submit.

It is notorious, beyond the need of specific citation, that the great business coalitions and industrial combinations which have characterized the situation of the last few years have commonly been the outcome of a long-drawn struggle, in which the industrial ends, as contrasted with business ends, have not been seriously considered, and in which great shrewdness and tenacity have commonly been shown in the staving off of a settlement for years in the hope of more advantageous terms. The like is true as regards further coalitions, further consolidations of industrial processes which have not been effected, but which are known to be feasible and desirable so far as regards the mechanical circumstances of the case. The difficulties in the way are difficulties of ownership, of business interest, not of mechanical feasibility.

These negotiations and much of the strategy that leads up to a business consolidation are of the nature of derangements of industry, after the

---

[11] Cf., *e.g.*, the accounts of the formation of the United States Steel Corporation or of the Shipbuilding Company.

manner spoken of above. So that business interests and maneuvers commonly delay consolidations, combinations, correlations of the several plants and processes, for some appreciable time after such measures have become patently advisable on industrial grounds. In the meantime the negotiators are working at cross-purposes and endeavoring to put their rivals in as disadvantageous a light as may be, with the result that there is chronic derangement, duplication, and misdirected growth of the industrial equipment while the strategy is going forward, and expensive maladjustment to be overcome when the negotiations are brought to a close.[12]

Serviceability, industrial advisability, is not the decisive point. The decisive point is business expediency and business pressure. In the normal course of business touching this matter of industrial consolidation, therefore, the captain of industry works against, as well as for, a new and more efficient organization. He inhibits as well as furthers the higher organization of industry.[13] Broadly, it may be said that industrial

---

[12] Witness the rate wars and the duplications of inefficient track and terminal equipment among the railways, and the similar duplications in the iron and steel industry. The system of railway terminals in Chicago, e.g., is an illuminated object-lesson of systematic ineptitude.

[13] The splendid reach of this inhibitory work of the captain of industry, as well as of his aggressive work of consolidation, is well shown, for instance, in the history and present position of the railway industry in America. It is and has for a long term of years been obvious that a very comprehensive unification or consolidation, in respect of the mechanical work to be done by the railway system, is eminently desirable and feasible, – consolidation of a scope not only equalling, but far outreaching the coalitions which have lately been effected or attempted. There is no hazard in venturing the assertion that several hundreds of men who are engaged in the mechanical work of railroading, in one capacity and another, are conversant with feasible plans for economizing work and improving the service by more comprehensive and closer correlation of the work; and it is equally obvious that nothing but the diverging interests of the business men concerned hinders these closer and larger feasible correlations from being put into effect. It is easily within the mark to say that the delay which railway consolidation has suffered up to the present, from business exigencies as distinct from the mechanical circumstances of the case, amounts to an average of at least twenty years. Ever since railroading began in this country there has been going on a process of reluctant consolidation, in which the movements of the business men in control have tardily followed up the opportunities for economy and efficient service which the railroad industry has offered. And their latest and boldest achievements along this line, as seen from the stand point of mechanical advisability, have been foregone conclusions since a date so far in the past as to be forgotten, and taken at their best they fail short to-day by not less than some fifty per cent, of their opportunities. Cf. Report of the Industrial Commission, vol. XIX., 'Transportation,' especially pp. 304–48.

Like other competitive business, but more particularly such business as has to do with the interstitial adjustments of the industrial system, the business of railway consolidation

consolidations and the working arrangements made for the more economical utilization of resources and mechanical contrivances are allowed to go into effect only after they are long overdue.

In current economic theory the business man is spoken of under the name of 'entrepreneur' or 'undertaker,' and his function is held to be the coordinating of industrial processes with a view to economics of production and heightened service ability. The soundness of this view need not be questioned. It has a great sentimental value and is useful in many ways. There is also a modicum of truth in it as an account of facts. In common with other men, the business man is moved by ideals of serviceability and an aspiration to make the way of life easier for his fellows. Like other men, he has something of the instinct of workmanship. No doubt such aspirations move the great business man less urgently than many others, who are, on that account, less successful in business affairs. Motives of this kind detract from business efficiency, and an undue yielding to them on the part of business men is to be deprecated as an infirmity. Still, throughout men's dealings with one another and with the interests of the community there runs a sense of equity, fair dealing, and workmanlike integrity; and in an uncertain degree, this bent discountenances gain that is got at an undue cost to others, or without rendering some colorable equivalent. Business men are also, in a measure, guided by the ambition to effect a creditable improvement in the industrial processes which their business traffic touches. These sentimental factors in business exercise something of a constraint, varying greatly from one person to another, but not measurable in its aggregate results. The

---

is of the nature of a game, in which the end sought by the players is their own pecuniary gain and to which the industrial serviceability of the outcome is incidental only. This is recognized by popular opinion and is made much of by popular agitators, who take the view that when once the game between the competing business interests has been played to a finish, in the definitive coalition of the competitors under one management, then the game will go on as a somewhat one-sided conflict between the resulting monopoly and the community at large.

So again, as a further illustration, it is and from the outset has been evident that the iron-ore beds of northern Wisconsin, Michigan, and Minnesota ought, industrially speaking, to have been worked as one collective enterprise. There are also none but business reasons why practically all the ore beds and iron and steel works in the country are not worked as one collective enterprise. It is equally evident that such correlations of work as are permitted by the business coalitions already effected in this field have resulted in a great economy of production, and that the failure to carry these coalitions farther means an annual waste running up into the millions. Both the economies so effected and the waste so incurred are to be set down to the account of the business managers who have gone so far and have failed to go farther. The like is obvious as regards many other branches of industry and groups of industries.

careers of most of the illustrious business men show the presence of some salutary constraint of this kind. Not infrequently an excessive sensitiveness of this hind leads to a withdrawal from business, or from certain forms of business which may appeal to a vivid fancy as peculiarly dishonest or peculiarly detrimental to the community.[14] Such grounds of action, and perhaps others equally genial and equally unbusinesslike, would probably be discovered by a detailed scrutiny of any large business deal. Probably in many cases the business strategist, infected with this human infirmity, reaches an agreement with his rivals and his neighbors in the industrial system without exacting the last concession that a ruthless business strategy might entitle him to. The result is, probably, a speedier conclusion and a smoother working of the large coalitions than would follow from the unmitigated sway of business principles.[15]

But the sentiment which in this way acts in constraint of business traffic proceeds on such grounds of equity and fair dealing as are afforded by current business ethics; it acts within the range of business principles, not in contravention of them; it acts as a conventional restraint upon pecuniary advantage, not in abrogation of it. This code of business ethics consists, after all, of mitigations of the maxim, *Caveat emptor*. It touches primarily the dealings of man with man, and only less directly and less searchingly inculcates temperance and circumspection as regards the ulterior interests of the community at large. Where this moral need of a balance between the services rendered the community and the gain derived from a given business transaction asserts itself at all, the balance

---

[14] Illustrative instances will readily suggest themselves. Many a business man turns by preference to something less dubious than the distilling of whiskey or the sale of deleterious household remedies. They prefer not to use deleterious adulterants, even within the limits of the law, they will rather use wool than shoddy at the same price. The officials of a railway commonly prefer to avoid wrecks and man slaughter, even if there is no pecuniary advantage in choosing the more humane course. More than that, it will be found true that the more prosperous of the craft, especially, take pride and pains to make the service of their roads or the output of their mills as efficient, not simply as the pecuniary advantage of the concern demands, but as the best pecuniary results will admit. Instances are perhaps not frequent, but they are also not altogether exceptional, where a prosperous captain of industry will go out of his way to heighten the serviceability of his industry even to a degree that is of doubtful pecuniary expediency for himself. Such aberrations are, of course, not large; and if they are persisted in to any very appreciable extent the result is, of course, disastrous to the enterprise. The enterprise in such a case falls out of the category of business management and falls under the imputation of philanthropy.

[15] The captains of the first class necessarily are relatively exempt from these unbusinesslike scruples.

is commonly sought to be maintained in some sort of pecuniary terms; but pecuniary terms afford only a very inadequate measure of serviceability to the community.

Great and many are the items of service to be set down to the business man's account in connection with the organization of the industrial system, but when all is said, it is still to be kept in mind that his work in the correlation of industrial processes is chiefly of a permissive kind. His furtherance of industry is at the second remove, and is chiefly of a negative character. In his capacity as business man he does not go creatively into the work of perfecting mechanical processes and turning the means at hand to new or larger uses. That is the work of the men who have in hand the devising and oversight of mechanical processes. The men in industry must first create the mechanical possibility of such new and more efficient methods and correlations, before the business man sees the chance, makes the necessary business arrangements, and gives general directions that the contemplated industrial advance shall go into effect. The period between the time of earliest practicability and the effectual completion of a given consolidation in industry marks the interval by which the business man retards the advance of industry. Against this are to be offset the cases, comparatively slight and infrequent, where the business men in control push the advance of industry into new fields and prompt the men concerned with the mechanics of the case to experiment and exploration in new fields of mechanical process.

When the recital is made, therefore, of how the large consolidations take place at the initiative of the business men who are in control, it should be added that the fact of their being in control precludes industrial correlations from taking place except by their advice and consent. The industrial system is organized on business principles and for pecuniary ends. The business man is at the centre; he holds the discretion and he exercises it freely, and his choice falls out now on one side, now on the other. The retardation as well as the advance is to be set down to his account.

As regards the economies in cost of production effected by these consolidations, there is a further characteristic feature to be noted, a feature of some significance for any theory of modern business. In great measure, the saving effected is a saving of the costs of business management and of the competitive costs of marketing products and services, rather than a saving in the prime costs of production. The heightened facility and efficiency of the new and larger business combinations primarily affect the expenses of office work and sales, and it is in great part only indirectly that this curtailment and consolidation of business management has an effect upon the methods and aims of industry proper. It touches the pecuniary processes immediately, and the mechanical processes indirectly and in an uncertain degree. It is of the nature of a partial neutralization of the wastes due to the presence of pecuniary motives and business management, for the business management involves waste wherever a greater number of men or transactions are involved than are necessary to the effective direction of the mechanical processes employed. The amount of 'business' that has to be transacted per unit of product is much greater where the various related industrial processes are managed in severalty than where several of them are brought under one business management. A pecuniary discretion has to be exercised at every point of contact or transition, where the process or its product touches or passes the boundary between different spheres of ownership. Business transactions have to do with ownership and changes of ownership. The greater the parcelment in point of ownership, the greater the amount of business work that has to be done in connection with a given output of goods or services, and the slower, less facile, and less accurate, on the whole, is the work. This applies both to the work of bargain and contract, wherein pecuniary initiative and discretion are chiefly exercised, and to the routine work of accounting, and of gathering and applying information and misinformation.

The standardization of industrial processes products, services, and consumers, spoken of in an earlier chapter, very materially facilitates the business man's work in reorganizing business enterprises on a larger scale; particularly does this standardization serve his ends by permitting a uniform routine in accounting, invoices, contracts, etc., and so admitting a large central accounting system, with homogeneous ramifications, such as will give a competent conspectus of the pecuniary situation of the enterprise at any given time.

The great, at the present stage of development perhaps the greatest, opportunity for saving by consolidation, in the common run of cases, is afforded by the ubiquitous and in a sense excessive presence of business enterprise in the economic system. It is in doing away with unnecessary business transactions and industrially futile maneuvering on the part of independent firms that the promoter of combinations finds his most telling opportunity. So that it is scarcely an overstatement to say that probably the largest, assuredly the securest and most unquestionable, service rendered by the great modern captains of industry is this curtailment of the business to be done, this sweeping retirement of business men as a class from the service and the definitive cancelment of opportunities for private enterprise.

So long as related industrial units are under different business manage-
ments, they are, by the nature of the case, at cross-purposes, and business
consolidation remedies this untoward feature of the industrial system by
eliminating the pecuniary element from the interstices of the system as
far as may be. The interstitial adjustments of the industrial system at large
are in this way withdrawn from the discretion of rival business men, and
the work of pecuniary management previously involved is in large part
dispensed with the result that there is a saving of war and an avoidance
of that systematic mutual hindrance that characterizes the competitive
manage merit of industry. To the community at large the work of
pecuniary management, it appears, is less serviceable the more there is of
it. The heroic role of the captain of industry is that a deliverer from an
excess of business management. It is a casting out of business men by
the chief of business men.[16]

The theory of business enterprise sketched above applies to such
business as is occupied with the interstitial adjustments of the system of
industries. This work of keeping and of disturbing the interstitial adjustments does not look immediately to the output of goods as its source of
gain, but to the alterations of values involved in disturbances of the
balance, and to the achievement of a more favorable business situation
for some of the enterprises engaged. This work lies in the middle,
between commercial enterprise proper, on the one hand, and industrial
enterprise in the stricter sense, on the other hand. It is directed to the
acquisition of gain through taking advantage of those conjunctures of
business that arise out of the concatenation of processes in the industrial
system.

In a similar manner commercial business may be said to be occupied
with conjunctures that arise out of the circumstances of the industrial
system at large, but not originating in the mechanical exigencies of the
industrial processes. The conjunctures of commercial business proper are
in the main fortuitous, in so far that they are commonly not initiated by
the business men engaged in these commercial pursuits. Commercial
business, simply as such, does not aim to guide the course of industry.

On the other hand, the large business enterprise spoken of above
initiates changes in industrial organization and seeks its gain in large part
through such alterations of value levels as take place on its own initiative.

---

[16] See Report of the Industrial Commission, vol. 1., Testimony of J.W. Gates, pp.
1020–89; S. Dodd, pp. 1049–50; N. B. Rogers, p. 1068; vol. XIII., C. M. Schwab, pp.
461, 450; H.B. Butler, p. 400; L.R. Hopkins, pp. 346, 347; A. S. White, pp. 254, 256.

These alterations of the value levels, of course, have their effect upon the output of goods and upon the material welfare of the community; but the effect which they have in this way is only incidental to the quest of profits.

But apart from this remoter and larger guidance of the course of industry, the business men also, and more persistently and pervasively, exercise a guidance over the course of industry in detail.

The production of goods and services is carried on for gain, and the output of goods is controlled by business men with a view to gain. Commonly, in ordinary routine business, the gains come from this output of goods and services. By the sale of the output the business man in industry 'realizes' his gains. To 'realize' means to convert salable goods into money values. The sale is the last step in the process and the end of the business man's endeavor.[17] When he has disposed of the output, and so has converted his holdings of consumable articles into money values, his gains are as nearly secure and definitive as the circumstances of modern life admit, it is in terms of price that he keeps his accounts, and in the same terms he computes his output of products. The vital point of production with him is the vendibility of the output, its convertibility into money values, not its serviceability for the needs of mankind. A modicum of serviceability, for some purpose or other, the output must have if it is to be salable. But it does not follow that the highest serviceability gives the largest gains to the business man in terms of money, nor does it follow that the output need in all cases have other than a factitious serviceability. There is, on the one hand, such a possibility as overstocking the market with any given line of goods, to the detriment of the business man concerned, but not necessarily to the immediate disadvantage of the body of consumers. And there are, on the other hand, certain lines of industry, such as many advertising enterprises, the output of which may be highly effective for its purpose but of quite equivocal use to the community. Many well-known and prosperous enterprises which advertise and sell patent medicines and other proprietary articles might be cited in proof.

In the older days, when handicraft was the rule of the industrial system, the personal contact between the producer and his customer was somewhat close and lasting. Under these circumstances the factor of personal esteem and disesteem had a considerable play in controlling the

---

[17] Cf. Marx, *Kapital*, bk. I. pt. II.

purveyors of goods and services. This factor of personal contact counted in two divergent ways: (1) producers were careful of their reputation for workmanship, even apart from the gains which such a reputation might bring; and (2) a degree of irritation and ill-will would arise in many cases, leading to petty trade quarrels and discriminations on other grounds than the gains to be got, at the same time that the detail character of dealings between producer and consumer admitted a degree of petty knavery and huckstering that is no longer practicable in the current large-scale business dealings. Of these two divergent effects resulting from close personal relations between producer and consumer, the former seems on the whole to have been of preponderant consequence. Under the system of handicraft and neighborhood industry, the adage that 'Honesty is the best policy' seems on the whole to have been accepted and to have been true. This adage has come down from the days before the machine regime and before modern business enterprise.

Under modern circumstances, where industry is carried on on a large scale, the discretionary head of an industrial enterprise is commonly removed from all personal contact with the body of customers for whom the industrial process under his control purveys goods or services. The mitigating effect which personal contact may have in dealings between man and man is therefore in great measure eliminated. The whole takes on something of an impersonal character. One can with an easier conscience and with less of a sense of meanness take advantage of the necessities of people whom one knows of only as an indiscriminate aggregate of consumers. Particularly is this true when, as frequently happens in the modern situation, this body of consumers belongs in the main to another, inferior class, so that personal contact and cognizance of them is not only not contemplated, but is in a sense impossible. Equity, in excess of the formal modicum specified by law, does not so readily assert its claims where the relations between the parties are remote and impersonal as where one is dealing with one's necessitous neighbors who live on the same social plane. Under these circumstances the adage cited above loses much of its axiomatic force. Business management has a chance to proceed on a temperate and sagacious calculation of profit and loss, untroubled by sentimental considerations of human kindness or irritation or of honesty.

The broad principle which guides producers and merchants, large and small, in fixing the prices at which they offer their wares and services is what is known in the language of the railroads as 'charging what the traffic will bear.'[18] Where a given enterprise has a strict monopoly of the supply of a given article or of a given class of services this principle applies in the unqualified form in which it has been understood among those who discuss railway charges. But where the monopoly is less strict, where there are competitors, there the competition that has to be met is one of the factors to be taken account of in determining what the traffic will bear; competition may even become the most serious factor in the case if the enterprise in question has little or none of the character of a monopoly. But it is very doubtful if there are any successful business ventures within the range of the modern industries from which the monopoly element is wholly absent.[19] They are, at any rate, few and not of great magnitude. And the endeavor of all such enterprises that look to a permanent continuance of their business is to establish as much of a monopoly as may be. Such a monopoly position may be a legally established one, or one due to location or the control of natural resources, or it may be a monopoly of a less definite character resting on custom and prestige (good-will). This latter class of monopolies are not commonly classed as such; although in character and degree the advantage which they give is very much the same as that due to a differential advantage in location or in the command of resources. The end sought by the systematic advertising of the larger business concerns is such a monopoly of custom and prestige. This form of monopoly is sometimes of great value, and is frequently sold under the name of good-will, trade marks, brands, etc. Instances are known where such monopolies of custom, prestige, prejudice, have been sold at prices running up into the millions.[20]

The great end of consistent advertising is to establish such differential monopolies resting on popular conviction. And the advertiser is successful in this endeavor to establish a profitable popular conviction, somewhat in proportion as he correctly apprehends the manner in which

[18] The economic principle of 'charging what the traffic will bear' is discussed with great care and elaboration by R. T. Ely, Monopolies and Trusts, ch. III., 'The Law of Monopoly Price.' Cf., for illustration of the practical working of this principle, testimony of C. M. Schwab, Report of the Industrial Commission, vol. XIII. pp. 453–455.

[19] 'Monopoly' is here used in that looser sense which it has colloquially, not in the strict sense of an exclusive control of the supply, as employed, e.g., by Mr. Ely in the volume cited above. This usage is the more excusable since Mr. Ely finds that a 'monopoly' in the strict sense of the definition practically does not occur in fact. Cf. Jenks, The Trust Problem, ch. IV.

[20] *E.g.* the prestige value of Ivory Soap.

a popular conviction on any given topic is built up.[21] The cost, as well as the pecuniary value and the magnitude, of this organized fabrication of popular convictions is indicated by such statements as that the proprietors of a certain well-known household remedy, reputed among medical authorities to be of entirely dubious value, have for a series of years found their profits in spending several million dollars annually in advertisements. This case is by no means unique.

[21] Cf. W. D. Scott, The Theory of Advertising; J. L. Mahin, The Commercial Value of Advertising, pp. 4–6, 12–13, 15; F. Fogg-Meade, 'The Place of Advertising In Modern Business,' Journal of Political Economy, March 1901; Sombart, vol. II. ch. XL–XXI.; G. Tarde, Psychologie Economique, vol. I. pp. 187–190. The writing and designing of advertisements (letterpress, display, and illustrations) has grown into a distinct calling; so that the work of a skilled writer of advertisements compares not unfavorably, in point of lucrativeness, with that of the avowed writers of popular fiction.

The psychological principles of advertising may be formulated somewhat as follows: A declaration of fact, made in the form and with the incidents of taste and expression to which a person is accustomed, will be accepted as authentic and will be acted upon if occasion arises, in so far as it does not conflict with opinions already accepted. The acceptance of an opinion seems to be almost entirely a passive matter. The presumption remains in favor of an opinion that has once been accepted, and an appreciable burden of proof falling on the negative. A competent formulation of opinion on a given point is the chief factor in gaining adherents to that opinion, and a reiteration of the statement is the chief factor in carrying conviction. The truth of such a formulation is a matter of secondary consequence, but a wide and patent departure from known fact generally weakens its persuasive effect. The aim of the advertiser is to arrest attention and then present his statement in such a manner that it is easily assimilated into the habits of thought of the person whose conviction is to be influenced. When this is effectually done a reversal of the conviction so established is a matter of considerable difficulty. The tenacity of a view once accepted in this way is evidenced, for instance, by the endless number and variety of testimonials to the merits of well advertised but notoriously worthless household remedies and the like.

So acute an observer as Mr. Sombart is still able to hold the opinion that 'auf Schwindel ist dauernd noch nie ein Unternehmen begründet worden' (Kapftalismus, vol. II. p. 378). Mr. Sombart has not made acquaintance with the adventures of Elijah the Restorer, nor is he conversant with American patent-medicine enterprise. With Mr. Sombart's view may be contrasted that of Mr. L. F. Ward, an observer of equally large outlook and acumen: –

'The law of mind as it operates in society as an aid to competition and in the interest of the individual is essentially immoral. It rests primarily on the principle of deception. It is an extension to other human beings of the method applied to the animal world by which the latter was subjected to man. This method was that of the ambush and the snare. Its ruling principle was cunning. Its object was to deceive, circumvent, ensnare, and capture. Low animal cunning was succeeded by more refined kinds of cunning. The more important of these go by the names of business shrewdness, strategy, and diplomacy, none of which differ from ordinary cunning in any thing but the degree of adroitness by which the victim is outwitted. In this way social life is completely honeycombed with deception.' – The Psychologic Basis of Social Economics, Ann. of Am. Acad., vol. III. pp. 83–4 [475–78].

It has been said,[22] no doubt in good faith and certainly with some reason, that advertising as currently carried on gives the body of consumers valuable information and guidance as to the ways and means whereby their wants can be satisfied and their purchasing power can be best utilized. To the extent to which this holds true, advertising is a service to the community. But there is a large reservation to be made on this head. Advertising is competitive; the greater part of it aims to divert purchases, etc., from one channel to another channel of the same general class.[23] And to the extent to which the efforts of advertising in all its branches are spent on this competitive disturbance of trade, they are, on the whole, of slight if any immediate service to the community. Such advertising, however, is indispensable to most branches of modern industry; but the necessity of most of the advertising is not due to its serving the needs of the community nor to any aggregate advantage accruing to the concerns which advertise, but to the fact that a business concern which falls short in advertising fails to get its share of trade. Each concern must advertise, chiefly because the others do. The aggregate expenditure that could advantageously be put into advertising in the absence of competition would undoubtedly be but an inconsiderable fraction of what is actually incurred, and necessarily incurred under existing circumstances.[24]

Not all advertising is wholly competitive, or at least it is not always obviously so. In proportion as an enterprise has secured a monopoly position, its advertising loses the air of competitive selling and takes on the character of information designed to increase the use of its output independently. But such an increase implies a redistribution of consumption on the part of the customers.[25] So that the element of competitive selling is after all not absent in these cases, but takes the form of competition between different classes of wares instead of competitive selling of different brands of the same class of wares.

[22] Fogg-Meade, 'Place of Advertising in Modern Business,' pp. 218, 224–36.

[23] Advertising and other like expedients for the sale of goods aim at changes in the 'substitution values' of the goods in question, not at an enhancement of the aggregate utilities of the available output of goods.

[24] Cf. Jenks, The Trust Problem, pp. 21–8; Report of the Industrial Commission, vol. XIX. pp. 611–2.

[25] Cf. Bohn-Bawerk, Positive Theory of Capital, bk. III, ch. V., VII-IX, on the value of alternative and complementary goods.

Attention is here called to this matter of advertising and the necessity of it in modern competitive business for the light which it throws on 'cost of production' in the modern system, where the process of production is under the control of business men and is carried on for business ends. Competitive advertising is an unavoidable item in the aggregate costs of industry. It does not add to the serviceability of the output, except it be incidentally and unintentionally. What it aims at is the sale of the output, and it is for this purpose that it is useful. It gives vendibility, which is useful to the seller, but has no utility to the last buyer. Its ubiquitous presence in the costs of any business enterprise that has to do with the production of goods for the market enforces the statement that the 'cost of production' of commodities under the modern business system is cost incurred with a view to vendibility, not with a view to serviceability of the goods for human use.

There is, of course, much else that goes into the cost of competitive selling, besides the expenses of advertising, although advertising may be the largest and most unequivocal item to be set down to that account. A great part of the work done by merchants and their staff of employees, both wholesale and retail, as well as by sales-agents not exclusively connected with any one mercantile house, belongs under the same head. Just how large a share of the costs of the distribution of goods fairly belongs under the rubric of competitive selling can of course not be made out. It is largest, on the whole, in the case of consumable goods marketed in finished form for the consumer, but there is more or less of it throughout. The goods turned out on a large scale by the modern industrial processes, on the whole, carry a larger portion of such competitive costs than the goods still produced by the old-fashioned detail methods of handicraft and household industry; although this distinction does not hold hard and fast some extreme cases the cost of competitive selling may amount to more than ninety per cent of the total cost of the goods when they reach the consumer. In other lines of business, occupied with the production of staple goods, constituent of cost may perhaps fall below ten per cent. of the total. Where the average, for the price of finished goods delivered to the consumers, may lie would be a hazardous guess.[26]

---

[26] Where competitive selling makes up a large proportion of the aggregate final cost of the marketed product, this fact is likely to itself in an exceptionally large proportion of goodwill in the capitalization of the concerns engaged in the given line of business; as, *e.g.* the American Chicle Company.

It is evident that the gains which accrue this business of competitive selling and buying bear determinable relation to the services which the in question may render the community. If a comparison may be hazarded between two unknown indeterminate quantities, it may perhaps be that the gains from competitive selling bear something more of a stable relation to the service rendered than do the gains derived from speculative transactions or from the financiering operations of the great captains of industry. It seems at least safe to say that the converse will not hold true. Gains and services seem more widely out of touch in the case of the large-scale financiering work. Not that the work of the large business men in reorganizing and consolidating the industrial process is of slight consequence; but as a general proposition, the amount of the business man's gains from any given transaction of this latter class bear no traceable relation to any benefit which the community may derive from the transaction.[27]

As to the wages paid to the men engaged in the routine of competitive selling, as salesmen, buyers, accountants, and the like, much the same holds true of them as of the income of the business men who carry on the business on their own initiative. Their employers pay the wages of these persons, not because their work is productive of benefit to the community, but because it brings a gain to the employers. The point to which the work is directed is profitable sales, and the wages are in some proportion to the efficiency of this work as counted in terms of heightened vendibility.

The like holds true for the work and pay of the force of workmen engaged in the industrial processes under business management. It holds, in a measure, of all modern industry that produces for the market, but it holds true, in an eminent degree, of those lines of industry that are more fully under the guidance of modern business methods. These are most closely in touch with the market and, are most consistently guided by considerations of vendibility. They are also, on the whole, more commonly carried on by hired labor, and the wages paid are competitively adjusted on grounds of the vendibility of the product. The brute serviceability of the output of these industries may be a large factor in its vendibility, perhaps the largest factor; but the fact remains that the end

---

[27] Cf. Ed. Hahn, Die Wirtschaft der Welt am Ausgang des XIX. Jahrhunderts. – 'In unserem heutigen Wirtschaftsleben ist der Gewinn durch den Zuwachs der Produktion, mit dem fruhere Jahrhunderte rechneten, ganz nod gar zuruckgedrangt, er ist unwesentlich geworden.'

sought by the business men in control is a profitable sale, and the wages are paid as a means to that end, not to the end that the way of life may be smoother for the ultimate consumer of the goods produced.[28]

The outcome of this recital, then, is that wherever and in so far as business ends and methods dominate modern industry the relation between the usefulness of the work (for other purposes than pecuniary gain) and the remuneration of it is remote and uncertain to such a degree that no attempt at formulating such a relation is worth while. This is eminently and obviously true of the work and gains of business men, in whatever lines of business they are engaged. This follows as a necessary consequence of the nature of business management.

Work that is, on the whole, useless or detrimental to the community at large may be as gainful to the business man and to the workmen whom he employs as work that contributes substantially to the aggregate livelihood. This seems to be peculiarly true of the bolder flights of business enterprise. In so far as its results are not detrimental to human life at large, such unproductive work directed to securing an income may seem to be an idle matter in which the rest of the community has no substantial interests. Such is not the case. In so far as the gains of these unproductive occupations are of a substantial character, they come out of the aggregate product of the other occupations in which the various classes of the community engage. The aggregate profits of the business, whatever its character, are drawn from the aggregate output of goods and services; and whatever goes to the maintenance of the profits of those who contribute nothing substantial to the output is, of course, deducted from the income of the others, whose work tells substantially.

There are, therefore, limits to the growth of the industrially parasitic lines of business just spoken of. A disproportionate growth of parasitic industries, such as most advertising and much of the other efforts that go into competitive selling, as well as warlike expenditure and other industries directed to turning out goods for conspicuously wasteful

[28] It might, therefore, be feasible to set up a theory to the effect that wages are competitively proportioned to the vendibility of the product; but there is no cogent ground for saying that the wages in any department of industry, under a business regime, are proportioned to the utility which the output has to any one else than the employer who sells it. When it is further taken into account that the vendibility of the product in very many lines of production depends chiefly on the wastefulness of the goods (cf. Theory of the Leisure Class, ch. V.), the divergence between the usefulness of the work and the wages paid for it seems wide enough to throw the whole question of an equivalence between work and pay out of theoretical consideration. Cf., however, Clark, The Distribution of Wealth, especially ch. VII. and XXII.

consumption, would lower the effective vitality of the community to such a degree as to jeopardize its chances of advance or even its life. The limits which the circumstances of life impose in this respect are of a selective character, in the last resort. A persistent excess of parasitic and wasteful efforts over productive industry must bring on a decline. But owing to the very high productive efficiency of the modern mechanical industry, the margin available for wasteful occupations and wasteful expenditures is very great. The requirements of the aggregate livelihood are so far short of the possible output of gods by modern methods as to leave a very wide margin for waste and parasitic income. So that instances of such a decline, due to industrial exhaustion, drawn from the history of any earlier phase of economic life, carry no well-defined lesson as to what a modern industrial community may allow itself in this respect.

While it is in the nature of things unavoidable that the management of industry by modern business methods should involve a large misdirection of effort and a very large waste of goods and services, it is also true that the aims and ideals to which this manner of economic life gives effect act forcibly to offset all this incidental futility. These pecuniary aims and ideals have a very great effect, for instance, in making men work hard and unremittingly, so that on this ground alone the business system probably compensates for any wastes involved in its working. There seems, therefore, to be no tenable ground for thinking that the working of the modern business system involves a curtailment of the community's livelihood. It makes up for its wastefulness by the added strain which it throws upon those engaged in the productive work.

# Introductory[1]

## Samuel E. Sparling

### GENERAL CONSIDERATIONS

A survey of our modern life impresses upon us the value and importance of organization in business, politics, and society. The nature and efficiency of this organization may be taken as a fair index to the progress made in these fields. The business man, as well as the student of economics, must assign to organization a leading position among those forces which have made possible our present industrial era. This is not alone true of the present, but likewise during other well-known periods of industrial activity business organization attained a high degree of development and exerted a far-reaching influence.

In discussing the problems of organization we shall keep before us the point of view of the organizer and manager of business undertakings.

Our primary aim shall be to outline our business institutions, as well as to point out the dominant business tendencies of today. Science is based upon accumulated experience. Classification is the result of a comparison of differences and similarities. If we cannot do this for business, it must be because chaos reigns there; but the most casual observation of business life shows us that this is not true. We may describe and classify the facts of business in such a way as to indicate their underlying tendencies and principles. In the conduct of business these principles are consciously or unconsciously utilized. Every business institution is related definitely with those which immediately preceded it, and in the same way business practice is related to the practice which preceded it. Business is an evolution, like government.

The purpose and significance of organization and management in business may be shown by a brief characterization of each. Organization may be defined as the act of bringing together related or interdependent parts into one organic whole. If we apply this general definition to

[1] [Chapters 1–2 of *Introduction to Business Organization*, New York: Macmillan, 1906, pp. 3–29.]

100

business, it would read as follows: Business organization is the bringing together of the related or interdependent parts of business into one organic whole. We observe that organization is the process of arranging, systematizing, and combining those elements which are related naturally and organically in such a manner as to make them a unit. In this way the constituent elements of insurance, transportation, manufacturing, and distribution are organized into definite business undertakings.

Such a relationship we call a business, a firm, or a house. For instance, the organization of a factory involves the selection of an administrative and labor force. Departments are created, and over each is placed a superintendent or manager. In a similar way the president of a railway combines those forces which relate to railway transportation. And thus throughout business there is going forward the selection and combination of those elements which are to constitute the organization; and the wisdom and skill exhibited in the selection and adjustment of those elements which naturally combine to form the organization are the recognized indications of ability in business.

The idea of management is readily expressed by the current phrase- business policy. Management properly begins after the organization has been perfected, and is therefore concerned with the development of a business policy. It is the actual conduct of business affairs. The manager has at his disposal various departments, and it is by directing these that the policy of the firm is developed. If business principles have any value, they should be uniform for similar conditions, for business administration consists in the application of well-recognized experience and practice to a specific business problem. The efficiency of management is ultimately measured by the profits of the business.

With this brief characterization of organization and management, we may now turn to a consideration of their value in business. Recent years have witnessed the rise of a class of business men whose talents have been devoted to the organization and management of business enterprises. They are called the captains of industry, because upon them falls the responsibility of promoting and organizing industrial undertakings. This organizing talent has created a series of intricate business institutions, and has won for itself a position of influence and power.

The manager of a business must secure the greatest efficiency and economy. In order to attain these, he must be fully acquainted with the elements that combine to form his organization and to shape his business policy. He must be familiar with the labor problem, the work of the various departments, the systems of cost-keeping, the legal aspects of trade

– in short, he must be familiar with the technique of his business and its relation to economic conditions.

There is a general impression that business is largely of a routine nature. While it is doubtless true that the work of the holders of sub ordinate positions in the larger organizations is routine, yet we should not fail to appreciate the fact that the higher positions give opportunities for creative work. It should be the aim of the manager to organize his business so that it will 'run itself.' When a business is so organized, the manager is then able to devote his time to larger affairs, leaving the details to be worked out by competent department managers. In other words, a properly organized business demands two kinds of talent: one class of workers must perform the clerical work, while a more select group is devising and initiating new methods and policies. In this way the application of correct principles of organization is utilized, and a high degree of efficiency secured.

This is amply illustrated by a study of the methods of well-known business houses. Efficient organization is vital to their continued prosperity. On the other hand it is well known that imperfect organization has often threatened their existence, and the failure to adjust the organization to changed business conditions has resulted disastrously in many instances.

It is generally asserted that the superiority of American firms over British is due to the more efficient organization of the former. Again, it is urged that the success of German houses in competing with English, and even American, firms is due, not only to the attention which they give to the technical phases of business, such as engineering, chemistry, etc., but also to a more thorough study of business organization and methods. Everywhere progressive firms are ready to utilize new methods, and to change their organization when it can be shown that such changes will yield better results. The more complex business conditions become, the higher the degree of skill required in directing the organization and management. A great business has been compared to a military organization, where all the parts are carefully grouped and officered. Each division is assigned to a particular work and discipline is carefully maintained.

We are accustomed to speak of business in its public and private aspects. We speak of the work of government as the administration of public business, while, on the other hand, we refer to the management of a firm as the administration of private business. While these two are quite distinct, in their purposes, they do, however, present many points of similarity in organization and methods. The object of public administration is to promote social well-being. It is not performing its work for financial profit, but rather to improve social conditions. In order to accomplish this end, taxes must be levied and expenditures made for public improvements, education, police, and other purposes. The successful prosecution of this work requires correct business methods.

The object of private administration, on the other hand, is, primarily, to secure present and prospective financial profit, and the success of the business is determined ultimately by this standard. While many private business undertakings are quasi-public in their character, such as lighting plants, water-works, and street railways, still, so long as they are privately managed, financial gain will be the controlling motive. Obviously, in many fields of administrative activity it is difficult to draw the line sharply between private and public business. In many instances the line can only be drawn vaguely, and then only by keeping before us the thought that public business has in view primarily social advantage, while private business has as its primary purpose financial advantage.

Business undertakings grow out of general economic conditions. In a primitive society we find only a few traces of definite business under takings. Each person provides for himself in his own way. The producer is virtually the consumer, and where the exchange of commodities takes place it is in the form of the simplest barter. In the more advanced stage of economic society wants become more varied – a fact which gradually leads to a specialization of effort and to the appearance of definite business institutions. The producer and consumer are more widely separated; hence, to accomplish the exchange of commodities, business organization becomes necessary. By way of illustration the grain business may be cited. The concentration of population in certain parts of the world, far removed from the grain surplus producing areas, has necessitated the development of systems of transportation, the establishment of mills, the organization of elevator companies and commission firms, in order to move the surplus grain and flour to the distant consumer. In the same manner the cotton, tobacco, or coal business is developed to bring these commodities from the producer to the consumer.

During periods of great industrial activity we find that the organization of business becomes more complicated. Before the development of the Roman law, we find few traces of the characteristics of business organization. We know something of the wealth and power of the merchant princes of the ancient cities, but we know little of the business methods they employed.

The Roman legal system gives us some idea of the nature of the business institutions of that day. It developed some of the essential features of partnership. But the business of the Roman was largely of a local character. With the German invasion the Roman commercial organization was virtually destroyed and the machinery of business swept away. In the eleventh century, however, commerce began to revive, and gradually manufacturing industries grew up in the cities, and mercantile institutions were established. Fairs were held in France and Germany and, in fact, throughout all Europe. These markets were the meeting-places of merchants, who often came great distances to attend them. The merchant princes of north Europe sent their ships to distant ports, and trade caravans crossed the country from market to market. By the fifteenth century the business structure became more complex and the area of commerce was extended.

The cities were the centers of manufacture and trade, and gradually grew in wealth and power. As a result of this widespread economic activity a type of industrial organization was developed which was virtually universal for the period. Producers and merchants organized themselves into groups or gilds for the manufacture and sale of particular wares. These gilds dominated the commercial life of that time. They framed the rules and regulations governing manufacturing and marketing. Under the gild system commerce greatly prospered, and the names of the merchant princes of that day are almost as familiar as those of its kings and rulers.

The age of discovery opened up new business possibilities and extended the commerce of Europe, thus calling for a readjustment of the commercial organization. Larger capital was required, and new investments were made in distant business ventures. All these involved greater risks, and, in order to minimize them, better legal protection became necessary. The need of some more elastic organization was fully recognized. New forms of investment required the capitalist to put his money into ventures where it was impossible for him to give the business his personal attention, and he was compelled to rely upon the honesty and business judgment of his managers. The partnership rendered his liabilities great, and any mismanagement might sweep away his private fortune. In order to limit the risks of investment where it was impossible for the investor to give to the business his personal attention, the corporation was gradually developed.

The corporation at first took the form of a joint-stock company, and was employed mainly to carry on business ventures in newly discovered countries. While the Romans had suggested the corporation, the commercial instinct of the Anglo-Saxon gave it the position of usefulness in commerce which it now holds. The discovery of new lands which fired the commercial spirit of Europe led to the organization of the great trade companies of England and Holland. They were organized essentially as corporations, and are still familiar figures in the trade and commerce of today. The East India Company and Hudson Bay Company go back for more than two centuries for their beginnings. In 1692 at least three of these companies existed in England, and similar corporations still exist. They were not only regarded as corporations for private business purposes, but were also employed for the administration of public affairs within the territory granted to them by the Government.

At the end of the seventeenth century the advantages of a corporation for business purposes were fully realized, and charters for the conduct of various kinds of business ventures were frequently sought. In 1720 about two hundred corporations existed in England alone. Blackstone in 1776 cited banking, insurance, public improvement, and municipal water-supplies as the legitimate fields of corporate activity. At the end of the eighteenth century this field was greatly extended, and as a result corporation law was more highly developed.

In the early part of the nineteenth century the full significance of corporate activity comes upon us with the rapid growth of industrialism which followed the utilization of coal and iron, the invention of the steam engine, and the development of electric power. We find that the older business methods and types of organization, such as the individual and partnership, were wholly unable to cope with the new business problems, and consequently were rapidly displaced by the corporation in all lines of business activity which involved great risks of investment and management. Thus, starting with the individual merchant, business activity has evolved the partnership and corporation to meet the increasing complexity of industrial processes.

The relation which business organization sustains to general economic society may be further illustrated by classifying the various business units in accordance with the accepted classification of economic science. Business organizations may be variously classified, but, by following the suggestion of the economist, we may divide them into the following divisions: 1, extractive; 2, manufacturing; 3, commercial; 4, transportation. The three classes most generally recognized are the extractive, manufacturing, and commercial or distributive activities. While these three groups correspond to the broad divisions of economic science, specialization within each field necessarily implies the existence of many separate business units which serve as connecting links.

An examination of the extractive business activities reveals a field divided into innumerable separate simple organizations. An extractive business is one in which raw materials of commerce are produced for the purposes of consumption or manufacture. The extractive business is confined to production. Its most important phases are agriculture, mining, and forestry. Agriculture relates to the cultivation of the soil. In its general aspect it comprises such special kinds of farming as wheat, fruit, cotton, tobacco, dairy, poultry, etc. These constitute the most important divisions of agriculture, and are indeed among the most important of our business life. The second division of the extractive field is mining. The function of mining is to bring to the surface the mineral deposits in order to utilize them in the arts and in commerce. The well-known mining operations are coal, copper, gold, silver, tin, zinc, and lead. The third division of the extractive group is forestry. In its broad sense its function is to make available the forest products, and upon it are built such manufacturing activities as lumbering, rubber, paper, and furniture.

An analysis of these various special under takings shows that each has peculiar limitations. They are essentially local, and are controlled in a particular way by soil and climate. If we take tobacco as an illustration, we find that its commercial value depends intimately upon soil and climate. Mining is peculiarly local. It will also be observed that these industries are subdivided into innumerable small undertakings. For in stance, general farming is carried on as innumerable separate enterprises. The difficulty of operating over a large territory compels this extreme subdivision. It will also he observed further that many of these activities are governed by the seasons of the year. In farming and lumbering we find intense activity in certain seasons, while in other periods almost none. They contrast sharply with the factory system, which goes on with uniform activity throughout the whole year. Again, viewed as separate business organizations, this type is comparatively simple in structure, but on the whole these enterprises represent in the aggregate great capital-ization, organized and conducted as separate undertakings.

The second division of our general classification includes manufac-turing. Manufacturing adds new value to a commodity by changing its form, and this new value is added mainly through the additions of labor, capital, and cost of management. A manufacturing plant is therefore an organization both technical and administrative, whose function it is to give to a product new value by changing its form. Manufacturing ends with the completion of the factory processes, and theoretically it has nothing to do with the purchase of the raw materials for the factory or with the distribution of the finished output. Of course, factory manage-ments do buy their raw materials, and distribute their finished products, but in so far as they take up this work they engage in commercial activity in addition to their manufacturing business. It will be found that the line between the factory and the commercial phase of manufacturing is not so sharply drawn in practice. Among the more important lines of manufacturing are farm implements, machinery, steel, hardware, dry-goods, refineries, packing-houses, tanneries, furniture, and chemicals. Manufacturing is characterized by great specialization. Furthermore, the factory operates throughout the year without any necessary interruptions, unless it is for business reasons. Scarcely any other business is so little influenced by nature. Consequently the capital invested may be constantly employed, while in many other business lines in certain seasons investments are relatively unproductive. However, in some lines of manufacturing the demand is dependent upon the seasons of the year, and this compels often the storing of large quantities for future distribution.

There remains a third class of business undertakings which is generally designated as commercial or distributive. It includes a wide and varied activity. For convenience, we may divide these activities into two general groups, marketing proper, and those undertakings which facilitate exchange, such as banking and credit institutions. By marketing, we refer to those commercial processes which are concerned with the distribution of the raw materials of production and the finished output of the factory. These business interests are engaged in distributing the various commodities among the consuming classes. Their function is to give additional value to these commodities through exchange. The particular function of distribution is to organize the market, and to establish a meeting-place for the seller and the consumer. In the field of distribution we find a vast variety of undertakings. These are based mainly upon agriculture, mining, and manufacturing. Among the more important raw materials to be distributed are cereals, cotton, produce, live stock, iron, coal, and petroleum. The distribution of the output of the factory includes dry-goods, hardware, machinery, woolen and cotton cloth, boots and shoes, and a great variety of other lines. The organization of the distributive machinery will naturally be determined by the relationship existing between the producer of raw materials and the manufacturer and the consumer. If the commodity passes directly to the consumer through retail stores, as is often the case in the local market, the distributing processes are correspondingly simplified. But if, on the other hand, the raw materials or manufactured wares are sent to distant markets, greater capital and a more elaborate organization are required.

The second phase of commercial activity includes banking and credit institutions. These comprise banking and loan firms and those agencies gathering commercial information and extending protection, such as bonding and insurance companies. Their function is to provide a safe depository for capital, to secure loans, and to assist in various ways in the work of distribution. A cotton merchant takes a consignment of cotton in some distant market, draws his draft upon his bank, which in turn undertakes to complete the transaction. In case credit is requested the dealer may use such agencies as Dun and Bradstreet to acquaint himself with the financial standing of the merchant. These commercial institutions provide banking facilities, extend financial assistance, and give credit information and assume in many other ways financial and commercial responsibilities.

Finally, the fourth class of business under takings is transportation. The function of transportation is to move the goods of commerce from place to place, and it should not be concerned with its marketing. It gives new value to the commodity by changing its place. It takes the surplus of the cereal belt and transports it to the markets of the East, and takes the product of the factory to the consumer. Among these are such familiar activities as railways, both general and urban, drayage and transfer, steamship and canal transportation. These great organizations have grown up mainly because of the needs of distribution and offer a wide and interesting field for the study of business organization.

These four main divisions, with their special groups, include the essential business activities of today. Other classifications might be made, but the one given will be generally recognized as corresponding in all essentials to present business practice. Through this classification we are able to observe how our ordinary business activities concretely embody the underlying principles of production, manufacture, and distribution. It places business upon a scientific basis.

## ELEMENTS OF ORGANIZATION

We have previously noted that the organization of business is the selection and arrangement of those elements which naturally combine to produce a business establishment or firm. Many of these elements are of a general character, and it is by their selection and combination that specific organizations are created. It is therefore desirable that the business man be familiar with these general characteristics of business organization.

One of the first problems of organization is the selection of the administrative and labor forces. Where large bodies of men are to be brought together, their selection becomes an important and often a very difficult problem, but it is impossible to lay down hard and fast rules governing the choice of men for the office and labor forces. In fact, the selection of employees is one of the best tests of the ability and judgment of the manager, for it indicates a quality of mind which is characteristic of successful business men.

In making the selection of his administrative and labor forces, the manager has in view certain personal traits and qualities which are considered everywhere as the basis of business success. The most important of these are the physical, intellectual, and moral qualities of the applicant. Naturally, the emphasis upon these qualifications will vary with the position; but, in a general way, it is obvious that a man of strong and vigorous physical powers will accomplish more in a given time than one who is not so endowed, and likewise an alert mind will be more efficient than a slow and sluggish one. Again, it is very generally recognized that good moral habits are desirable in business, especially where great responsibilities must be assumed. For this reason immoral habits absolutely debar one from positions of trust and responsibility with the best firms. In more recent years some of the great railway systems have enforced strict orders against cigarette smoking and drinking on the part of their employees when on or off duty. Gambling on the part of the employee is not tolerated by business firms. On the other hand, regular habits of life are encouraged, and many commercial houses even keep watch over the companionship of their employees and the manner in which they spend their leisure time.

The importance of these simple considerations is apparent when we measure their value in the light of business efficiency. Everything that tends to promote efficiency is vital. The efficiency of any body of men goes back essentially to the physical, intellectual, and moral capacities of each individual. A great railway system or manufacturing plant is efficient or weak in pro portion as these qualities have been regarded in the selection of the labor and administrative forces.

The careful policy pursued by the best firms In selecting their employees is fully demonstrated by the character of the questions asked those seeking employment. Of course, the nature of the inquiry depends upon the character of the business, and of the position, but even in the lower ranks searching questions must be satisfactorily answered. Obviously the more highly developed the organization is, the more careful must be the attention given to this side of the problem. A manufacturer must give greater attention to the selection of his force than the managers of the more simple business organization.

The primary purpose in guarding the selection of employees is to harmonize talent and fitness with the employment or the position. The value of these considerations is still further emphasized by the policy pursued by many business houses in providing many things for the convenience and pleasure of their employees, for the reason that in the end it will make them more content, and consequently more efficient. Where the welfare of the employee has been disregarded, legislation often compels the firm to maintain a wholesome physical and moral environment, and while this policy is pursued on the ground of public policy, it indicates in a general way the value of these qualities in promoting business efficiency. These regulations generally relate to the ventilation of factories and offices, the labor day, and the employment of women and children. The best business houses recognize that a wholesome environment both in and outside of business is of primary importance.

The problem before the manager, therefore, in the selection of his clerks and employees is to find those men who will work together under one supervision without friction and waste. A general rule of great value is that specialization shall be carried out so that the employees shall not divide and dissipate their energies. The division of labor is an economic and administrative necessity. Accountability must be clearly and accurately defined. The energy and efficiency of the force must be sustained, and the personal interest of the employers kept foremost in the minds of the employees. Responsibility in private administration is as essential as in public administration. The clerk must turn out accurate work with the same precision that the factory employee turns out a piece of machinery. This skill and precision are secured by applying the principle of the division of labor to business, so that each clerk or laborer is confined to those operations which require the exercise of special talents and skill.

A recent report of Bradstreet relating to business failure throws some light upon the qualities necessary to business success. The statistics show that a large percentage of the failures may be traced to poor business judgment, and not alone to the lack of capital. A lack of capital has brought about one failure in three, incompetency one in five, while extravagance and speculation each one in one hundred. These ratios indicate the value of a high standard of judgment in business practice. These failures must be charged in the main against business managers, and not against the working force, and they indicate the value of a thorough knowledge of business elements as a preparation for success.

It is obvious that complete obedience in the performance of duties is required of all employees. The individual must subordinate his own personal desires to the rules and regulations of the firm. In short, anything that will destroy the *esprit de corps* of the clerical and labor forces will bring disaster to the business. Insubordination endangers efficiency. The interests of the business are paramount, and all the efforts of the force must be so concentrated and utilized as to produce the largest efficiency. Private interests must be forgotten and indifference weeded out.

The management is always alert in recognizing individuality and personal efficiency in the ranks of the service. The work of the employees is carefully studied and observed, and systematic and orderly habits are always rewarded.

In summarizing these considerations, too much stress cannot be placed upon a wise and careful selection of the administrative and labor forces. The physical, intellectual, and moral qualities of the men are paramount. These combinations produce strength and efficiency, and, combined with executive ability and judgment, we have the foundations of a successful business organization. Such a force will prove strong at all times, and will be resourceful in the development of methods and effective in their execution.

There are other elements relating to business organization which must be considered. In the interests of economy and efficiency, great improvement has been made in recent years in office aids and facilities. It has been amply shown that the office is capable of handling a larger volume of work by equipping it with those aids and appliances which will relieve the force, in so far as possible, from the care of details. This is good business practice where it can be done more systematically and accurately by the use of improved records and devices.

In the first place, more attention is given today to the arrangement of office space, and particularly in dividing it so that the business processes go on naturally and logically. Much greater attention is now given to the selection of office furniture and equipment for the records of the business. It is quite obvious that these aids and appliances will differ with the business. The attention given to this side of the office organization has resulted in larger efficiency and has greatly reduced the expenses of management.

No better illustration of this new movement in business is found than in the recent development of the card system as applied to office organization. In every well-organized office of to-day this system is employed in keeping the records, and is utilized in every department of business. This development has been phenomenal during the last few years. Another appliance which is very widely used to-day is the cash register, which minimizes the work of the bookkeeper, and provides an excellent check upon the clerks. Again, the use of tubes and trolleys in the large department and retail stores for the delivery of goods and cash affords another excellent illustration of the value of mechanical aids in the organization of the business. This remarkable development has greatly influenced the character of business organization in very recent years. It has greatly aided in the efficiency of the organization as well as resulting in much greater economy. Wherever mechanical devices and aids can be used greater accuracy and economy will result. It enables the manager of the business to keep closer watch over the details and gives a more accurate control over the operations of his organization.

It is a well-recognized fact that the division of effort and centralization have gone on rapidly in the business world. The growth of large firms has made necessary the organization of departments in order to exercise control over all the parts of the business. Consequently the extent to which the principle of the division of labor can be applied to any given business will determine the efficiency of the organization. The differentiation of functions within the business organization indicates a high degree of development, provided that unity and harmony, economy and energy, are not sacrificed. This principle of special effort, combined with central supervision and control, is of far-reaching importance in business. The principle may be violated by too much or too little specialization, and it is the duty of the manager to separate his business processes and to constitute them into separate departments. He must group those operations of a similar kind into one department.

We have briefly summarized some of the more important elements in order that their value as the general groundwork of the business structure might be suggested. It is out of these simple elements that every business organization is constituted. They are of universal application throughout the business world. They combine to produce the simplest business unit, or apply to those organizations involving the harmonious action of thousands of men which reach out over the continent and even across the seas. They are in themselves so simple and universal that at times the business manager may fail to realize their far-reaching importance. But it is upon the clear and careful application of these principles that the efficiency and success of business is dependent.

# The Nature of Corporations[1]

## John P. Davis

All human activity has its social as well as its individual aspect. Man is so essentially a 'social animal' that his every act, however insignificant, has its effect, directly or indirectly, on his fellows. All men sustain social relations to all other men. The effect of the social relations – social growth, stagnation, or decay – is a product of two factors, the content (function) of the human activity and the organization (form) within which it is exerted. The existence of each factor implies the existence of the other. Social functions are exercised only through the machinery of social forms; yet social forms, though indispensable to the exercise of social functions, are continually suffering modification to meet the demands of new or altered social functions. In general, function and form – each depends upon and reacts on the other; progress and retrogression in each are reflected in some degree in the condition of the other. The corporation is a group of natural persons embodied in a certain class of the many forms of organization within or through which certain classes of social functions are exercised. The delimitations of form and function will appear in the following review of the several generic attributes of the corporation:

## 1. *Associate Activity.*

The corporate form is one within whose limits associate, as distinguished from individual, activity[2] is exercised, and comprehends both the inter-relations of the associated members and their relations with other organs of society. The early distinction of corporations as aggregate or sole is

---

[1] [Chapter 2 of *Corporations*, New York, G.P. Putnam, 1905, vol. 1, pp. 13–34.]

[2] The use of corporations for associated social activity has been more generally recognized than any other feature of them; unfortunately most writers have not succeeded in discovering, or at least have failed to consider, any other feature. E.g., Professor Giddings, in his Principles of Sociology (p. 187), recognizes corporations as forms of association, but discusses no other quality of them.

manifestly illogical and has been almost entirely abandoned in practice.[3] There are probably no corporations sole in the United States, with the possible exception of church parsons in Massachusetts.[4] If there are any, their powers and duties may be fully interpreted by the laws of trust and trusteeship. It is significant that the later textbooks on corporations give no space to the subject of the corporation sole. The inclusion of certain individuals in a classification of corporations was undoubtedly considered necessary on account of the present in some public officers (or offices) of attributes common to them and to corporations, such as the legal limitation of activity (found in all public offices) or of limited control over property held for public purposes. From another point of view, the extended use of the term is explained by a particular application of the theory of artificial personality – a legal exaltation of the purpose for which property is held or powers exercised above the natural personality of the person or persons holding the one or exercising the others.[5]

Again, while the functions of corporations aggregate and corporations sole may be the same, the latter lack the continuity of existence that is so prominent a characteristic of the former. When it is said that the king never dies and that he thus resembles a corporation, the actual continuous group life of the latter is confused with the continuity of existence of the public office not possessed by its successive incumbents.[6] Groups may, but individuals may not, have continuous existence; social functions of both groups and individuals may endure continuously.

---

[3] 'The idea of a corporation ante has been claimed as peculiar to English law, but the novelty consists only in the name; and it has been justly remarked that, "as an little of the law of corporations in general applies to corporations sole, it might have been better to have given them some other denomination."' – Dr. Wooddeson, Vinerian Lectures, vol. i., pp. 471, 472. 'There are very few points of corporation law applicable to a corporation sole.' – Kent, Commentaries, vol. ii., p. 273.

[4] 'The number of corporations sole in the United States must be very small indeed. It is possible that the statutes of some states vesting the property of the Roman Catholic church in the bishop and his successors may have the effect to make him a corporation solo; and some public officers have corporate powers for the purposes of holding property and of suing and being sued.' – Blackstone, Commentaries, Book I., p. 468, note of editor (Cooley).

[5] This idea is elaborated fully in Pollock and Maitland's History of English Law, vol. i., pp. 469–95.

[6] 'The law has wisely ordained that the parson, quaternes parson, shall never die, any more than the King; by making him and his successors a corporation. By this means all the original rights of the parsonage are preserved entire to the successor; for the present incumbent, and his predecessor who lived seven centuries ago, are in law one and the

Holding property for particular public purposes with incapacity to use it for other purposes or to alienate it does not alone constitute the holder a corporation, though it is one of the attributes of a corporation that its use of its property is limited by the terms of the charter to which it owes its creation and in accordance with whose terms it must exercise its activity. So-called corporations sole differ from true corporations, not in function but in form; the former lack the internal social structure of the latter.[7]

## 2. *Creation by the State.*

The corporate form or sum of peculiar relations subsisting between the members of the corporate group and between them and other members of society is created by the state, or, after spontaneous origin and maintenance by the force of custom, is approved with the same legal effect as if originally created by it. Neither the group nor its functions, but only the internal and external personal and group relations under or within which the group exercises its functions are created by the state. The progress of civilization demands an increasing exercise of associate activity, but not necessarily in the corporate form. As compared with the state, a primary, sovereign group, the corporation is a secondary, derivative, subordinate group. Likewise ecclesiastical corporations, under the earlier conception of the church as society primarily organized on its religious side (whether or not coextensive with the state) were sub-groups of the church, deriving from it their internal and external social relations. To be sure, all social activity, whether of individuals or groups, is limited and conditioned by the system of law under which it is exercised, for the state is itself, like the corporation, a group (though superior to all others), acting through or within certain self-imposed forms; but the corporate form brings to the

same person; and what was given to the one was given to the other also.' – Blackstone, Commentaries, Book I., cap. 18. This is verbal jugglery.

'It is true the Common Lawyers of England have been used to speak of Parsons, Vicars and even Wardens of Parish Churches, as Corporate-bodies. Sir Thomas Littleton speaketh after that manner. But I do apprehend that the reason thereof is, because Parsons, Vicars, or Church-wardens, have a Perpetual succession, like as Politick bodies have; and. therefore, that this way of speaking of them as of corporate-bodies is founded rather upon Resemblance than Reality.' – Maclox, Firma Burgi, p. 47. See also reference to the case of Overseers vs. Sears, *infra*, p. 23, note.

'One general figurative notion of incorporeity hath produced many fictions,' – Madox, as quoted by Gross, Gild Merchant, vol. i., p. 104, note. The reference there given is 'Addit. MS., Brit. Mus. 4531, fol. 122.'

[7] See discussion of functions of corporations, infra, p. 31.

members of the group in possession of it internal and external relations different from the usual and regular social relations imposed on individuals by the existing system of law and artificial and exceptional as compared with them.[8]  Not only is the corporate form artificial and exceptional, but the field of group functional activity is narrowed or widened, or otherwise artificially and exceptionally created or modified, by the act of the state.  Nor need the corporate relations owe their existence to a direct and special creative act of the state; they may be created through any subordinate agency of the state that the state may see fit to select, or by virtue of 'general incorporation' laws, which have the effect of causing the erection of the peculiar legal relations on the performance of certain preliminary acts by incorporators.[9]  Some fields of social activity, such as the construction and operation of railways[10] and

---

[8]  Of course, whether given legal relations are regular or exceptional depends on the nature of the system of law under which the relations are recognized or created and enforced; some systems, such as that of early Rome, have been based on a composite unit, as the family or some other group; others, such as the Imperial Roman law and the (English and American) law since the destruction of feudalism, have been based on the simple unit, the individual. The members of a corporation act not as units not as parts of a composite unit, and their social relations are to that extent exceptional as compared with the regular social relations of individuals regarded as social units. It is sometimes prophesied with a considerable degree of assurance (as in the quotation in the note on page 32, infra) that society is to attain in the near future a stage of development in which the social unit will be aggregate or composite instead of individual, as at present, and that the corporation is the institution through which socialism, in a more or less modified form is to be made effective. Unfortunately for such views, the historical development of corporations has not as yet afforded them much support. If the corporate form were always used as one might expect from a consideration of its adaptability, it might serve as a stepping-stone to socialism, but as a form of social activity it has been perverted to highly individualistic uses, and has actually produced more exaggerated individualism. The use of corporations has tended to result; not in co-operative commonwealths, but in trusts. There is much more reason to expect that if socialism comes at all it will derive its organization from above, not from below-from the subdivisions of the state and not from corporations – in other words, it is more likely to be state socialism than co-operative socialism.

[9]  Blackstone, Commentaries, Bk. I., pp. 473–4.

[10]  This is a broad statement of the fact as to railways. The exercise of the right of eminent domain is delegated to corporations alone. Some exceptional circumstances might enable individuals to construct and operate railways, but, speaking in general terms, the function is restricted to corporations. When railroads are sold at forced sale under decrees of foreclosure or on executions, it is held that an individual may purchase and operate the property, but that he may not succeed to the corporate franchise. Opinions in some cases seem to contemplate only a temporary operation of the property by the individual purchaser. At all events, individual ownership and operation of railways are regarded as justifiable only under extraordinary circumstances and when absolutely necessary to the attainment of justice.

the formation and management of banks, may by modern law be occupied only by groups of persons organized in the corporate form. Whatever may be the purposes of granting special group forms or of contracting or expanding the field of group-activity, the act is always that of the supreme social group organized as the state or church. This attribute of corporations has always been fully recognized by courts of law, and the enforcement of the rule of strict construction of corporate powers and acts has been consistent with the recognition of it.[11]

### 3. *Voluntary Inception – Compulsory Endurance.*

The assumption by a group of the corporate form and the acceptance by individuals of membership in the group are voluntary, as distinguished from the compulsory political status of citizens in the state and its subdivisions.[12] But this is not equivalent to saying that persons not members of the group may be voluntarily exempt from the external effects of the organization and activity of corporate groups. One must be a citizen of some state, though not necessarily a member of any corporation; in either case, however, his conduct must conform to the conditions imposed by the organized authority of the state, its subordinate institutions and the autonomous corporations created by it. There is a

---

[11] Beach on Public Corporations, I., p. 92, and cases cited. Dillon on Municipal Corporations, i., § 91. Sedgwick on Construction of Statutory and Constitutional Law, 338. American and English Encyclopaedia of Law, *sub verbo* 'Corporation.'

[12] It may be objected that the consent of the citizens of a municipality is not necessary to its incorporation, and that acceptance by them of a municipal charter is not necessary to make its provisions operative. Though that is now the well-settled rule with relation to public corporations, it is so generally regarded as repulsive to the spirit of English and American political institutions that some preliminary act in the nature of consent or acceptance on the part of the prospective citizens of the municipality is required before the law of incorporation is permitted to take effect. It is true, in general, that municipalities have exhibited a strong and increasing tendency to cease to be corporations and to become more truly sub-govern mental administrative bodies. This tendency has been expressed in the enactment of general incorporation laws, the more particular classification of municipalities, the increased interference by legislatures in the government of municipalities, and the modification of the doctrine of consent to be incorporated. Municipal self-government is being rapidly transformed into a mere determination within narrower limits of the means of executing laws imposed by state governments. The decadence of city government in England in the seventeenth and eighteenth centuries was evidenced by the multiplication of local commissions acting under the supervision of the central government. American cities seem to be passing at present through a similar phase of development, – which indicates as far as the present study is concerned, a decadence of corporate municipal life and a corresponding expansion of state government.

particular sense in which even the state organization may be described as voluntary; even if imposed by external force, it may be said to depend for its continued existence on the consent of the subjects upon whom it is imposed; but a society must have a political organization of some kind, – the 'right of the state to be' has been placed beyond question. Once organized, the state may coercively organize sub-groups of its citizens for the exercise in detail of the functions of government, but such coercively organized groups are riot true corporations, though the name is often applied to them; legal writers have well described them as quasi-corporations, because they have many of the attributes of corporations, though lacking in the essential elements of voluntary inception and autonomy.[13] After the corporate form has been assumed by a group, it is compulsory, from the side of the state, upon all its members until forfeited for misuser or non-user or regularly put aside in the manner provided by the state at the time of its creation or afterwards; from the side of the corporation, however, the corporate form may not be assumed or retained against the sovereign will of the state. The doctrine that 'a charter is a contract' is vicious; the conception of a bargain between a state and a group of its citizens is illogical; the only final guaranty of the protection of rights and of the performance of duties is a sound social sentiment. The prevalence of corporations is therefore characteristic of a state of society in which individual (and not state) initiative is relied on and individual responsibility is expected to serve as a regulating force. In rapidly developing communities the individual initiative has often been unduly encouraged by making the maintenance of corporate relations (once assumed) less compulsory. Perpetual-lived corporations are usually born in epochs of social expansion; under settled social conditions, corporations having a definite and shorter term of life are usually created.

### 4. *Autonomy, Self-Sufficiency, Self-Renovation.*

The group of members within the corporation is (a) autonomous, (b) self-sufficient and (c) self-renewing.

(a) Within the limits of the particular corporate form and function imposed or granted by the state, the corporate group controls the conditions (of both form and function) of its own activity without direction, interference or revision by other persons or groups of persons, including

---

[13] See preceding note.

the state itself.[14] In this respect the true corporation is distinguished from purely administrative or subgovernmental bodies, which possess and exercise only enough discretion to execute properly duties for the most part directed, controlled or revised by superior social groups. Thus the autonomy (and thereby the corporate character) of American municipalities is greatly decreased by the interference of state governments in their local affairs, by frequent modifications of their charters, the creation of state commissions for local purposes, and the almost excessive use of the writs of injunction and mandamus by the courts. Though the courts theoretically recognize the element of autonomy by refusing to compel by mandamus the performance of other than purely ministerial acts or to prevent by injunction a reasonable exercise of a corporation's powers within the terms of its charter, the present tendency of legislation and judicial interpretation is to lengthen the category of ministerial acts and to interpret the 'reasonable' more strictly. The limits of municipal activity are being narrowed, though the actual volume of activity within the narrower limits may be increasing. From the standpoint of historical social development, this characteristic of corporate relations has been most important; it is a proposition not difficult to establish that the early stages of nearly all the movements in the direction of what is comprehended in 'personal liberty' have been organized in the corporate form.[15]

(b) During the period of existence granted to a corporation by the terms of its charter, its general powers must be sufficient to assure it existence and maintenance, and the ability to effectively exercise the particular powers granted it and the duties imposed upon it, independently of

---

[14] It is not necessary to assume that the state has made a contract with a corporation, the terms of which are expressed in the charter granted, in order to insure autonomy or stability of corporate life. It is entirely a question of public sentiment. In no other country could corporate powers and duties be as easily modified or destroyed by law as in England, for Parliament is supreme; but the social sentiment in favor of 'vested interests' is so strong that English corporations have always enjoyed an exceptional degree of independence. Rarely have corporations been deprived by Parliament of their powers, even after long-continued misuse or abuse of them, without being provided a liberal pecuniary compensation for then; yet no contract relations between England and the corporation could be considered to have existed.

[15] See Mrs. J. R. Green's Town Life in the Fifteenth Century, vol. ii., pp. 437–48, for the part played in the movement by mediaeval towns in England. See also The Genesis of a Written Constitution, by Wm. C. Morey, in the Annals of the American Academy of Political and Social Science, April, 1891, vol. i., p. 529 et seq., for the connection between the organic structure of the English trading and colonial companies and the constitutions of the United States and several States.

external social agents, except in so far as all members of society are dependent upon their social environment. Such powers, if not expressly granted, are uniformly held by the courts to have been granted by implication, some being considered as of the essence of the corporate organization itself and others as incidentally necessary to the exercise of the particular activity of the corporation described by its charter. For example, if a corporation should be permitted to elect officers necessary to perform its functions only when directed by some external agent so to do, it would not be self-sufficient; it might actually cease to exercise its functions for want of the necessary official organs through which to act; such a body would be merely an abortive, not a true corporation. In 1684, Charles II, by the threatened use of the writ of *quo warranto*, compelled the London Livery Companies to surrender their charters and accept in place of them new charters in which it was provided by a special clause that the wardens' and clerks' names were first to be presented to the King for his approval, and if rejected, that the courts of assistants were to elect others, and so on, from time to time, until his Majesty should be satisfied, any election contrary to such provisions to be void; the King also reserved the power of removing any warden, assistant or clerk; the wardens and commonalty were to be subject to the lord mayor and court of aldermen of the City of London (themselves to be appointed by the Crown), who were to approve of all persons admitted to the clothing or livery.[16] The exaction of these concessions by Charles II and the attempt to enforce them by James II were readily recognized as tyranny, and had much to do with the expulsion of the Stuarts and the Revolution of 1688.

(c) A corporate group without power to renew its membership during the term of existence granted to it in its charter might cease to exist and thus fail of its purposes for want of members. The existence of a group at all implies a necessity (real or assumed) of plurality of persons for the due performance of some social function; if there were no such necessity, there would be no group. If by the grace of the state the group become a corporation by the assumption of a peculiar form, its character as a group does not cease to be necessary for the exercise of its social functions. The diminution of a very large number by the loss of even a single member might, in an extreme case, so impair the group (as such) as to make it inefficient for its work. The purpose of conferring the corporate form,

[16] Herbert, *History of the Twelve Great Livery Companies of London*, vol. i, p. 218.

however, is not to destroy the character of the group as such, but to make
it more efficient by providing it with a form appropriate for its peculiar
activity. Failure to provide adequate means for the renewal of a corporation's membership, therefore, would be inconsistent with the original
purpose of conferring the corporate form. If at the same time the
necessity of autonomy and self-sufficiency be given due weight, the
means of renewal must be within the group itself,[17] – it must be self-
renewal. Thus it is an established principle that the loss by a corporation
of an 'integral part,' in the absence of power to supply it, works its
dissolution. It has also been held that when no provision is made in a
charter for the filling of future vacancies, the power to do so by co
operation is conferred by implication.

The three attributes here considered under one head (because each
involves and implies the other) are in some cases very difficult to identify.
They are all, however, found developed in some degree in every corporation, as well as in many bodies not usually regarded as corporations.
When they are not highly developed, the corporation proper is not
easily distinguished from the purely administrative body; indeed, it must
be admitted that a critical analysis of most so-called quasi-corporations
would reveal in them the presence of the three attributes. The question
is one of degree of development; the corporation is in distinct, effective
and clearly perceptible possession of them; the purely administrative
body has them indistinct, rudimentary and almost imperceptible, and
ordinarily depends on the state for complementary activity to enable it
to exercise its functions. The necessity of autonomy and self-sufficiency
is the basis of the doctrine enforced by the courts (as an exception to the
general rule of strict construction of corporate grants and powers) that
such a construction, if possible, shall be applied in the interpretation of
corporate powers and duties as shall permit the accomplishment by the
corporation of the original purpose of its creation.[18]

---

[17] In The Overseers of the Poor of the City of Boston vs. David Sears et ux. (22 Pickering,
122) it was contended by counsel that 'the corporation [Overseers etc.] thus created is
more analogous to a sole than to an aggregate corporation. The two kinds run into each
other and the demandents [Overseers etc.] are to be regarded as a sole corporation, or
a quasi sole corporation with some of the incidents of an aggregate corporation. It is a
necessary and inseparable incident of an aggregate corporation that it have the power
of perpetuating itself by choice of members. Here the corporators have no such power,
but they are chosen by the inhabitants of Boston; and they have a civil death annually,
as the sole corporation dies a natural death.' See page 15, supra.

[18] Beach on Public Corporations, 1, 93, and cases cited. Dillon on Municipal Corporations,
i., § 87, and cases cited. Field on Private Corporations, 66, 67. Taylor on Private Corporations,
121.

## 5. *Compulsory Unity.*

The creation of a corporation contemplates that in all its relations with other organs of society it shall act and be acted upon as a unit. Accordingly it is provided by its charter (supplemented by its by-laws) with a means of determining the group-will of its members, with agencies through which the group-will shall be executed, and with agencies through which other social organs shall maintain their relations with it. In the element of compulsory unity, corporations are distinguished from most other associate bodies, and resemble most nearly the state itself. Blackstone very aptly called them 'little republics,' though he would have been more faithful to history if he had called republics 'big corporations.' This is one of the sources of the theory of 'artificial personality'; the corporation is said to have a common name, and to be, 'for certain purposes, considered as a natural person,'[19] 'vested by the policy of the law with the capacity of acting in several respects as an individual.'[20] There is nothing harmful in the recognition by the state in its system of law that a sub-group of it has distinct characteristics like men, if the fact that it is still a group be not lost to view. Though unified in action, the corporation is none the less a group; on the contrary, its unity of action preserves it as a group; if each member persisted in following his own will in preference to finding a common ground on which a group-will might stand, the group would not act as such, but would be inactive, and lawyers would readily determine it liable to forfeit its charter for non-user. The fact that the common group-will may not coincide completely with the will of any one member ought not to exempt the members from responsibility for the effects of its execution. It is purely a legal fiction that a corporation is an 'artificial person,' – 'a conception, which, if it amounts to anything, is but a stumbling-block in the advance of corporation law towards the discrimination of the real rights of actual men and women.'[21] The other source of the theory is formed in the nature of the functional activity of the corporation, which will be considered below.[22]

It must be admitted, however, that the theory has been discredited in practice, in the rejection or modification of so many of the principles founded on it that it is quite unnecessary to refer to them in detail. One

---

[19] Angell and Amso on Corporations, pages 19–20.

[20] Kyd on Corporations, page 13.

[21] Taylor on Private Corporations, § 51.

[22] Infra, pages 27, 29.

such principle has been the source of an unusual amount of confusion; it is a logical deduction from it that the members of a corporation have no right in debts due to it and are not liable for debts owing by it, – '*si quid universitati debitur, singulis non debetur; nec, quad debit universitus, singuli debent.*' The principle has been so extensively applied that the corporate form has come to be used for the advantage of the limited liability afforded by it more than for any other purpose.[23] Yet there is nothing in the corporate form itself that affords a justification for the presence of this predominant element; though some social functions may be regarded as to such an extent public in character as to justify the setting a limit to the pecuniary risk of those who perform them, regardless of the social form (whether corporate or not) in which they are organized. The pernicious movement has decreased the personal responsibility on which the integrity of democratic institutions depends, and has introduced into both investments and social services a dangerous element of insecurity. Limited liability of members was not a feature of early corporate life in England, and its undue prevalence in this century has been due to an overestimation of the importance of national internal development.[24] More settled economic conditions have already resulted in some improvement, and the element of personal responsibility is gradually pushing its way back into the management of corporations so far that limited liability, instead of being an advantage, is often regarded by promoters and investors as a positive detriment.

### 6. *Motive in Private Interest.*

A corporation is composed of persons having a private or particular (or local), not merely public or general, interest in the subject-matter of the group-activity, whether it be political, social (in the narrower sense), religious on economic. This is partly deducible from the voluntary inception of corporate relations, for if such relations are voluntary in their

---

[23] 'The distinctive feature of the modern trading corporation is the limited liability of its members.' – A. T. Hadley, Railroad Transportation, p. 43.

[24] The sentiment is fairly expressed in the following words: 'It is a well-known fact that many of the enterprises which have greatly developed the resources of the country, and which have been of great benefit to society, would never have been undertaken without corporate organizations. No new enterprise is a cinch, it is more or less uncertain and speculative, and where it involves large expenditures of capital, unless the men who undertake it ran know the limit of their liability, it will remain undeveloped.' – 'Suggestions for Amendment of the Laws Governing Corporations in the State of Michigan,' by Jay P. Lee, in Publications of the Michigan Political Science Association, No. 3, pp. 74, 75.

inception, only those will desire to assume them who have the satisfaction of a private interest as their motive. A county is not regarded as
a corporation proper, but only as a quasi-corporation; what the citizens
of a county do as such, they do as members of the inclusive society of the
state, and their acts are limited (theoretically, at least) to such as it is
necessary for them to do as members of the general society of the state,
and do not include such as they have merely a particular, private or local
interest in doing. While the same may be said of the citizens of a municipality, there is a field of activity in which they are considered to be
actuated by a particular, private or local interest not shared by society in
general. Lower in the scale, members of a so-called private corporation,
such as one for purposes of trade, are actuated almost entirely by private
interest. In some cases, however, associations upon which a compulsory
organization has been imposed by the state have become corporations by
such a perverted use of the machinery of the imposed organization as to
make it a fit form for the exercise of activity dictated by the private
interests of the associated persons; such was the origin of the old English
corporation of the Merchants of the Staple or Staplers. But 'public' and
'private' are relative terms. What is a public and what a private interest
is determined only by the stage of development that has been attained by
a particular society. In a rapidly growing community, a body of citizens
so influenced by patriotic sentiment as to establish a business enterprise
largely for the purpose of 'booming' their country may be said to: be
actuated by something more than mere private interest; while a similar
venture, under mature and settled social conditions, would have little of
the public element in it. Public and private, social and individual, interests
are always found in combination, and sometimes so blended and confused
that it is extremely difficult to determine which is predominant.
Legislatures and courts of law, in the application of the principle, have
often been driven to assume apparently inconsistent attitudes towards very
similar states of facts, though the correctness of the principle has not been
denied. The principle must be adhered to, even if in many cases so hard
to apply. In the corporation proper, then, private and particular interest
is permitted to seek its own satisfaction, and public and general interest,
if at all, will be consulted from the side of the corporation, only incidentally, collaterally or secondarily, as set forth in the paragraph following.

### 7. *Functions Public and Appropriate for Associate Activity.*
The social functions performed by corporations have had two enduring
qualities. They have been (a) such as were considered under succeeding
sets of social conditions conducive to the welfare of the public and of

society in general rather than to the particular welfare of the persons performing them, and (b) such as were more advantageously performed by associate than by individual activity. The first has reference to the relations of the activity of the corporate group to the society of which it is a part; the second, to the relations of the group to the conditions under which its activity must be exercised. The standpoint of the first is society in general; of the second, the corporate group.

(a) What now appears at first blush to be a too restricted view of corporate functions would probably have been accepted as sufficiently comprehensive before the beginning of the nineteenth century. The unprecedented growth of private corporations since 1830 seems to discredit the statement made, but it is believed that even private corporations find justification for their existence in the general opinion that public welfare is materially promoted by the more facile exercise in corporate form of social functions whose exercise is prompted by the pursuit of private interest.[25] Nor is the limitation in consistent with the statement made in paragraph six above. The corporate form has always been intended and used to promote public welfare through private interest by affording to private interest a social mechanism through which adequately and effectually to express itself in social activity. The almost insuperable difficulty in the use of the corporate form has been to reconcile the private motive and public purpose of the activity exercised within it. But the difficulty is due not so much to the corporate form itself as to the character of the activity; indeed, it is urged with much force that the use of the corporate form has a tendency to ameliorate the unfortunate social conditions incidental to some kinds of social activity.[26] The class of social evils usually included in discussions of the 'railway

---

[25] See note on page 26, supra. 'The purpose in making all corporations is the accomplishment of some public good. Hence, the division into public and private has a tendency to confuse and lead to error in investigation, for unless the public are to be benefited, it is no more lawful to confer exclusive rights and privileges upon an artificial body than upon a private citizen.' – Mills vs. Williams, II Iredell's (N. C.) 558.

[26] 'The corporation is the ally, the agent, the representative of plutocracy…. Plutocracy has appeared in a new guise – a new cost of mail, – the corporation. The struggle of democracy against plutocracy will be between democracy and the corporation. The people are beginning to recognize their old plutocratic foe in its new corporate form.' (W. W. Cook, The Corporation Problem, p. 249.) Plutocracy in the form of the individual is largely beyond the reach of legislatures and the law. But plutocracy in the form of the corporation is open to attack. It can be regulated, restricted, and annihilated. Plutocracy acting through corporations is obliged to he cautious and conservative…. The plutocrat gives bonds to keep the peace when he acts through the corporation.' (Ibid., pp. 252, 253.) 'It is better to have the large corporation than to have the trust.' – Ibid., p. 243.

problem' are evils due more to modern methods of transportation under modern social conditions than to the peculiar legal form in which the men engaged in transportation are organized. Ownership and operation of railways by individuals would entail greater evils than their ownership and operation by corporations.[27]

This attribute of corporate functions is another source of the pernicious legal theory of 'artificial personality.'[28] The function performed by a person is personified, and the sum of rights and duties involved in the performance of the function is separated in abstract thought and law from the succession of natural persons or groups of per sons in whom they are reposed. Then the persons or groups are known to the law as corporations to the extent of their connection with the social functions in view. Hence the division of corporations into aggregate and sole. The early English parson was the *persona ecclesiae*; the church was personified in him; the land, of which he had a limited use, was in reality the property of the church, or the property of society devoted to particular religious services performed by the parson.[29]

The private corporation pure and simple is a product of social, political and industrial conditions largely peculiar to the nineteenth century, of which democracy and individualism are the foundations. Repugnance to class distinctions and the belief in the equality of men combined with the tendency to restrict the area of state activity at the end of the eighteenth century opposed the creation of corporations because they involved class privileges, inequality and the limitation of individual activity; powers that could not be safely (as a matter of theory) left to the exercise of the state could with no greater degree of safety be reposed in corporations. But if certain functions were dangerous to the liberty of the individual when exercised by the state, they were none the less necessary to be exercised, and the nearer they were to the individual, the less dangerous they seemed to be; accordingly corporations became more numerous in the early part of the present century. But again, inconsistently enough, class distinctions must not be maintained and the assumption of the corporate form and the exercise of corporate powers must be free to all; general incorporation laws were accordingly justified by social theories. The distinction between public and private functions

---

[27] Cf. A. T. Hadley, 'Railroad Transportation,' p. 48. Cf. also R. T. Ely, 'The Future of Corporations,' Harper's Magazine, vol. lxxv., pp. 260, 261, (July, 1887).

[28] See page 25, supra.

[29] See Pollock & Maitland's History of English Law, vol. i. pp. 483–6,

is never easy to determine and it is not made easier by democratic theories of society and the state; all functions have tended to reach the same level, and 'incorporation for any lawful purpose' not been freely permitted to all. A false definition of public and private functions has been the cause of the confusion. The 'private corporation' is a contradiction in terms, and has no place in a sound organization of society. The present tendency in the business world (as well as in the courts) is to distinguish more clearly between the various purposes for which corporations are organized and to estimate the responsibility of the organized persons accordingly.

(b) The importance of the second attribute of corporate functions has been only gradually developed and appreciated in the progress of society. Before the present century, even partnerships were unusual and, when they existed, were usually composed of members of the same family. The object of mediaeval corporations was primarily to provide and limit the conditions of individual activity and only secondarily to afford a means of expression for unified associate activity. It is only in the nineteenth century that the latter object has been magnified (concurrently with a depreciation of the former) to such a degree as seriously to menace the stability and permanence of the individual as a social unit.[30]

The principle of association may make itself manifest in two degrees: (a) in the imposition by a group of the conditions of activity on its individual members and (b) in the absorption by the group as a unit of the activity of its members. (a) The activity in the first case is so closely appropriate for associated persons that it will not be discussed. (b) Whether absorption by a group of the activity represented by its membership is advantageous is a question to be determined by the ratio of the unit of greatest efficiency of the activity itself (corresponding to the unit of production in economics) to the unit of means of exercising

---

[30] 'The modern form of corporation prevailed because it was found to be the best form of ownership for the large permanent investments under concentrated management which are required in modern industry.' – A. T. Hadley, Railroad Transportation, p. 46.

'As John Stuart Mill says, [the union of capitalists and laborers] must be brought about by a development of the partnership principle. No one...can tell exactly what form this will take, but some things seem already clear. Corporations will play an important part in this development, as they gradually become more democratic in their tendencies. Corporations and co-operative enterprises will become more and more nearly assimilated until they can scarcely be distinguished.' – Richard T. Ely, 'The Future of Corporations,' Harper's Magazine, vol. lxxv., p. 260 (July, 1887). See comment on this view in note on page 17, *supra*.

the activity; in general, when the former exceeds the latter, association will be necessary. The ratio of the two factors varies in successive stages of society and the necessity of association varies accordingly. In some cases both degrees of association have been manifested in the activity of the same corporation; in the fifteenth century, fishing vessels were frequently owned by a borough and used by the burgesses in common, each conducting his business for himself, but according to the ordinances of the corporation, and using the corporation vessels in common with his fellows. The principle of joint-stock management of the entire activity of the corporation was first fully applied in the East India Company, and in that case it was a gradual evolution; originally an 'open' regulated company with several groups of investors, it later by degrees came to be a complete joint-stock company with one body of investors under unified management.

The corporate function has both attributes. However fully developed either attribute may be, the function is not truly corporate if the other be wanting.[31]

After the foregoing somewhat extended discussion of the nature of the corporation, the following is offered as a definition: A corporation is a body of persons upon whom the state has conferred such voluntarily accepted but compulsorily maintained relations to one another and to all others that as an autonomous, self-sufficient and self-renewing body they may determine and enforce their common will, and in the pursuit of their private interest may exercise more efficiently social functions both specially conducive to public welfare and most appropriately exercised by associated persons.

---

[31] 'To render such an establishment [of a joint-stock company] perfectly reasonable, (a) with the circumstances of being reducible to strict rule and method, two other circumstances ought to concur. First, (6) it ought to appear, with the clearest evidence, that the undertaking is of greater and more general utility than the greater part of common trades; and secondly, (c) that it requires a greater capital than can easily be collected into a private copartnery. If a moderate capital were sufficient, the great utility of the undertaking would not be a sufficient reason for establishing a joint stock company; because, in this case, the demand for what it was to produce, would readily and easily be supplied by private adventurers. In the four trades [of (a) banking, (b) fire, marine and capture insurance, (c) canals, and (d) city water supply] both these circumstances concur.' – Adam Smith, Wealth of Nations, Book V., cap. I.

# Internal Organization;
# Defects of Ordinary Types of Management[1]

## Frank M. Mason

The subject matter of the preceding chapters has been in the main historical and general. Emphasis has been laid more particularly on the broad principles of economic doctrine that have to do with the forms of business enterprise, the factors affecting the productivity of labor and capital, the conditions deciding the most effective size for the industrial unit, the general principles that bear upon business activity in its broader aspects. The account has been far from complete. An exhaustive treatment of this phase of our subject would take us far afield, and would have to cover the whole range of political economy, finance, banking, foreign trade, commercial law, economic resources, labor problems and accounting. To select the prime essentials out of this encyclopedic mass of factors that have a bearing more or less direct on business organization, and to preserve the principles involved even in a brief and unelaborated form does not lie within the scope of this work. Those who are desirous of making a more complete study of the wider problems that touch so many sides of economic activity are referred to the multitude excellent separate works on each subject. The branches of study of this general nature that have been considered in the previous chapters are those which seemed to be most directly and intimately connected with the problems of business organization.

Leaving, now, the historical and general phase of the subject, which may be loosely described as dealing with business activity as affected by outside forces, let us turn to the more specific, and in many ways more difficult problems connected with the internal management of business enterprises. In a sense this may be called a study of the ways and means of making larger profits. It involves a consideration of the methods of organization that will result in a larger output with the same expenditure

---

[1] [Chapter 5 of Frank M. Mason, *Business Principles and Organization*, Chicago: Cree Publishing Co., 1909, pp. 87–132.]

of labor and capital, or at least an increased output with a less than proportional increase in the labor and capital expense; the methods of avoiding waste and of detecting the weak places in a system; the building up of defective departments;. the establishment of cost systems, order and tracing systems, and other methods of checking up that will reveal the points of strength and weakness; organization of selling departments, advertising systems, and problems of general executive policy.

In the beginning, emphasis must be laid on the fairly obvious fact that there exists no perfect body of rules that apply inflexibly to all forms of business organization. Most business concerns have been built up gradually, and the particular skill, training and experience possessed by the men at the helm will often have a tremendous influence on the efficiency of the final form of organization, whether it resembles one that would work well under average conditions or not. The customs of the firm may be so fixed, the methods so well threshed out by long practice, the knowledge of the management's policy so well diffused throughout the works, that more would be lost through a radical change than would be gained by a system theoretically more perfect. In many concerns, and particularly in small ones, the special skill and personality of men at the head will often compel variations from the type that has been found best in the general run of cases.

There is at present a tendency among men who have become skilled in reorganizing run-down concerns to attach a minimum of importance to the personal factor in management, and to form their reorganizations in as perfect and scientific a manner as possible. They say, and truly, that the pet plans and policies of men in authority have proven the ruination of many an otherwise sound concern; that a theoretically perfect organization is not dependent on the health and continued ability of one or two men; and lastly, that in one case you are going by guesswork and taking a chance, whereas in the other there is no uncertainty. It is undoubtedly true that in the past too much emphasis has beet placed upon management by the individual, upon trusting one man to carry all the ins and outs of a business in his head, and too little reliance has been placed in a scientific organization. The individual ordinarily has little influence on the efficiency of large organizations of long standing; but in a small concern, and in one that is newly formed, where lines of policy and of management have not as yet been definitely determined, a man of force and character, one of exceptional ability in broad grasp and outlook, will often accomplish more as the autocratic head of the business than the most perfect system could do with the man subordinate to it.

The business man who is looking for general principles that will apply with invariable success will meet again and again with instances of plans and systems that will seem to him to involve some universally applicable rule. One finds men everywhere who have read about, or seen in operation, some system or some feature of organization which they have found admirable, and which they proceed to use wherever an opening seems to present itself. The human mind is strongly disposed to generalize; and in business, particularly, nearly everybody has some pet theory, some universal panacea, for the ills that business management falls heir to.

Most men regard that form of organization that is typified by the army, as the perfect one. The ideal division of men into regiments, and companies, the exactly defined duties and authority of the commanders and officers, the precise discipline that insures explicit obedience to all commands of the superiors, suggests to most people the perfection of organized and concerted action. Yet in many business houses too great adherence to the military type has resulted in mistakes in management, because in many cases the necessity for strict control and sharply marked lines of authority is less than for specialization of functions and for the careful combination of different sets of laborers. Now and then some business man comes across, in his records, some significant or striking feature of his production costs, and he begins to think that keeping sets of figures represents efficient organization. While this may represent a sound principle up to a certain point, and in certain ways, it cannot take the place of other factors that have to be combined with it to make it even useful. If carried out too far, and applied indiscriminately to every line of work, it may become about as valuable a business asset as a collection of canceled postage stamps.

To many men the word 'system' has a magic sound. So much improvement has been accomplished through bringing method and order into a complex set of operations that before had represented only doubt and confusion, and so great a factor is it in checking loose and slipshod work, that there are many who regard everything done systematically as being done economically, no matter how the principle is applied. But like everything else that furnishes a rule to success in business, even system cannot be carried so far as to be an end in itself, but must be used with discrimination.

An example that will illustrate how a mistaken elaboration of a systematic way of doing things may lead to needless expense may be taken from the filing system of a certain mail order house. Country customers of this concern often send in letters containing lists and specifications of a large number of articles. These letters frequently had to be sent out to different departments, sent back with notations or remarks by the department chiefs, and sometimes kept in one part or other of the establishment while the specifications mentioned were worked out. It was found that many difficulties arose under this plan. The letters were often missing from the files when wanted; and then if the filing clerk could not remember who had it last, a long search through the different departments became necessary. Often times an important letter was lost or mislaid. If the notations were more than could be placed on the blank part of the letter, the necessary information became illegible or was left off altogether.

The difficulties were done away with in the following manner: On each letter, as it was received, a specially prepared tag was pasted, on which was stamped the date when it was received; it was supplied with a serial number, spaces in which to note to which department it had been sent, and to place the date showing when it had been answered and when the order had been filled. In the mailing department an order book was started; in this were entered the date, the serial number, and the name of the writer of each letter as it came in; also the department to which it had been referred. Every time the letter comes back to the office or is sent to an other department, the entry in the order book is changed. Thus a careful record is kept of every letter, and the head men can tell in an instant who has had the letter and where it is. An immense amount of time is saved in this particular house to the men who before were compelled to drop important work to run around in a blind search for lost and mislaid letters. The scheme adopted saves money also in that important orders are no longer lost. But would the same system be equally effective if applied to all businesses? As a general rule letters are not liable to be sent out to different departments, do not run the same risk of being lost or mislaid, and, if wanted, are usually to be found in the files where they were placed when received and answered. In most cases, therefore, this system of pasting on letters tags to be filled out, and of recording them so minutely in an order book, would be a hindrance rather than a help, and would cause needless expense. Yet more than one country merchant has come in, has admired the smooth-running and obvious advantages of this arrangement as applied to this particular house, and has enthusiastically in stalled a similar system in his own establishment, in spite of the fact that the conditions are different; and the only advantage gained has been the feeling of satisfaction that comes to him from thinking that his business had been improved by the use of system.

All this is not intended to be construed as an argument that no general principles can be applied to organization. The emphasis given here to the diversity of condition and the difference in the purposes of business enterprises is intended chiefly to warn the student of business principles against the tendency to generalize too much, to become biased in favor of one remedy or another without regard to their relative importance. Yet in spite of the great difference in the purposes for which business enterprises are organized, and the great differences in the conditions with which they are surrounded, there are certain factors of organization which apply to all undertakings in some measure or other. We know, for example, that no business can be run unless it is organized in some way or other. There must at least be some definite method or plan, some mapping out of work, some assignment of duties, or nothing will be accomplished. The work may be poorly assigned, the men chosen to do it may not be the ones best fitted to carry it out, the assignment of duties may result in a slow and cumbersome method of attaining results; but if some plan had been laid out, if the working force know at least approximately what they have to do, an organization of some kind will result.

It is clear from the foregoing that there must be some authority, someone at least at the head, to map out the plan of work, assign duties, and in some measure or other assume responsibility for the work that is being undertaken. We may go even further, and say that, in general, there ought to be definitely marked outlines of authority. The example of a military organization has taught us a great deal of the value of discipline, the effectiveness in administration of placing responsibility, the definiteness of control that is gained by subdividing authority and responsibility. It is fairly clear that in a large organization the man who has control of the general policy cannot be responsible for the successful carrying out of the petty details the authority and responsibility must, therefore, taper down. The job boss in whose hands is placed the turning out of a small and definitely marked out piece of work, can not be held to account if the work given to him to do should turn out to be part of an unprofitable under taking. At the same time, the individual workman who bungles will hardly expect to hear from the president of the company; he is directly responsible to his job boss alone. The smaller men in authority should be relieved from responsibility except in the fields for which they are fitted. The constant disputes that always arise over methods and ways and means must have a court of appeal, which is provided by the man to whom responsibility for the performance of that particular section of work has been delegated.

Another lesson taught us by the army is in the value of having a properly trained supply of new men to fill superior places that may become vacated. In the army the captain of one moment may have to be the colonel of the next; and in an industrial army the machine room without a foreman may become as helpless as a company without a head. Tapering authority never leaves affairs in such a state that the place of anyone cannot be filled without stopping the machinery of business.

The accurate placing of responsibility is another important factor in organization. There is a great incentive to careful and energetic work if a man knows that everything he does is brought to the scrutinizing attention of his superior, when he knows that credit will be given him for work well done and a black mark be placed against his name if he has failed.

Another great factor in organization, that binds the whole mechanism together, is the introduction of order and method in all parts of an undertaking, sometimes called system. It relieves the man at the head from the details of execution, and lets the man of special skill devote his entire energies to the work for which he is best fitted. It prevents the man who is worth $10,000 a year from spending an hour of his time every day opening the mail. It brings to men work fully prepared and ready for their attention, so that they can devote their whole time to the application of their particular function. When every thing is moving in a regular and accustomed routine, the waste of time and effort that is involved in starting something new is avoided. System attempts to provide for everything in advance; and instead of making important steps depend upon some man's fallible memory, it makes automatic provision for everything necessary. It arranges the processes so that the greatest use is made of the property devoted to the undertaking and the labor and capital need not remain idle.

In addition to system there must be provision for carrying it out. The discipline that aims at holding all to the chosen system of working is as important as the keeping to a definite plan. Rules and regulations must be provided and enforced, while the proper training and instruction in the features of the system is essential to an understanding and an intelligent application of its principles. Nor can it be assumed that after a system has been installed it can be left to take care of itself. Especially when an establishment has been reorganized upon a new and scientific plan, if minute care is not taken to see that plans and specifications and the details of the new system are strictly adhered to, it will be found that the workmen, the job bosses, even the foremen, are slipping back into their old habits. Watchfulness and carefully planned supervision are necessary to keep the working force and the superior officers up to the mark and to provide against dishonesty, against errors of judgment and errors from carelessness.

Again, experience has shown that careful records must be kept, that the cost and profits of each article be clearly shown, that the expenditure and results from each department be carefully checked up, so that the business man may clearly see which articles he is making the most profit on, and which department is running least economically. Valuable analyses of costs, operation by operation, should show not only where the profit and where the loss comes from, but should supply invaluable data from which to proceed to the task of reducing costs. The larger and more complex the organization, the greater is the importance of securing accurate cost accounts; for as an establishment grows in size and complexity it becomes increasingly difficult for the man at the top to analyze conditions from observation alone.

In days gone by, one heard many tales of the shrewd business man who kept all the odds and ends and details of his establishment in his head and had little need of carefully analyzed cost systems or figures of any kind. That was indeed possible when his only competitors were less clever men who used the same rough, happy-go-lucky system that he used, and when the man who had any organization at all was so much ahead of those who had less or none. The conditions of competition, and the growing knowledge of the essentials of careful organization, are tending more and more to cut down the difference between the cost of production and the selling price.

When this margin was a wide one, an ordinarily shrewd guess often did not fall far enough from the truth to hit outside the profit making limits. Nowadays the anxiety to save a profit that is constantly growing smaller makes rough judgments fatal. Figures of cost of production, covering cost of labor, of machines, and of running departments, must be accurately compiled; these figures must show unerringly the points of high and excessive costs at every stage of the manufacture or business. The failure to gauge a business upon mathematically accurate data may easily result in a mistake that will turn a fast disappearing profit into a loss.

A discouragingly large proportion of the systems of organizations now in existence are permanently prevented from reaching a high state of efficiency, owing to the disputes, disagreements, and constant ill-feeling that pervades all the parts of the body. Disagreement between employers and men are regarded by many able thinkers as inevitable. It is said that the interests of the two classes are permanently opposed to each other, and that the best we can look for is a sort of armed neutrality between the two opposing forces. What the workmen want from their employers more than anything else is high wages, and the workmen feel happiest as a rule when they are doing no more than other laborers in similar lines and yet receive higher pay. On the other hand, employers are most concerned to turn out their products at a low labor cost, and the majority of them experience a feeling of satisfaction if their own workmen are receiving lower wages than those of their competitors. As we shall see later both these conditions should be viewed with apprehension, for they contain the elements of discord, of dissatisfaction on both sides, and lead to working at cross-purposes, to lack of harmony, and to lowered efficiency in the whole establishment.

The question of bringing perfect harmony between employers and men, of keeping both sides satisfied, of making both feel that their interests are identical, and of bringing about a condition of cooperation, is too involved and intricate to be discussed at length in this place. There are a number of theories and a large number of schemes now in operation in actual establishments designed to bring about a spirit of 'team-play' between employers and employees, some of which we shall have to consider carefully. It is sufficient to point out at this place that one of the important ends to be achieved by an effective organization is an enthusiastic and unselfish working together of all its parts. It is obvious that the larger the establishment, the greater is the difficulty of bringing this about.

One of the advantages of a small concern lies in the fact that the employer can come into personal contact with all of his men. He knows their family history; he knows the difficulties they have to meet; he can sympathize with them in their troubles, and if a dispute arises he can see their point of view. In a large establishment, all this is changed. The men, instead of having dealings with the 'boss' or the 'governor,' which are often terms of affection, now regard themselves as being employed by some vast machine, which they know as 'the company.' The company is looked upon as a machine, as an artificial sort of being that recognizes such things as system, discipline, hard work, but that has no place for any thing like mutual interest, working in harmony, esprit de corps. Many managers of even large establishments have attacked this problem of bringing harmony into the interests of employers and of men, with varying degrees of success. Gradually some principles have been evolved which are forming valuable contributions to the science of business organization. At any rate, we can now say that any type of management in which each side spends a large part of its time thinking over and talking over the injustice and the hard treatment which it receives at the hands of the other, must be avoided. The best type of organization is one which calls forth that hearty cooperation on the part of all its members which can only be secured through a genuine, lively and loyal interest in the success and progress of the whole undertaking.

The foregoing paragraphs outline in brief but pretty definitely the factors that should be included in successful organization. They are a definite purpose, superior direction, definite and fixed responsibility, system, and rules and regulations. To this we must add accurate records and statistics, including an effective cost system; and last, but not least, co operation, harmony, 'team-play.'

These are the factors that must enter, in some proportion, into the successful management of almost any enterprise; but when we come to determine the comparative importance of each factor, or to consider whether there may not be factors which are essential to some lines of enterprise but not to others, we begin to realize that the purposes, conditions, and materials with which we have to deal are in no two businesses alike. If we were to attempt to make complete analysis of all the factors by which business success can be achieved, it would he necessary to consider every factor of every business now being conducted, and that, too, not, alone but in connection with all the conditions by which it is surrounded and all the influences by which it is affected and to which it has to adapt itself.

There are certain principles, as we have seen, which can invariably be applied in some proportion or other, some features which all organizations have or ought to have in common. As we cannot deal with these principles as they work out under all conditions, we shall have to simplify our task by making use, as far as possible, of types. Probably the most general type and the one with which the largest number of people are familiar, is that of a manufacturing industry. In applying our general rules for organization and profit-making, there are several advantages in using the manufacturing industry as a model on which to rest our principle.

1. Not only is it the one with which most people are familiar, but it is the one that varies the least from all forms of business enterprise.
2. The principles discussed in connection with our typical ease can generally be applied to other branches. It will be necessary in the course of our discussion to point out wherein variation in conditions results in different application of principles to different lines of enterprise. It may, indeed, be come necessary to devote special attention to certain lines of business which are themselves more or less typical.
3. In the manufacturing industry the most scientific investigation and experience in regard to the factors that make for efficient organization have been carried on and in this field the most trustworthy results have been secured: If we use this as a type, therefore, we shall tread on more solid ground.

Perhaps it will clear the atmosphere a little, and make our way ahead more plainly visible, if we first consider some of the faults that are to be found in ordinary types of organization. The most general fault of the customary system of management is that the form is not adapted to the conditions and purposes of the business and results to be achieved. It has already been sufficiently noted that the nature of the organization required to manage different types of business must vary enormously. In some enterprises, time is a very important factor. In this case there is need for a better command of affairs by administrative officers, clearly marked-out lines of authority, more definitely placed responsibility, and greater attention to discipline. If, for instance, one were called upon to clear away from a railroad line a mountain of earth caused by a landslide, it is probable that a body of men would be collected and these men would be divided into companies, each, with a foreman, and each company be divided into squads, each with a job-boss. All these kinds of units would be headed by men in absolute authority over their units and with no relation to those engaged in other parts of the work that would cause complications or delay. The end to be achieved here is best effected by a system of management that insures quick obedience to command and effective control.

In the example cited above the advantages of military organization are obvious. It is perhaps not so obvious that a force of workmen organized to do precisely the same kind of work under different conditions might be more effectively organized in a different way. Suppose that, instead of a track to be cleared away there is a great canal to be constructed – one that will require thousands of men, and many years of time. In this case, it will be advisable to bring about an organization in which less attention is paid to the sharp division of lines of authority, and more to a careful division of labor, to segregating the different functions of the men so that each one will have the task for which he is best fitted. There are to-day many industrial organizations in which the employer forces into prominence the chief features of the military system, when the purpose in view is much more influenced for good or ill by other forces, when the need for sharp control is less than for specialization of function and the harmonious combining of the different parts. In a great industrial establishment, for example, where machines are manufactured that have a very close competition both as to quality and as to price, the success of this organization depends very little upon sharp division of lines of authority and control, but more largely upon the ability with which the advantages of the division of labor are utilized.

There are numerous examples of this; take the making of shoes. Here there is a division into departments, but the different departments are not engaged in the same line of work nor could the foreman of one department interchange with the position of a foreman of another. The making of the product has been split up into its smallest parts and in each of these small processes – the workers are trained to the highest degree of efficiency. In the well-organized shop the workman has sifted from his duties all but the one in which he is supreme. Military virtues are here desirable to the extent that the workman is responsible to his foreman, but this feature is only incidental; it is not the factor that determines whether or not good shoes are to be turned out at a low cost.

The success or failure of the industry would not depend upon instant obedience, upon a definite line of succession in authority, upon interchangeability of position in case of emergency. Rather would it depend upon the narrowing down of processes to make the most of each man's skill and dexterity, upon study and care in purchasing, upon saving time in putting the different parts of the products into the, workers' hands, upon keeping every man and every machine fully occupied; so as to save interest and rent, upon maintaining an efficient sales agency and advertising policy so as to secure ready market for the product.

It is true that, even in an establishment of this kind, the workers are responsible to the foreman, and the foreman himself must therefore have all the abilities of the workingmen must be able to do everything he asks them to do, must see that their work is brought to them and taken away; and in addition, must have tact, energy, foresight, good health, and a number of other qualities. Many of the men who have carried on investigation and experiment in the field of factory organization point out the fact that the duties that must be performed by a foreman constitute in themselves a violation of the principle of division of labor. The man who has all the qualities that go to make up a good foreman is very difficult and sometimes impossible to find, for the duties which he has to perform are of almost infinite variety. Based upon these theories, which are on the whole sound, has been built a system of organization which is almost in direct antithesis to the military type at every point. Briefly stated, the idea is that the duties of the foreman even are divided up among a number of men, and the workman instead of being responsible to a single superior for the faithful performance of all the duties that are assigned to him, is responsible to six or eight 'functional' bosses. To each one, of course, he is responsible for that part of his work over which the boss is placed.

This form of organization, known as functional management, will come up for fuller discussion later. It is sufficient to note here that wherever it can be successfully applied, experience seems to show that functional management results in a considerable economy and lowering of cost; so that, as we shall see, in the thousands of cases where it could be successfully applied but is not the organization is defective in that it does not take advantage of all its opportunities of economy and profit.

Another fault of the ordinary type of management is that there is no method of securing uniform efficiency in the different departments. In a large concern, it is generally true that one or two departments have been built up to a high degree of efficiency through the energy or special ability of some leader of more than ordinary force of character. As a rule, this leader has risen from some humble position in the ranks until he became the head of his particular division. In this department the greatest economy has been brought about in the use of tools and machinery, the men have been selected from the best types and trained to work at their maximum of efficiency, while systems of stock keeping and cost accounting have been introduced, so that wasteful methods have been eliminated. It may even happen that the profits of a whole establishment are based upon one or two sections that are managed scientifically, while the other departments are running at a loss or at best are not much more than holding their own. A great part of the loss from this state of affairs, which experience has shown to be only too common, can be eliminated or at least discovered, by a system of cost accounting installed throughout the whole establishment, by which separate accounts are kept for each department exactly as though it were an independent concern. Expert reorganizers have run across strange illustrations of the fallacies that manufacturers have been led into through the lack of uniformity in the development of the several divisions of their works, when the efficiency of the different departments was not measured with mathematical accuracy.

Not long ago a certain bicycle firm, taking account of its sales and expenses for the year gone by, found that there was a net profit of $100,000. Now the department that had to do with the manufacture of pneumatic tires was believed by the foreman of that division, and by the head of the concern himself, to be the one that was responsible for half the profits. It was decided, therefore, to build a separate plant in which to carry on the making of tires, while the other parts of the manufacture were continued in the old establishment. At the end of a year, to the astonishment of all concerned, the new factory went into the hands of a receiver, while the old was in even better shape than before. The services of an expert reorganizer were secured, and all the accounts of both the old plant and the new were carefully examined and compared. The new factory, run on the same lines as when it had been merely a department of the old, showed a loss of $25,000. In other words, the old concern had been making $125,000 a year out of the departments that were retained when the new plant was built, and losing $25,000 a year in its tire division.

The problems connected with bringing each department up to a fixed standard of efficiency must be left for fuller discussion. The first step toward remedying the fault just illustrated is to find out accurately just which parts of an establishment are showing the best results and which are below the standard. This is secured by a departmental efficiency record in which output, number of employees, pay-roll and costs are collected and compared.

A case contrary to our Illustration of the bicycle factory, namely, one in which most of the profits of a whole establishment come from the superior efficiency of a single department, is surprisingly common, even among concerns which are supposed to be well managed. It frequently happens that the able foreman who has brought his particular section up to a high point has been made manager of the whole establishment on account of the special ability shown in his line. An enterprise under such a management will usually show that the one department in which the leader has grown up reaches a high degree of excellence, while the others are indifferently conducted. The manager's success in one department, gained through an intimate acquaintance with all the smallest details of that division and personal training of the workmen, could not be transferred to other parts of the works indiscriminately. It is because there are so few really efficient men, who are generally at the head of great concerns where, they cannot come into personal contact with the men and the small details of the separate departments, that the need for a scientific and fundamentally correct system of management is so keenly felt.

The old idea of organization made it a question of men alone, and regarded it as an axiom that if the right man be found the methods could safely be left to him. The scarcity of 'right men' and the necessity of spreading the activities of such a one, when found, over so wide a field, brings it about that adherence to the old idea will, in nine cases out of ten, result in glaring examples of inefficiency in those – departments with which the 'right man' is not intimately acquainted.

The combination of competing firms often furnishes pertinent illustrations of how a single department may frequently provide most of the profits of the whole establishment, while the rest of the plant is at best merely not causing a loss. For many years there were two furniture manufacturers who carried on business in competition with one another in the same field; and in spite of very obvious disadvantages that resulted from their pulling in opposite directions, they could not be brought together.

The real obstacle to amalgamation lay in the fact that each of the heads of the two concerns carried out a line of policy absolutely different from that of the other, and each thoroughly and heartily believed that the other was wrong. Each of these men occupied the position of owner and manager of his company through the special ability which he had shown while in the ranks; but while one had forced to the top through the skill he had shown in advertising, salesmanship, and the marketing of products, the other had come up through the manufacturing end of the establishment. They were finally persuaded by mutual friends and well-wishers to combine. When their books were gone over and compared by an expert cost accountant, it was found that each man had plenty of ground for thinking the other weak and inefficient. The man who had risen from the factory end, it was found, was making his furniture fully 30 per cent cheaper than his rival; the salesman manager, on the other hand, was making up the difference by his superiority in advertising, selling, intimate knowledge of the market demands, and efficient organization of the commercial end of the undertaking. The combination of the two firms suited in an economical organization in each establishment of the department which before had been poorly conducted, and a consequent saving to the new concern of the large percentage of profits that had been lost when each was independent.

In discussing the defects that are found in the ordinary type of organization, it is, of course, understood that every. management must have, in some degree or other, the special factors which we noted earlier as being essential to good organization. To summarize again, we may call them definite structure, lines of authority, definite and fixed responsibility, system and rules and regulations; accurate records and statistics and an effective cost system; and, lastly, harmony and cooperation between employers and men and between different departments. The defects due to a lack of one or more of these factors in an organization have already been partly indicated in the description of them and will appear in greater detail when we come to discuss the best types of organization. The defects discussed under the head of the adaptability of the type of organization to the purposes and conditions of the business, and the unevenness in the efficiency of the management of different departments, are intended in a more general way to outline the task before us. It may be worth while, now, to descend to particulars and to note the faults to be found in the details of the average business.

The average business will be found to include:

1. Superintendent, foremen, job bosses, and workmen. The relation of these to one another and to the business as a whole, constitute the problems of management.
2. A system of manufacturing, of handling raw material or products, or of carrying on the work for which the business is organized.
3. A commercial end, by which we may designate sales organization, advertising, and methods of creating and reaching the market.

First we have to consider the superintendent. Enough has been said already to indicate the difficulties which are met with when the entire responsibility for the efficient management of all the departments in an establishment rests on the shoulders of one man. It is obvious that an effective management must devise some plan by which the efficiency of all departments is automatically brought up to a certain set standard, and whereby the maintenance of this standard of efficiency rests upon something more solid than the personal skill or intuition of a single super-intendent alone. In the functional type of management, this result is best accomplished through a. so-called 'planning department,' hereafter to be described, where the system for the operation of all departments is origi-nated and sent out, and the results are recorded. In the ordinary or military type, the superintendent should come into touch with the foremen of all the departments in such a manner that the skill, foresight, and ability of the superintendent, supplemented by the intimate acquain-tance with details and personal contact of the foremen, may combine to bring the efficiency of all departments up to a uniform level. This plan, simple enough on paper, meets with many obstacles when tried in actual experience and cannot be put through by a cheap or inefficient man. A strong and capable superintendent is, as a rule, cheap at almost any price. The advantages of having a capable superintendent who surrounds himself with efficient foremen to advise him upon important subjects, will bring to a concern unexpected advantages besides those which are obvious. It gives the foremen an opportunity to add to their knowledge of the affairs of the business and gives them a broader outlook upon the results to be accomplished, so that they are better able to work toward the end in view. Then, again, a foreman who is called into consultation with his chief is stimulated to good work by the opportunity thus afforded to bring his results to the immediate notice of his superior. In the ordinary system, the foremen peg along by themselves; they are frequently actuated by feelings of jealousy toward one another; by grumbling and fault-finding they weaken their own efficiency and that of the entire plant. With proper management they can be moved to cooperate with their superintendent; with each other and with the men under them, for the good of the firm.

Next to consider are the foremen. The question of securing efficient foremen, or of getting the work that belongs to them efficiently done, is becoming increasingly prominent as the most difficult problem in the science of business organization. With the tendency of the age toward specialization in work, it is becoming more and more obvious that the great variety of qualities demanded in a foreman, and the large range of duties that he is called upon to perform, present an almost insurmountable obstacle to the problem of securing the most efficient and economical performance of a foreman's functions. These are the men who come into daily touch with the workers at machine and bench; to them belongs the responsibility of securing the maximum results from the labor force; on them falls the task of bringing out the greatest possibilities of the machines – matters which can be determined with mathematical accuracy (as we shall see later), and with which very few of the ordinary type of foremen are acquainted. Yet in the ordinary run of establishments the foreman is simply a machine hand or job boss, who has been promoted because of his energy, his desire to please, or because he has long years of service behind him.

The person selected for this important position may have only a knowledge gained from the running of his machine, when as a matter of fact he should be thoroughly skilled in the methods of modern scientific machine practice, should be in touch with the most modern mechanical processes, should know the best methods of handling men and of getting the best results from them, and should be able to supervise the timekeeping and fix the rates of pay. More and more it becomes evident that profits depend upon the selection of foremen of a much higher grade than has in the past been recognized as necessary.

The standard set is high, and there are few men who can perform efficiently and economically all the duties that their position calls for. At least it may be said that is most concerns the foreman should be selected with much greater attention to the fitness of their qualities and training for the work that they have to perform. Some experienced students of this subjects, indeed, maintain that the variety of work that falls to the lot of the foreman is so great that it is impossible for any one man to put it through in the most efficient manner. In the best organized establishments of to-day there is an increasing tendency to take away from the foreman many of his functions, such as determining the speed of the machines and the types of tools to be used, fixing the rates of pay, and other things. This plan of dividing the functions of the foreman up into separate operations and putting each function into the hands of a man who is skilled in his line, will bring great economies where it can be instituted. It seems limited in its application however, to manufacturing concerns of considerable size where great masses of product uniform in type and pattern are turned out. In many cases the more elaborate plan cannot be carried through, and as a matter of fact it is only rendered necessary by the weakness of the ordinary type of foreman. In the average establishment the same economies can be achieved is the foremen are selected with care, of they are trained sedulously in the various duties they have to perform, if they are stimulated to so their best in cooperation with the superintendent and the other foremen, and if they are made to feel that good work will be instantly recognized and rewarded.

Last come the workmen. Probably there is no problem connected with business organization that needs so much attention and careful study as the scientific management of the workmen. There is no question that the average man, whether he be millionaire or day laborer, is inclined by nature to take it easy. It is only as a result of example of external stimulant of a powerful kind that a man can be induced to work at a more rapid rate. The result is that in a surprisingly large number of cases the workmen are loafing along at an easy gait and efforts made by the managements to get better results are so poorly directed that the workmen increase their efforts only in the direction of making a brave show of working at top-notch speed. The common tendency to 'mark time' is, as a rule, considerably increased wherever a large number of men work together at similar work and uniform standard rate of pay per day. Whenever this happens, the better and more energetic men are forced almost to slow down their gait to that of the weakest and lest efficient. The workmen as a rule, are inclined to look with suspicion upon any man does twice as much as the average his work will tend to throw an average man out of employment. Second, the presence of a man who is doing extra well furnishes to the employer an argument why all the other men in the shop should follow his example. Then, too, when a naturally energetic man works for a few days alongside of a lazy one who is getting the same pay, he cannot help feeling that half of his hard work is going for nothing.

The remedy for this state of affairs will occur to anyone; namely, that the reward should be proportionate to the work performed. This desirable state of affairs has been sought generally by the installation of piece-work system. In theory, payment by piece work is intended to give the workman a direct share in any increased production which he may bring about, by more intelligent or increased exertion. As applied in most shops, the piece-work system results in high labor cost to the employer, little or no increase of wages to the employee, and consequently very little satisfaction to either side.

Thus we see that whether the labor force is working under ordinary day work or on piece system, there is an equal temptation to idleness and an equal tendency to reduce the profits of the employer through high labor cost. Manufacturers, business men, and students of labor problems all over the country are showing a lively awakening to the great losses that have been needlessly suffered under the prevailing system of paying wages, and the different plans that have been devised to remedy the situation under varying, conditions will demand careful consideration. Under conditions as they exist to-day the foreman sets prices by methods strictly their own; the employer suffers continued losses through high labor cost and limited output and the workman idles away his time at machine and bench as the only way open to him to get even with the management for its unfair treatment.

The defects of business organization which are connected with manufacturing, with handling the stock, or with carrying on the work for which the business is organized, may be traced to three sources; namely, carelessness or ignorance in regard to system, to accounting, and to manufacturing methods. Let us begin with those specific faults of system which are connected with the handling of the raw material or product in the establishment.

Almost every business man makes a practice of taking an inventory of his stock on hand at least once a year. This is usually accomplished by a complete or partial shutting down of the business for several days, and does him little good except to show him what stock he has on hand and how much he has made or lost at the end of the year's operation; yet it is not only entirely practicable, but very profitable, to make an inventory each month of the stock bought, sold and on hand. Such a system will prevent large purchases of goods which must remain on hand for a long period of time, unnecessarily increasing the amount of working capital required and the charges for interest.

Another fault of system is connected with the tracing of products in their progress through an establishment. Few concerns realize the necessity of keeping accurate records, showing exactly which point has been reached by the unfinished product, how far it has advanced in its way toward completion, and how soon it may be finished. Yet the failure of more than one concern has hinged upon its tardiness in filling orders and fulfilling its contracts as to delivery, which might have been avoided by careful attention to a system of tracing stock. Like the monthly inventory system, this plan also will affect a saving in the amount of capital invested it will show, for example, if any products are lying idle because no provision has been made to finish them and in any case a good tracing system tends to keep stock moving.

Something has already been said as to the great importance of the cost system in keeping the efficiency of different departments up to a uniform level. But a thorough-going application of system to the problems of cost of manufacture must not stop here. Most types of management are lamentably lax in the matter of keeping accurate records of the work per formed by the individual laborers. Yet if this be not done, the business man will find himself up in the air at the very outset of any reorganization aimed to reduce cost of production. A campaign of this kind must usually start by increasing the efficiency of the working force and eliminating the inefficient men. If the individual records of the men are not kept, there is no basis except guesswork on which to start campaigns of improvement.

Another advantage of great importance to be gained by keeping individual records for the work men is the effect of such records upon the workmen themselves. The man who knows that an accurate tabular account of his value or his incompetency is kept and carefully inspected by his superiors, will be under a much more powerful incentive to do good work. If, in addition, increase of pay and chance of promotion are made directly contingent upon good records as shown in the cost sheets, the tendency toward idleness or slovenly work, even under an unsatisfactory or antiquated system of pay, will be materially reduced.

It is hardly necessary to point out that every manufacturer, in these days of close competition, should keep an accurate itemized account of the cost of every article, turned out. The advantages of so doing are too obvious to need comment and yet how many failures are caused. by nothing less than the selling of products at prices lower than the actual cost to make up the goods. Manufacturers should be able to tell at any time the cost of any article made; should have records showing how much an unfinished article has cost up to the present and how much more it will cost to finish it. It is by such records alone that he will be able to keep within proper limits his costs of production.

Defects in manufacturing methods, such as can be brought into a general discussion of business principles, must be limited to a consideration of how to get the best results from the cooperation of machines and men and in assembling the final product. A lack of scientific management in the matter of cost system and payment of wages will invariably lead to weaknesses in the economical handling of machines and tools and the processes of production. It is astonishing to find out what a lack of information there exists in regard to the amount and kind of work that may be turned out from the proper use of machines. In fact, there are very few establishments in the country where sufficient experiments have been carried on to show exactly at what speed, with what power and under what conditions a machine will turn out the most work. In most cases this very important matter is left in the hands of the foremen, who, without knowledge or experience as to the methods of finding out what must be done, make what they think a shrewd guess and let it go at that. Even worse, the foreman sometimes leaves the whole matter to the individual preference of the workmen. If defects of this kind were not so widespread in general, one would wonder that ninety or ninety-five per cent of the manufacturers of the country do not go to the wall. For success it must be remembered no company need be better organized than its competitors. The methods of accurately determining just how much work a machine is capable of turning out under best conditions need not be discussed at this point. It may be well, however, to point out by an example or two just what is meant. Suppose that a foreman superintends twenty men shoveling sand, and wants to get the best results from the use of the shovels. Now, one might think that good results would accrue from letting each man use a shovel of the size and shape that he might prefer. Experience has shown, however, that the best results are obtainable only by experiment. The men should be provided with shovels of different sizes and shapes, and each of these should be employed for a certain length of time. On each variation of pattern and size, accurate time measurements with a stop watch, measuring say the time required to fill a wheelbarrow, should be recorded. The comparison of all the statistics so gathered will show what should be the shape of the shovel, and how much it should hold if the maximum results are to be secured. A certain contractor in Massachusetts carried on experiments for three years with different shapes and sizes of shovels, and discovered that one containing 22 pounds measured the scientific load on which the average man can do his maximum. It need not be pointed out that, side by side with this process of selecting the proper shaped tool to be used, there should go on the process of selecting also the proper men. This may be done by keeping individual records of the work of each man, as already pointed out.

In the case of machines of more complexity than we find in the simple pick or shovel, the securing of scientific results is not so easy, but is correspondingly more important. The difficulties are increased here by the large number of variables that have to be considered. In recent years, extensive investigations have been made in regard to machines for metal cutting. It was found that the variables to be considered in this case ran about as follows: 1, shape of cut; 2, kind of metal being cut; 3, shape of tool; 4, kind of steel in tool and metal; 5, depth of cut; 6, power of machinery; 7, rapidity of turn; 8, effects of soda water or other cooling chemical.

From what has been said, it may. easily be seen that the ordinary type of foremen, anxious as he may be to do well and, to make a good showing, has no means of securing the necessary training and experience to bring about the proper results. When such matters as cutting speed, depth of cut, angle of cut, and other important variables are left to guess work, it is no wonder that upon scientific investigation, losses of fifty and sixty per cent in the efficiency of machines are found. For many types of machinery, careful investigations by skilled engineers have already been made out and results tabulated. The foremen should be acquainted not only with the methods of securing scientific data of this kind, but should be trained to recognize the value of and use such results as have, come or may come to their hands.

The situation relative to the use of the proper machining methods is well illustrated by the experience related by Mr. C. U. Carpenter, in his book on 'Profit-making in Shop and Factory Management.' 'I recently installed,' says Mr. Carpenter, 'in certain factories several large boring mills and heavy planers, built by two of the highest grades of manufacturers. In order to test the amount of knowledge possessed by the manufacturers of these machines they were called upon for advice as to the best results that could be secured from them when working under differing conditions. Simple questions were asked as to the speed and depth of cut possible in order to secure the best results. These builders of the tools could not give a definite answer that would be of any material assistance to anyone needing light. They knew that their machine tools ran as fast and would turn out as much work, etc., as any in the market; but when it came to the question of shapes of tools, depth of cuts, results upon differing grades of metal, results from the use of water and composition on the tool, and so on, they floundered hopelessly. The lack of knowledge of the best results obtainable is not by any means con fined to the older types of shops. There is many a factory to-day which to the eye presents a modern appearance, with its new buildings, well-ventilated and cleanly, its fine equipment in machinery and tools, and its show of bustle and hustle, which yet needs the doctor's care badly.'

With foremen so utterly unversed in the fine points of their work, can it be wondered at that expert organizers often find differences of 30 per cent and more in the working efficiency of the machines under different men, and report establishments where the best guess made as to conditions of maximum output falls twenty or twenty-five per cent short of what it should be.

There is little need to dwell at length on the shortcomings that make their appearance in. the commercial ends of a business – the buying, and particularly the selling, departments. Business enterprises differ so greatly in this respect that it is difficult to pick out any features that will be common to all. To some kinds of business houses the buying and the selling are the whole thing – the retail department store, for example, is organized for no other purpose than to buy and sell again, its services consisting only in adding utilities of time and place to an already manufactured product. Nevertheless it is true that there is hardly any business enterprise which does not find the purchasing of raw materials, machinery, furniture, and so on, and the selling of a finished product very important parts of its functions. In the early days of the handicraft system it was the practice for the customer to bring raw material and pay for having it worked up. Nowadays all business enterprises buy something and sell something again.

In regard to the buying department, the defects in most concerns can, as a rule, be reduced to two. First, it is liable to degenerate into a 'dickering' department, filled with men who have great faith in their powers of bargaining, but who unconsciously cost their company thousands of dollars through developing the wrong kind of qualities and knowledge. Strange to say, the importance of the purchasing department is underestimated more than that of any other in the majority of cases, in spite of the fact that one would think that heads of business firms ought to be more keenly alive to opportunities for effecting economies and saving profits in the buying of materials than in other less obvious ways. Clearly it is impossible for one man to possess all the technical knowledge necessary to enable him to select just what is required in relation to the ends to be accomplished and the surrounding conditions yet we find employers curiously indifferent on this important point, and buyers as a rule concentrating their energies on driving a close bargain, with little regard for the value to the firm of the articles for which they are bargaining.

What is needed in many cases is a full and complete system of instruction sheets for buyers, compiled and inspected by the heads of the departments who are most intimately acquainted with the nature and specifications of the articles needed. The buyer should have full and complete information as to where he can find out what he needs to know, and the value of his work should be judged not by what kind of a price he has secured but by the closeness with which he has approximated meeting the specifications required in the article purchased. By these means mistakes such as the one made by a buyer for a certain manufacturing plant will be avoided. This man had a great deal of confidence – not unjustified – in his ability to force down prices. Instructions were sent to him to purchase a large lot of steel shafts of certain size to be used in the manufacturing of a machine product which his firm was turning out. He proceeded on most approved lines to secure bids from several different firms; and by playing one off against the other, he finally purchased them at a very low price, and moreover secured an immediate delivery shortly after that he was called into the manager's presence to receive, as he supposed, commendation for his good work. What was his surprise, therefore, to be met by a sour countenance and the cold statement that the firm was out several hundred dollars on his bargain, for the simple reason that soft steel shafts would have served the purpose as well as the high grade hard' steel ones purchased. The manager blamed the buyer for not knowing what was wanted, and for making no effort to find out; the buyer blamed the department head who had sent instructions so vitally defective.

Both were right. Information as to purchases should be set down clearly and unmistakably, and in such a way that the buyer can co-operate with every department intelligently. On the other hand, the buyer should be trained to consider that the most important part of his duties consists in following instructions intelligently, in being pertain that his information as to purchases is absolutely accurate and in keeping in touch with the various departments so that he will know at least the outline of the processes of production and what kinds of materials will meet conditions.

Another important part of the buyer's duty is to keep in touch with what there is in the market, how it may be secured, and what relation these products may have to the needs of his firm. The buyer, as well as the management itself, should be extremely well posted in regard to the latest processes of manufacture and the latest improvements in tools and equipment. The makers of tools and raw materials are ordinarily under a double temptation to persuade the buyer to stick to the old ruts and follow precedents slavishly.

In the first place, if improved processes have created a demand for a new kind of tools and equipment, the makers of these things are naturally anxious to dispose of the old stock and will make the strongest kind of appeal to the ambition of a buyer who wishes to acquire a reputation as a shrewd and clever bargainer.

Second, raw material and tool and equipment manufacturers seldom find it to their interest to encourage the adoption of new processes, or a demand for new tools. They have money tied up in old patterns, in old stock, in machines going through the process of manufacturing, and in their own equipment. Changes of a radical nature would prove a serious matter to them.

Moreover, it is too often true that the progressive firm, the one which stands immediately in readiness to adopt improvements and make desirable changes, finds itself alone in the field. Until the demand of this firm for new tools and equipment has been supplemented by that of sufficient others to compel the manufacturer of such products to turn them out on a large scale, every effort will be made to induce the progressive management to stick to the old. If improvements are to be put through, the buyer must be taken into the manufacturer's confidence, must be made to see exactly what it is intended to accomplish, and must be fortified against the attempt of other firms to sell him something different and against his own ambition to make his name famous as a shrewd bargainer.

Another mistake often made in connection with the purchasing department is that of giving to this department charge of the receipt and storing of materials. It is true that in many eases departments cannot be sharply divided off in :such a way that there is a separate division for every small function of a firm's necessary operation; but the importance of separating the purchasing department from that which has charge of the receiving and storing of the incoming stock is not often realized. The accounts of the purchasing body and that of the receiving department must be kept absolutely separate if the management desires to avoid not only confusion and waste, but absolute dishonesty. If the purchasing body is given charge of the care of material, the opportunity for graft is too immediate and too tempting for even the most honest to resist. There is not only in some cases the danger of having things carried off and 'lost,' – I almost said strayed or stolen, but it becomes the easiest thing in the world to devise an amalgamated system of bookkeeping .by which things are really paid for, apparently received, but actually never seen in fact. The experiences of receivers and expert accountants teem with instances in which the whole purchasing department of an apparently well-managed concern is honeycombed by a system of private rebates, corruption money, and 'doctored' accounts. There should be a divorce effected between the purchasing department and receiving department to prevent such collusion; and this rule should be followed, no matter how small the plant.

At the other end of the commercial function of a business appears the side which has to do with the marketing of the product. The most crucial defects connected with the marketing of the product appear in the methods of the sales department. Few business men are aware of the possibilities that lie in the scientific development of this end of the concern. The prevailing impression is that salesmen are born and not made. It cannot be denied that this impression is not without foundation. A certain great politician once said of his father that he was the best silk salesman in Massachusetts. It was true that he knew very little about silk fabrics, but he had about him that impressive personality that individual magnetism, that pushing force of character, which made people want to do what he wanted them to do.

If the sales manager can collect, organize, and send out a force of such men, well and good. The trouble is that most managers, in attempting to do this, run across the same sort of difficulties that would be met by a man attempting to organize a company of ex-presidents, or that Frederick of Prussia encountered when trying to form a regiment of eight-foot soldiers. The ordinary salesman must form an effective member of a fighting or a selling force, not because he is a giant, but because he has the training and knowledge and skill requisite for fighting or selling. Few sales managers realize the gulf of difference there is between a man who merely quotes prices and waits for something to happen, and the man who sells the goods over, his competitor's head because he can talk the business. Innate selling ability need not be entirely disregarded in hiring men. The organizer of an army, though he cannot rely on eight-foot regiments, does not on that account accept weaklings; but an inborn selling personality must be bulwarked by a thorough training in all the talking points of the product to bring the best results. The good salesman should know all the faults, and the good points as well, of rival products; he should know beforehand all the objections he will have to meet; he should have from the experience of all the best men who have been over the ground the most successful methods of displaying the merits of the goods to a prospective customer.

Lack of system in this department, as in many others, is often the stumbling block in the way of best results. The manager who will employ a new salesman, give him a few samples and a price list, and send him out to do business, need not wonder if the territory is not being covered or the customers not being reached. The first requirement is thorough and organized training of the selling force. Next, the records returned by the salesmen should show at once whether the ground is being covered, whether all possible customers are being handled, and whether competition is being met. In far too many firms the salesmen are encouraged to compete against one another, under the false idea that such a system will so stimulate them that the largest volume of sales will be recorded. This system often brings it about that the salesmen become jealous and distrust each other. They have no idea at all of pulling together for the good of the company, and worst of all they keep jealously to themselves whatever knowledge they have gained, which for the company's good ought to be shared by all. The results that have been achieved by scientific development of proper methods of sales management have proved that this subject is worthy of the most careful and painstaking study.

The defects of business organization that have been outlined show that, from a broad point of view, the problem before the business man is twofold in its scope. Before he can apply his knowledge of how to correct faults, he must first know what is wrong. The every-day business man plunges along in the dark, unprovided with the information that proper organization, system and methods would bring to shed light on his path. His buying department may be in the worst kind of confused and leaky condition, but he does not know it; the factory methods may be costly in the extreme, but he may not know why, or how to better them; his salesmen may be blandly quoting prices, while his competitor writes down the orders secured by a trained selling force. Worse than the man who realizes where his losses come from but does not know how to stop them, is the executive who does not realize the inefficiency that prevails in all the divisions of his establishment, and who cannot see beyond the fact that profits are on the thin edge which divides a plus quantity from a minus quantity.

Such a one should go into his business thoroughly. He should attempt to discover, first, if all the factors that go to making a strong organization are present in his concern. Then he should trace out, one by one, the weaknesses that are found in so many of the average plants. Lastly, he should compare his business with a successful one in the same line, choosing for this purpose one in which the foremen are trained in the latest and best methods of handling men and machinery in which the workers are happy in giving their best energies to further the company's progress; and in which 'system' in cost methods and reports not only discovers the weak places, but points out the lines of progress, prosperity and profits.

# The Organization of Great Corporations[1]

## William W. Mulford

If you are a corporation wage earner, and seven out of every ten of the wage earners of the United States are, then you surely have a fellow feeling for the office boy who, as the story goes, when asked 'Who is the responsible party here?' replied 'I don't know who's responsible, but I'm always to blame.'

Was the boy at fault, or was the root of the trouble deeper, possibly in the organization itself? The 'Trusts' are with us because they fill a specific requirement. They are well worth while and when their virtues outweigh their faults are greatly to be desired. How firmly they are entrenched may be judged from the statistics which Mr. Winchell, president of the St. Louis and San Francisco Railroad, has given us:

There are more than one million corporations doing business in these United States; of all the capital employed, 82 per cent is in the carrying on of the business of incorporated concerns; corporations employ 71 per cent of all wage earners, pay 72 per cent of all the wages, and buy 75 per cent of all the materials used in manufacturing enterprises of the country.

For the industrial world these figures challenge attention. It was my honor to know Dr. Orton, a 'Louis Agassiz man,' one time president of the Ohio State University. In discussing the economic conditions of the day about the time the first steel corporation combinations were being formed, I asked, 'Dr. Orton, what do these combinations of big corporations lead to?' to which he replied, 'I am very optimistic on the outlook. They lead to socialism.' 'But, Dr. Orton, you are not a socialist, and I am not a socialist !' And as I recall it, this was his reply:

Well, I am an old man, I can prophesy. You are a young man. It will not do for, a young man to prophesy. We are neither of us socialists

---

[1] [*Engineering Magazine*, vol. 40, 1910, pp. 240–48.]

in the sense of the fanatic so-called German student, nor in the sense of the labor-union demagogue, but there is a right form of socialism. You have seen the oil business gradually absorbed under the control of one great corporation, or call it 'trust' if you like. You have seen the same thing in the sugar business. And now the iron men are attempting to work out their industrial problems. Your will see a great corporation formed, call it 'Steel Trust' if you like. This will be dominated by one strong man, possibly a narrow man, certainly a far-seeing man of strong will and determination. But he will die. Another man with perhaps a little broader humanity and not so strong will power take his place. But he, too, will die. The time will come when the men with money, the men of brains, and the men of sinew will realize that they are themselves the foundation strength of the steel business. The industry will have developed from the 'one-man' policy to the broader and stronger determined by the will of the majority of the true masters of this particular industry.

I believe that you will live to see the time in this country when not only the Declaration of Independence, and the Constitution of the United States, but also the Recognition of Industrial Organizations are the prominent forces in the land.

The outlook following the financial storm is brighter than it has been for many a long day. Even in the silver lining of the storm-clouds it, is apparent that the right development of the corporation is a vital question for business prosperity, if that prosperity is to have any permanency. Now is the time to take another buckle in our belts, study the compass, set our course truer, and prepare for a longer, surer run. The prevailing idea seems to have been that the corporation officials, 'captains and lieutenants of industry,' were definitely divided into two classes; first; the builders up, creative men, orderly men, planners, and executors of great undertakings of great enterprises, of great organizations; second, the tearers down, those who by destroying one combination possibly establish another, those who profit by destruction, those who gather in the forced temporary profits from economies brought about by cutting down maintenance so as to show increased earnings and 'getting out from under' before the investors are 'wise.' Experience teaches us there is a third class of equal importance, the confusionists, those who thoroughly tangle up affairs through a maze of multiple corporations, through a labyrinth of combinations of controlling interests. Any worker can choose which of these classes he prefers to join, but he may find it difficult to keep in that class, no matter how earnestly he strives. The game, though only in its infancy, is keenly interesting, pace set is strenuous, 'it is not so much where you are, as which way you are going that counts.' This is equally true, for the individual labor union and the corporation.

'Education is the only interest worthy the deep, controlling anxiety of the thoughtful man,' so Wendell Phillips told us. Possibly in a broad sense a corporation is only the curriculum of the great live American university of today.

A composite photograph of the forms of organization of the many corporations has its educational value, because the mastering of economic conditions through common business customs, whether it is pioneer work, development work, or the carrying on of an established enterprise, requires an organization of forces which is briefly the means of accomplishing and adjusting the division of labor. If it is desired to establish in any industry co-operative methods that save waste and increase profits and efficiency, it is necessary to acquire more than the first rough use of the power of organization.

The kinds of work are so many, are so diversified – there is such a wide difference between the ways of the easy-going chap and the ways of the martinet (though both frequently are eminently successful in their management of corporations and men) that at first it would hardly seem possible that the form of organization of the great corporation was already assuming uniform shape.

Like all wholesome American business methods it is a matter of evolution. The better forms have been adopted after careful studies of those already used in doing similar work. These are changed, modified, or revised to meet the conditions and requirements of the particular work; then improved and simplified in order to obtain greater efficiency and to yield larger results. Certain customs are common to many of the successful big corporations. This has gradually brought about a standardization of their forms of organization. Certain fundamental principles are so clearly recognized that they can well be considered as established. These are summed up and expressed in what is known as the 'three-column form.'

Broadly speaking, there are three distinct branches in the work of all large corporation organizations, Financial, Operating, Commercial; all other positions or departments are either subordinate to these, or are practically consulting authorities. This holds true whether in industrials or railroads, whether in the single corporation or in the series of corporations, and whether the departmental. the bureaucratic, the divisional, or the functional form of organization is used.

A chart of the usual 'three-column form' of organization is shown below.

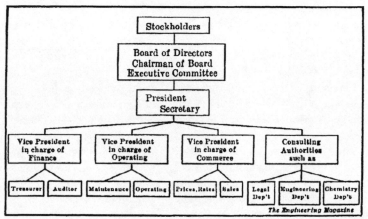

TYPICAL ORGANIZATION CHART FOLLOWING THE THREE-COLUMN FORM.

The reason why the three-column form of organization holds true in so many apparently distinctly different kinds of organizations seems to rest upon the underlying principle of an old saying – 'Even in a Democracy there must be a leader.' This is equally true in carrying on a business. There is always a fixed policy to be carried out, although that policy may be of the *laissez faire* variety. There must be a leader; and furthermore each department, or bureau, must have a head, and these are the lieutenants of the commander in chief. But organization is the antitheists of administration. Under the three column form of organization the distinction between administration and organization is so clear that it is instinctively understood by every employee.

The reason why the financial, operating, and commercial divisions rather than any others are the chief is that the form of organization is not determined by the size of the department, the number of employees, or the volume of work, but by the relative importance of the work and its relationship to the policy of the company. The salient questions of finance, operation, and commerce affect directly the policy of the corporation, and are wholly dependent upon one another. First, the money must be provided. Second, the work must be done. Third, the product must be sold. The best sales man cannot sell unless he has the goods to sell. He knows what the market requires, and what prices he can obtain. He knows how to create selling methods. With that given, the skilled operating man knows how to manufacture what is demanded, or to perform the service that is required. With these two given, the financial man must not only provide for the money but must ascertain beforehand whether the monetary market warrants furnishing or withholding the supply, for financial emergencies must be prepared for well in advance. These are the vital features of any business policy. In the three-column form, the vice-president in charge of finance, the vice-president in charge of operating, the vice-president in charge of commerce, are on an equality; they are peers, and have an associated authority and responsibility.

For this creature of legislation, the corporation, the board of directors is the sovereign power, subject only to the laws of the land. Following the chart, the chairman of the board is the highest official of the corporation. Frequently there is an executive committee of the board of directors. This, however, is usually only a division between the active and inactive directors; possibly it is more courteous to call them 'less active directors.' Again following the chart, the board of directors, or the executive committee of the board, selects the president who is chosen to carry out their policy. Therefore with a given policy, which he is pledged to follow, the president becomes the chief executive of the corporation. He appoints as his executive staff vice-presidents and consulting authorities, in accordance with what he deems to be the essential requirements of the business or work.

The three-column form of organization makes it possible to separate the work of direction and deliberation from the details of execution, and also makes the executives of the great vital departments parties to these deliberation in their positions of staff officials. In this rests its greatest strength.

By increasing the number of vice-presidential staff positions little or nothing is gained. For instance, it is necessary to have the treasurer's and auditor's departments absolutely separate, for the one is a check upon the other. If both the treasurer and auditor are members of the official staff, and unless they work in wonderful harmony, it means that many questions relative only to these two departments arc brought before the staff, seriously increasing its routine work and hampering its work as a whole.

Where there are bureaus of information, these are each under the control of a chief, and may either be staff positions similar to the other consulting authorities, or may be, as is frequently the case, a branch of some specific sub-department.

By decreasing the number of vice-presidential positions the balance between finance, operating and commerce is destroyed. In certain classes of work, or in the early stages of development, any one of the three vital divisions may temporarily overshadow the other two; this, however, in no case alters their relative importance. The corporation may be so small that one official may hold and direct much of the work personally, thereby combining several positions. The ability of the individual together with his capacity for work determines how far this can be successfully carried. For instance, one important railroad had a departmental organization where each department reports to the president. In this case the president practically holds the two positions of president and general manager. Another much more extensive railroad property, which uses the three-column form to its full extent, makes the division the unit, and places all, the powers of a general manager in the man at the head of each division. In the series of corporations, the sub-corporation is sometimes, the unit. The determination of what the unit may best be is found by carrying the adjustment of responsibility, authority, and the division of labor down through the organization.

What the unit maybe has an important bearing on the method of training the men. The career of the young employee is of great moment to a corporation intending to continue its business for any length of time. While there is no patent on ignorance still there are may ignorant men. Men have to be trained and the training has to begin early and extend through many branches of the service in order that they may become competent and efficient. Even when the right material has been developed the best of, men cannot produce results under a faulty or vague organization with its inevitable lack of exact responsibility.

The employee must not only know his duties and what is expected of him, but also rather than have obstacles placed in the way he should be able to obtain in a convenient manner, in so far as they affect his work, all the information, statistics, data, and even an understanding of the policy of the company, if he desires to seek them. Unless this is done, it is impossible to avoid duplication of work; or what may be more discouraging, the employee may suddenly find out that half of the work he has done has already been done by others and probably, because they had more time for it, in a more thorough way. Here is where system be comes manifest. Here is where true *esprit du corps* is nurtured or destroyed. Here is where man's originality is crushed, or he gains the joy of achievement. If he is to 'play up, play up, and play the game,' he must know the rules of that game.

For the individual competition is keen, he must make good every day, all days, month in and month out. If a man resigns, his place is at once filled for there can be no vacancies in a good organization except at the bottom. The pace set is often terrific, heart breaking, soul-racking, frequently leading only to nervous breakdowns. When this occurs the organization is somewhere at fault.

Together with the striving for place, there is the ever increasing pressure for results. An editorial writer in an able article in a recent *Railroad Age Gazette* speaking of the units of work in use, in common railway work, points out how 'reputations are made and blasted in terms of these units or "results" while real causes and effects are lost sight of,' but that is the unit of work not of organization and is 'another story.'

In a series of corporations, especially, the bureaus of information for specific subjects or the departments for particular branches of the business are of inestimable value. Frequently they cause trouble and confusion, showing that the organization is at fault. But under the three-column form of organization they naturally take their proper places, establishing their true relationship to the organization.

Extravagant ceremony and superabundance of 'red tape' are often mistaken for system. It is the mistake of being too highly organized, and can defeat the very end for which the organization was created. It is quickly apparent when an organization is too rigid, and the three-column form is undoubtedly the most flexible and elastic of any so far devised. An old privileged workman when told that the new president of his company in a popular address defined 'organization as the handmaiden of administration,' said 'I make no odds about the handmaiden's looks, nor about her merry widow hat, but did he say whether her dress was of red tape?'

When an organization is successful there is no false motion. 'The man who does things' is usually the man who can so adjust his organization that he is securing the greatest efficiency, that each man is doing the work in which he is most proficient, and that no two are working at cross purposes or causing duplication of work. The form of organization is among the problems of today, and full success for the head of any organization depends largely upon his ability to choose able lieutenants.

If you turn to the 'Official Guide of the Railways' which is the railroad man's handbook, you will find the form of organization and its personnel as shown in the official roster of each road. It is quite remarkable how closely they follow the three-column form of organization. This form, so successfully used by Mr. Cornelius Vanderbilt and on the New York Central and Hudson River Railroad and Mr. Cassatt on the Pennsylvania System, was so skilfully made use of by Mr. Harriman in his great combination of Railroad corporations that Judge Lovett's announcement of the official organization of the Union Pacific merely emphasizes its value Mr. Julius Kruttschnitt, in a paper read before the New York Railroad Club, shows how thoroughly the organization of the operating division has been worked out, together with its relation to the traffic or commercial division. An interesting point in Mr. Kruttschnitt's paper is his comment regarding the meetings held by the various operating heads of the several properties. 'They are legislative bodies assisted by the individual general managers as expert advisers and subject to the approval or veto of the director of maintenance and operation.' In this is shown their educational feature or, to use his own expression, 'a means of disseminating education to officials.'

In the telephone organization only two of the three great divisions of the three-column form of organization are predominant factors, finance and operating. And because there are only two, the power swings like a pendulum from one to the other, for a few years the one dictates and then the other. The commercial division has not been given an equal standing with the other two. It is said that this is because business has always come to them as fast as it could be conveniently taken care of and that they have not had to seek a market except occasionally for a by-product. How ever that may be, it is true that if a balance in power is to be maintained between finance and operating, it can only be accomplished through the recognition of the commercial division as their peer. Mr. George W. Perkins in his article 'Humanizing A Corporation' in *Appleton's Magazine* wrote:

The formation of the United States Steel Corporation meant that individual ownership of some of the most prominent steel industries of this country ceased. To men and students of affairs the real problem that faced the new corporation was this: Could men on salaries and wages successfully carry on this vast organization, directed only by other men on salaries – with no proprietorship above them save a vast and scattered body of security holders?

The far-reaching and efficient plan arranged by Mr. Perkins making it possible for those employees who so desired to become shareholders, and in that way partners, so to speak, with the corporation has proved highly successful. The results form a most important chapter in the educational work of organizations.

There are specific kinds of work which require rather remark able organizations, for instance, that of a great mail-order house, or that of a great engineering undertaking such as the building of the Panama Canal, or that of the 'Base Ball Trust' which is said to be the most effectively organized 'trust' in this country. There are some forms of organization which show clearly the imprint of West Point training.

The importance of the form of organization is constantly increasing. Certain men of large affairs when considering granting a loan, or taking up an issue of bonds, investigate thoroughly the form of organization to know the relative authority and responsibility of the personnel; whether it is a one-man corporation where one individual dominates, or whether a group of broadly and thoroughly trained men are in charge. What authority have the lieutenants; are they automatons, or men of vigor and character? For the investor, next in importance to the story told in the company's balance sheet is the story told in the form of organization.

There is a vast difference between running an organization (or a government) by the mass of employees, such as trade-unionism suggests, and running it through a well-perfected, well-balanced organization which recognizes the rights of the public, the rights of the investors, the rights of the employees. The public as represented in the prices charged for the service they receive, the commercial division; the investors in the dividend and interest returns on their money, the financial division; the employees, in rendering maximum efficiency and receiving credit for work well done, the operating division. Under the well-balanced organization there can be no privileged body of men who can dictate terms to the rest of creation. The true three-column form of organization is for the trust a safety guard against trouble from misguided labor agitation, from retaliatory legislation, from financial dilemma.

The rapid growth and far-reaching consequences of our industrials, our railways, our quasi-public corporations, show the importance of this problem. Involved in it are not only the questions of civil service, of labor and capital, but also of maintaining what Toynbee called 'equal industrial opportunity.' The individual is the atomic unit of the organization. In recognizing and respecting 'the rights of the individual as a person,' well balanced industrial organization becomes the cornerstone of the science of sociology.

# Interdepartmental Relations[1]

## Lee Galloway

*Course of an order for goods.*
Let us now consider the system by which the orders secured by the sales department from customers are converted into finished goods and how they are sent back to the purchaser. We shall assume that the sales department is located at the main office with a sales manager in charge and a corps of clerks as assistants. Under the manager come the district sales offices, each having a certain territory within which are located the traveling salesmen, the local stores or other means by which the company's product is disposed of.

Let us assume that the main office is located in Philadelphia and the district sales offices in various cities; one in Boston to take care of the New England states; one in Albany covering the territory of New York and perhaps that of northern Pennsylvania; another in Cleveland to care for the Ohio, West Virginia and Western Pennsylvania territory.

The district managers have under them the 'drummers,' who are either located at some important centers, or travel over the territory at important intervals. Each branch office may keep on hand a small stock of goods to be used as samples, or may run a store of consider able size. This branch system is also used in the instruction of salesmen, which is treated of under 'Salesmanship' in a succeeding chapter.

We are now interested in the course which an order takes through the factory and how it reaches the purchaser by whom it was given. We will suppose that the salesman has overcome all difficulties and secured his order. Various forms are used in sending the order to the factory, depending upon the character of the goods. The following will serve as a sample:

---

[1] [Chapter 10, *Organization and Management*, New York: Alexander Hamilton Institute, 1911, pp. 161–74.]

---

Date.....................
The A. B. Company,
            Philadelphia, Pa.
Gentlemen:
    Please furnish to the Purchaser Company at 100 Blank
Street, Chicago, the following:
Quantity.        Quality.        No.        Further Details.
Method of Shipment......Mail.....Express.....Freight.
Terms....................when shipment must be made.

---

The orders received every day in the order department of the branch
house are sorted. A careful record is made showing the number of sales,
the various kinds of products and the different sales managers under
whom the goods were sold. If the branch has the product in stock it will
fill the order directly; if not, the order goes to the home office, where
orders are grouped and the factory notified as to what should be manufactured.

When the order is received by the order department, it will be sent
immediately to the shipping department, a duplicate going to the
stores department. This duplicate serves as authority for the delivery
of the finished goods by the stores department to the shipping
department. When the goods are turned over for shipment an
inspector sees that the packing is done properly and that the final
shipment is made in accordance with the order department's instructions.

In case the required goods are not in store but must be manufactured, the direction of the order takes an other course. A copy is sent first
to the superintendent of the production division. If the order calls for
standard products he decides upon the number of parts that must be
made, and notifies the different departments concerned in their
production.

If, however, the order is for a new style or new product, the engineering
department is consulted by the sales manager. A design is made and a
factory order number is assigned to it, which number is retained until the
finished article appears in the store room.

As an illustration let us take an ordinary steam valve. The parts of
this article are one wooden handle, two brass discs, one cast iron
body, two screws. The superintendent will order these different parts

from the store room to the assembling room. The washers will be ordered from the press-room, the steel stems from the machine shop, the wheels for the valves from the carpenter shop, the brass discs from the brass foundry and the iron body from the iron foundry. If the screws are not in stock the purchasing department will be ordered to buy them. The order will go through the shop bearing the order number which has been given it. Each department will turn out its part of it and send it to the stores department. Perhaps there may be departmental store rooms; if so, then the inspector examines it at that stage of manufacture before the workmen get their pay. The stores department then turns the parts over to the assembling department. Having been put into its final form, the valve is returned to the stores department for finished goods, and after a final inspection is ready for the shipping department, the district sales manager and the customer for whom it is made.

The forms that are used for carrying the work through the various processes which have been referred to are generally stock forms. They may vary in details in different businesses, but in general outline they are very simple.

Thus instead of sending an order through the factory calling for 200 valves, the order goes through calling for these six different parts – namely, 200 washers, 200 wheels, 200 stems, 400 screws, 200 cast iron bodies, 400 brass discs.

*Drafting department.*

Reference was made to the close connection between the engineering and sales departments. There also exists a vital relation between the engineering department and the shop itself. The character of the design is important, since all the processes necessary to produce the product will be shaped by it. Hence a design should not be decided upon until a thorough investigation has been made regarding its fitness for the market and the factory conditions governing its manufacture. Among the latter factors to be considered are the ease and cheapness of manufacture, the use of standard and stock parts, and the working relations between the several departmental authorities. One of the great drawbacks to economy, efficiency and progressiveness in many organizations, is the hostility that exists between the various departments. This hostility can be broken down to a large extent by having the draftsmen mingle constantly with the shop foremen, not only to establish a personal touch between the two departments, but that the draftsman may absorb all the shop and foundry practice possible.

Designs that prove a practical success soon gain the respect of the mechanic. Nothing gives a manager more assurance that to feel that every design represents the combined knowledge of the two departments. The shop men, from their shop experience and knowledge of past mistakes, can offer much that is beneficial. Such conferences will also facilitate better routing of the work through the shop. There may be a still further development due to this inter-departmental intercourse, namely a thorough and profitable consideration of the re-design of the regular product. Goods of special sizes and quality can often be changed to a standardized product. Here again the sales department must aid the engineering end of the business by attempting to change public taste so that a standard article will be accepted in place of the individualized sort. Again, if the draftsmen are in close touch with the factory, they will be readily impressed with the necessity of designing parts that can be easily and cheaply machined and assembled, taking into consideration the types of machine tools that must be employed.

The confidence and cooperation of the shopmen can be further gained by having a rule that all drawings must be O.K.'d by the shop foreman before they are placed in the shop. The sustained interest of the foremen may be maintained by a system of reports which they must make based upon their actual experience while the product is passing through their hands. These reports may contain criticisms of the design or new suggestions.

In order to give regularity and vitality to such intercourse between the departments, some system of consultation should be devised. One eminently practical and successful manager appointed a committee consisting of the head designer or draftsman, the head of the tool room, the factory manager, the important machine-room foremen and the head cost man. At times this committee was aided by the presence of the foundry man, the pattern maker and the stock man. Before this committee came all ideas pertaining to the new design or re-design of an old product. 'The experienced shop manager,' says Mr. Charles U. Carpenter, 'has only to consider the usual maddening program of errors in data, mistakes in design, faulty judgment regarding economy of manufacture, lack of standardization of parts, and last, but by no means least, the covert hostility of the shopmen to the new productions of "that drafting department," to realize the possibilities which lie in developing methods which will insure accuracy, economy, standardization, and the interest of the machine foreman in the successful and economical production of any particular design.' Standardization of design, as an important element in management, is treated in Chapter VI of Part II.

*Tool room.*
The relation of this department to the remainder of the factory is most
vital. The tool room has been termed 'the heart of the shop.' No
factory, any more than the artisan, can do its best work with poor tools.
The tool room is therefore responsible for the determination of what the
maximum efficiency of a factory is. Not until the tool room is in a
relatively perfect condition can there be established a basis for the determination of all these individual standards by which the efficiency of the
various producing factors can be measured. The possible output, the
lowest cost of production, a wage standard – all depend on the accurate
determination of the lowest possible time in which each piece of work
can be done. Upon the tool room falls the burden of starting the
productive forces, labor and machines, at a rate consistent with the
above requirements.

To begin with, then, the tool room must meet certain tests. Has it a
knowledge of the best results that can be obtained from the high-speed
cutting tool steel? Does it know the proper shape and size of the cutting
tool? Has it a knowledge of the character of the steel worked upon? Has
it determined the greatest capacity of the machine tool used with
reference to maintenance expense and depreciation?

The tool room is in reality a factory within a factory. It is a place for
making tools that are to be used in the building of the finished machine
for the market. All the methods, therefore, that apply to the organization
of the factory proper will apply to the production of tools.
Standardization, duplication, subdivision of labor – all apply here in
principle as well as in the main organization.

*Local management versus direction from a distance.*
The relations which have been considered so far in this chapter have
pertained chiefly to departmental functions. The method of
management as a system of control has only been referred to indirectly
by the mention of branch offices, etc. The changes which are going on
in the method of management are in harmony with the general tendency
to concentrate the control of industrial enterprises in the hands of a few.
Local management has disappeared in many large companies; that is, the
functions of management are largely performed at a main office, more
or less distant from the factory, the latter being left in charge of a resident
superintendent, who carries out the instructions of the main office and
uses such equipment and materials as are given to him.

Local management exists where the different functions are performed
by departments and divisions located at the factory. This condition of

affairs is said to exist until the balance of power has been absorbed at a main office, which by the character of its orders show that the directing authority has been changed from a local to a centralized control. A main office may per form only a few of the functions or it may exercise all of them. The practice differs with the different companies. The advantages of this separation of the management from the factory lies in the fact that the business transactions are more readily carried on at a business center or a large city, and if the company owns more than one factory, centralization and specialization in management are to an extent productive of considerable administrative economy. Many of the functions can be as well performed away from the mill as at the mill. The telephone, the telegraph and the mail express have made this possible and easy. But, on the other hand, main office management tends to become formal and automatic. Indirect, impersonal and mechanical management has all the disadvantages incident to control on the basis of knowledge not obtained through the senses and by contact.

Some examples of separation may be seen in the movement to a main office of those functions which were associated originally closely with the factory. Briefly these functions are: the supply of equipment and raw material, the employment of labor, the manufacturing of goods, the storing, warehousing and ship ping of same, and the maintenance of the plant. While it is not uncommon to find the executive and selling functions located at the factory, these will be the first to be moved when a separation is decided upon. The following illustrates this separation:

I. *Functions performed at the factory:*
Equipment.
Supplying raw material.
Purchasing.
Employment.
Manufacturing.
Stores and warehouse.
Transportation.
Maintenance.

*Functions performed at main office:*
Executive.
Administrative.
Selling.

II. *Functions performed at factory:*
Purchasing.
Employment.
Manufacturing.
Store and warehouse.
Maintenance.

*Functions performed at main office:*
Executive.
Administrative.
Selling.
Supplying raw material.
Transportation.
Equipment.

III. *Functions performed at factory:*
Employment.
Manufacturing (part).
Stores and warehouse.
Maintenance (part).

*Functions performed at main office:*
Executive.
Administrative.
Selling.
Supplying raw material.
Purchasing.
Manufacturing (part).
Transportation.
Maintenance (part).
Equipment.

*Character of the controlling authority and its relation to the business.*
The control of owners is more frequent to-day than it was a few years ago. The advantages of a control in which the owner feels a personal interest and pride are shown in the greater vigor, freshness and energy of those concerns which approach most nearly to this form of control. The organization which is controlled by a salaried manager, to whom profits and loss are only of an indirect interest, tends toward formality and unprogressiveness. A salaried employee may have character, skill and ambition, but he lacks the interest in the company which the owner has. If the employee has a stimulus which calls forth his personal effort in addition to and distinct from his activity due to a desire to advance in the company and to retain his position as a means of livelihood, there is an approach to the more desirable condition of ownership control.

Many forms of stimulus have been tried, few have been rewarded by success. The prevailing tendency to-day, aside from any disciplinary features of the organization is to rely upon human selfishness, ambition and social necessities to urge the employee to an exertion deemed satisfactory to his employers.

### Committee system.

One method that is proving to be more and more a success is the committee system of management. It is an attempt to apply the same democratic principles of government to factory management that have proven themselves so successful when applied to the national and state governments. The primary idea is to enlist the cooperation of the men in the shop in forming plans and differing suggestions for the good of the company. By frequent meetings and a thorough airing of opinions an esprit de corps and a feeling of responsibility for the success of the business as a whole is established. In its method this system is the opposite of the military method of management. The committee system is especially well adapted to furnishing a means by which the discontented can give expression to their feelings, and affords a valuable aid to the management in locating the cause of any disaffection. Furthermore, it is claimed for this system that it provides a method of overseeing whereby an executive totally ignorant of shop and sales processes is provided with reliable data concerning any weak spots in the production, buying or selling departments.

### Committees.

The purpose of all committees is to act as advisory bodies only. The members of the committees should be composed chiefly of the foremen. The chairmen of the most important committees should in most cases be the factory superintendents. In cases where there are assistant superintendents, these may act as chairmen of the less important committees. In practice it has been found that five or six men form the ideal committee. Yet in some cases when it is deemed advisable to have some of the superior officers or factory experts present the committee may be enlarged, but in no case should the foremen be excluded.

The principal committee is the 'main factory committee.' Before this body come all the general questions pertaining to the shop. The superintendent acts as chairman. The secretary should be a stenographer and should be selected because of his ability to absorb the knowledge of conditions and to express an intelligent opinion upon them. Such a man will prove an invaluable aid to the executive. Other members of this committee should be selected because of their intelligence and progressive tendencies. The following personnel has been proved to be effective by some successful managements: Chief designer of product, chief designer of tools, head of the cost department, and two or possibly three foremen.

One of the special functions of this committee is to advise upon promotions. The superintendent, of course, acts as a final authority in such cases but the fact that no 'boss' is to have a chance to recommend a relative or friend unquestioned by the management, frees the minds of the workmen from feelings of unfairness and injustice.

The meetings of the committee should be regular and certain, and although the exact number depends upon the nature of the business, yet in most cases meetings should be held as often as twice a week. The next committee, or rather set of committees, which follow the main factory committee in importance, are the subsidiary committee or committees. These appear when a company makes not only a main product but also some subsidiary product. Their duties will in general be of much the same nature as those of the general factory committee, but the scope of their work will be limited to the line of production in which they are engaged.

Each committee should be composed of the foremen in that particular line of production together with some of the main factory committee. It has been found advisable to have the same secretary serve on as many committees as possible.

*Meetings of the job bosses and foremen.*
An extension of the committee system is seen in those factories where the foremen hold meetings at frequent and regular intervals with their job bosses. Objection to these meetings is raised by some authorities on the ground that it takes the men away from their work and retards production. In reply to this objection sup porters of the system propose that the meetings be not too frequent (twice a month is sufficient) and that they be short and to the point. They claim that any loss due to slackened production will be more than compensated through increased harmony and the dependence which can be placed upon the bosses. In the last analysis they say it rests upon these men to carry out the plans of the management. The bosses control the labor situation in the shop arid strongly influence the attitude of the laborers toward their work. Furthermore, these meetings not only afford a good schooling for the bosses, but they offer the superintendent an excellent opportunity for judging the men from whom he must select his future foremen.

The general foremen's meeting is another of those meetings which are thought by some to be unnecessary; on the other hand, many important firms consider it to be one of the most important means of efficient management. The purpose of this meeting is to furnish an expert body before which the various shop practices and policies can be discussed. A foreman in defending some act of his department which has retarded progress will not be inclined to use falsehoods or extravagant arguments if he knows his statements are to be listened to by a body of men well acquainted with all the conditions.

The basis of discussions in the majority of such meetings will lie in the consideration of the departmental records. It is in the defense of these reports by the different foremen that many new plans are suggested which are later developed to the great benefit of the company.

Many devices might be suggested as aids in presenting matter to the various meetings of this kind. One method has been the use of a folding blackboard. Orders from an executive officer pertaining to some work which is especially desired to be developed under certain conditions is outlined upon this blackboard so that each foreman knows exactly what is expected of him in carrying out the plans. By this means the foreman is urged to do his best for he knows at the next meeting this blackboard will stand as a mute witness of his success or failure in the presence of his fellow foremen and his superior officers.

*Work of the committees.*
The work which will form the basis of each committee discussion must be in harmony with the purpose of each committee. The following, however, will be suggestive in showing the fundamental problems which must in some form or other be considered:

1. Routine work and report of progress.
2. New designs and inventions.
3. Cost reductions and economy.
4. Plans to standardize products.

# Modern Organization[1]

## Charles Delano Hine

### THE UNIT SYSTEM ON THE HARRIMAN LINES

Organization has been termed a smaller sister of sociology, the science of human nature. Industrial organization, including that of transportation and commerce, reflects and typifies in a greater or less degree the sociological development of a people.

Society for centuries has been emerging from political feudalism and despotism. The emergence from Industrial feudalism and despotism is coming apace. The first working conception of the corporation was that of government. In the Middle Ages governments were such close corporations that the common people as shareholders had little voice in the management. Progressive grants of liberty have made their proxies more effective. Since history repeats itself, the modern industrial corporation is passing through stages of development similar to those which have characterized the evolution of the greatest of corporations – governments.

Corporations, like most individuals, acquire money or its equivalent by the economical expenditure of money or effort. It is always easier to expend than to acquire. The problem, therefore, is so to limit expenditure that a satisfactory margin of acquisition may be preserved. This requires the most effective team work on the part of the individuals who compose the officers and employees of the corporation. Organization as a science teaches the art of so uniting and directing these working forces as to produce the most desirable composite effect.

An interesting concrete example of modern scientific organization is furnished by the most extensive railway system in the world, the Union Pacific System Southern Pacific Company, popularly known as the Harriman Lines. These lines comprise about 18,000 miles of railway extending from Omaha, Kansas City, and New Orleans on the east to

---

[1] [*Engineering Magazine*, vol. 42, 1912, pp. 481–7, 720–22, 869–72; vol. 43, 1912, pp. 44–8, 217–21, 348–52, 588–91.]

Seattle, Portland, San Francisco, Los Angeles and Mazatlan, Mexico, on the Pacific coast. The gross annual earnings aggregate about $225,000,000. The pay rolls carry from 80,000 to 100,000 employees. The operating activities of this vast system, including maintenance and new construction, have been controlled since 1904 by Mr. Julius Kruttschnitt with the somewhat awkward title of Director of Maintenance and Operation, awkward and really misleading because it is difficult to conceive of continued successful operation without satisfactory maintenance. The headquarters of Mr. Kruttschnitt, who is known as the von Moltke of transportation, have lately been removed from Chicago to New York in order that he may be in closer touch with his fellow members of the various boards of directors of the constituent corporate properties.

As a result of studies and recommendations made by the writer in 1908 under the direction of Mr. Kruttschnitt, there has been progressively inaugurated during the last three years a unit system of operating organization. This unit system of organization first installed in January, 1909, on the Nebraska division of the Union Pacific Railroad at Omaha, is now in successful operation on twenty-seven operating divisions and on six general operating jurisdictions, a total of thirty-three units so organized. On many of these the application of the underlying principles has been consistent and earnest, with corresponding and gratifying beneficial results. On a few the application has been too timid and perfunctory to secure very perceptible benefits. In no case, however, has evidence materialized of any positive loss of efficiency. There has in the few cases mentioned been a negative neglect to vitalize the latent possibilities of the new system. The personal patience of Mr. Kruttschnitt is as enduring as his official policies are far-sighted. Realizing that however sound in principle might be the new organization, its very novelty would excite the opposition of the ultra-conservative, he declined to order its adoption but placed upon me, as his special representative, the duty of gaining official converts to the cause. This peripatetic missionary work has involved traveling some 50,000 miles per year, and holding countless meetings and conferences. So fine is the spirit of official loyalty on the Harriman Lines, so splendid is the personnel, that the fatigues of strenuous travel are forgotten in the pleasant associations and delightful friendships that have resulted. To question motives or to permit honest differences of official opinion to affect personal relations would be to preserve a relic of that semi-barbarous feudalism which the new organization seeks to eradicate.

The number of assistant general managers may vary with the size of the jurisdiction, but is normally eight, including the man previously the assistant general manager, who to avoid misunderstanding is reappointed as the senior or number one on the new list. Thus far the list has not included any superintendents of dining cars as contemplated by the complete plan. Meanwhile it is probable that the title of the superintendent of dining cars will be changed to 'chief commissary' to avoid confusing him, the head of a department covering the whole road, from the division superintendent covering only one division.

The number of assistant superintendents on an operating division varies from one on a very small division, to twelve on one very large division. The normal number is six, including the man previously the assistant superintendent, who to avoid misunderstanding is reappointed as the senior or number one on the new list. It is now desired to increase this normal number to eight by taking in the division storekeeper, as has been done on one division, and the station inspector or division agent.

A district comprising two or more divisions and under a general superintendent, is a more or less incomplete unit sometimes created intermediate between a general manager's property and a superintendent's operating division. This is organized under the unit system by following the form of circular for the general manager's office, *mutatis mutandis*, and appointing two or more assistant general superintendents, the normal number being three.

Any study of the underlying principles of the unit system must take into account a most distinctive characteristic of a railway, namely, its physical extent. The head of a manufacturing plant, of a bank, or of a department store, could in a few hours' time personally see every employee of the establishment and observe most of the constituent activities. After a railway once begins business no division superintendent even can hope ever to see all of his trains assembled or all of his employees congregated in one place. So few can come to him that he must go to them. This results in an anomalous condition. While the superintendent or other official is on the road, the routine business at headquarters most be transacted or the company's interests will suffer. Under a feudal conception that because the superintendent is an official he can be in at least two places at the same time, it is the custom on most railways to have the chief clerk at headquarters sign the name of the absent superintendent to official communications. This dishonest violation of the fundamental laws of matter is supported by the same subtle arguments, the same legal fictions, with which the learned men of the Middle Ages sought to bolster up the untenable conception of feudal authority. As a government of laws replaces a government of men, so must what is known as 'government by chief clerks' be eradicated from corporate administration. When the superintendent is absent from head quarters the chief clerk perforce handles communications to such subordinate officials as the master mechanic, the division engineer, the train-master, etc., officers all receiving large salaries than the untitled chief clerk and presumably men of wider experience and better qualifications than he. Sooner or later every chief clerk oversteps the tenuous line and in the name of routine business is consciously or unconsciously restricting the authority or activity of those who are in reality his official superiors. Here comes in an amiable failing of human nature, against which it is the province of organization as a science to impose a check. Every official flatters himself: 'My chief clerk never does that. He knows me too well and appreciates my unwillingness to stand for such things.'

It is an interesting fact that the official who is most zealous in defending his own chief clerk is often one quickest to squirm under the acid test of an inquiry as to the sense of proportion maintained by the chief clerk of the official next above. Singularly enough, promote the official to position higher up, make the offending chief clerk his own, and the marplot becomes a model of discerning judgment. The conclusion is obvious that such an universal state of affairs must indicate the viciousness of a fallacious system rather than the shortcomings of a particular set of individuals.

The unit system of organization eliminates 'government by chief clerks' by insisting that no person shall sign the name or initials of another. A man's name is his birthright, as his signature is his patent of enlightened manhood. The underlying sociological principle is that the individual is the indivisible unit society. Since the business must go on and no person may sign for another, it follows that a sufficient number of duly qualified officers appointed. By giving all the uniform title of assistant this or that, every one is available for prompt comprehensive action should occasion so requires. An attempt at description in a title may be too restrictive by inferentially debarring all features not specifically included. In dealing with human nature a reasonable degree of elasticity is preferable to that rigidity which is often so essential in treating material things. Engineers from familiarity with working applications of the laws of matter often unconsciously impose too rigid requirements upon society. Engineers who design and construct public utilities must study the psychology of the crowd.

Apart from the basic objection to the chief clerk system is the practical disadvantage of having outside matters decided and acted upon a man whose experience has usually been limited to the inside of the office. This lack of sympathetic viewpoint with the difficulties of outside problems is often the cause of unnecessary expense on the outside. The sailor at sea, the traveling salesman on the road, the soldier in the field, the railroad man on the line, all have their troubles with the man in the office. Human nature is the same whether engaged in navigating the ocean, selling goods, making campaigns, or producing transportations. The unit system minimizes the undesirable features of the necessary partial control from a central office by insisting that such outside direction shall be exercised only by officials duly qualified by outside experience.

This requirement is worked out in practice by having normally at headquarters the senior assistant who is in effect though not in name the chief of staff. At the headquarters of an operating division he is, as stated, the man who was previously to reorganization *the* assistant superintendent of the division. The former chief train dispatcher of the division is usually started near the foot of the list of assistants. His duties are unchanged and he remains at headquarters handling such endless details of operation as directing the work of train dispatchers and telegraph and telephone operators, assigning locomotives, distributing cars, manning trains; in fact, he is the incarnation of detailed administrative activity. At a normal division headquarters, then, there are two assistant superintendents on duty, one as chief of staff, the other as chief dispatcher, one the senior and the other a junior, one a distinct head of the office, the other in effect his senior's aide. Both assistants being clothed with authority, either can act on any problem that may suddenly develop in an unforeseen absence of the other. On divisions of very light traffic one assistant at headquarters may be sufficient.

No distinct grade of senior or chief assistant is created in any unit. Normally number one, the real senior, is 'on the lid,' as it is termed, at headquarters, and is excused from outside road duties. In case of his prolonged absence, the head of the unit, the general manager, or the superintendent, as the case may be, designates the most available of the other assistants to remain at headquarters and sit on the lid. An unwritten law here operates to make such designated assistant the chief or senior of all the others for the time being. No formal announcement of such designation is necessary. A railroad does not change its physical location frequently, as does a fleet or an army, and the chance of confusion of relative rank is remote. Advantage is taken of this elastic feature of assignment on some divisions to rotate various assistants through the senior chair in order to gain the splendid comprehensive training for higher positions which the position affords. Assistants thus favored are unanimous in expressions of appreciation for the valuable knowledge and experience acquired.

The feature of consolidating office records in one common file is taken from the civil courts. At a city hall or a court house there may be a dozen judges occupying the benches of the various courts, but there is normally only one clerk of the court, with the necessary deputies, one office of record for all. When one judge wishes to know what another judge has done he does not write a letter and open up a file, as does frequently one corporation official across the hall from another. No, the judge sends to the clerk's office and gets the complete record in the case. Under the unit system the official sends to the file room for all the papers. The consolidated file is perhaps the most universally popular feature of the unit system. It is estimated that its introduction in the operating department of the Harriman Lines has thus far resulted in the elimination of over half a million letters per year. These unnecessary letters were harmful rather than, helpful since they retarded administration. Often by attempting to think for the other man they dwarfed individual initiative.

Each assistant when at headquarters signs communications to subordinates in that branch of work in which he is technically expert and for which he is held responsible by the head of the unit. For example, the maintenance assistant superintendent issues instructions to his roadmasters or track supervisors; the mechanical assistant to his engine-house foremen or car-repair foremen; the transportation assistant to his yardmasters, etc., etc. Each, however, after signing is supposed to send his communication over the desk of the senior assistant, both for the latter's information and for review and coordination. This has proved a valuable check upon official caprice in issuing unnecessary instructions. More energy is now expended in seeing that instructions already issued are carried out, and less in promulgating those that in themselves may unconsciously confess a laxity in previous enforcement. It is obvious that under this system the senior assistant has a most comprehensive knowledge of the affairs of the unit. The head and the other assistants come and go between the road and the office. The senior assistant has a practical grasp of operation that enables him to aid the head of the unit in balancing its component elements, in minimizing departmental jealousies, and in engendering a spirit of team work. The consolidated file is helpful in producing a get-together feeling.

When the head of the unit or any assistant is on the road, he is represented at headquarters not by a chief clerk but by a chief of staff, the senior assistant, who transacts business in his own name. This somewhat elaborate covering of headquarters results as intended in more traveling and in better outside supervision by the other assistants. Their increased availability for outside work is the strongest of the several strong features of the system, and will be more fully discussed hereafter.

## BROADENING THE IDEALS OF SUPERVISION

On most railways, if the division engineer, while riding on the rear of the train to inspect track, should tell the young flagman that the latter had not gone back far enough to protect the train, friction might result.

If the flagman, mayhap of brief service and little experience, did not tell the division engineer, an old and tried officer, to go to blazes, the train-master perhaps would do so. The feudal notion 'you have interfered with my man' would prevail, rather than the broader concept of the best interests of the company and the public. Let the division engineer invoke the more formal procedure of reporting the flagman. The train-master might take such action as an implied reflection upon his own efficiency and unconsciously constitute himself attorney for the defense. The papers would grind through the official baskets, and perhaps weeks later return to the division engineer in such manner as by inference to discredit his judgment. The natural effect is for the division engineer to lose interest in the efficiency of flagmen and to confine his attention to his own specialized activity. His salary and expense account continue undiminished, and the company and the public lose just so much of his possible efficiency.

Under the unit system of organization, the old division engineers is an assistant superintendent. Unrestricted by the limitations of a descriptive title, the presumption is in his favor rather than in that of an inexperienced employee. For the bundle of letters resulting from a written report, which are in the nature of a technical appeal to higher authority, there is substituted a man to man contact, the rough and ready justice of the police court, which is usually a pretty good brand of justice. Were the division officials a set of callow youths with immature judgment an undesirable condition might result. Fault finding and nagging might replace the comprehensive supervision that is desired. No such effect, however, has been encountered. The officials concerned have shown themselves possessed of that poise which is to be expected from years of experience in directing their fellow men. So far from uniformity of titles producing a conflict of authority, the result has been the opposite. The difficulty on the Harriman Lines has been rather in getting the officials to interest themselves along broader lines of activity. It is much better that the departure from the ideal should be in this direction, since no fatality to the general scheme is involved. The broadened usefulness must be a matter of gradual development. It was recognized in the beginning that maximum improvement could be obtained only with a new generation of officials. Experience, however, has vindicated the wisdom in making a comprehensive start and securing whatever gain may be practicable. Perhaps the most creditable feature of the installation of the new system is the fact that results have been obtained with the official talent at hand. No importations of enthusiasts and no infusion of fresh blood, have been found necessary. The good old wheel-horses have shown their ability to move somewhat faster when the way is made easier; when the ruts of narrowing specialties and the hurdles of departmental prejudices have been removed. The changes have thus been made without demoralizing the service. This consideration for the individuals concerned has increased rather than decreased the *esprit de corps*.

Under the old order of things, if a train happened to arrive late with the master mechanic on board, he would be interested only in knowing that the locomotive and equipment were in good shape; that the engine-men, firemen, and car inspectors had performed their duties properly. Whether or not the conductor had been slow in going for orders at each telegraph office; whether or not the train dispatcher had used poor judgment; whether or not station forces had been alert in handling train baggage; whether or not there had been team work as between train men and engine men, would be questions of little moment to the master mechanic. In fact, if interrogated on the subject his tendency would be to minimize the shortcomings of the mechanical activities by emphasizing the derelictions of the other employees. He became unconsciously a breeder of friction. As an assistant superintendent, he can be held responsible for a judicious enforcement of all regulations, for an almost unconscious development of harmonious efforts on the part of all concerned. The more easily that he produces this composite efficiency, the more fully does he meet the test of his own capacity for true leadership. That traditional horse which the world has been leading to water, will, with proper handling, be drinking before he has time to realize the impossibility of such desirable consummation being enforced.

Again, the old trainmaster, now an assistant superintendent., after an all night chaperonage of a freight train, may pull up at a water tank at 7.15 a.m. If by chance he then observes a section gang beginning to think about going to work, he need not, and does not, because of being an assistant superintendent, read the riot act to the belated section foreman. A considerate inquiry as to 'what are your working hours?' or 'what time does the roadmaster (or track supervisor) expect you to turn out in the morning?' is all that may be necessary. There may be a good reason for the seeming departure from normal conditions. The presumption must be in favor of the faithful old employee. The moral effect of the official inquiry, if considerately made, will be far reaching.

The examples cited from actual practice indicate the extreme difficulty of adequate supervision of so extensive a plant as a railway. They also illustrate the necessity for that human touch which alone can restore that feeling of individual responsibility which is so vital for the successful administration of the modern corporation. All normal men have an inherent respect for duly constituted authority. This natural feeling of respect is alienated when authority is exercised at long range by untrained office meddlers. It borders on the cowardly to ascribe to the labor unions alone the responsibility for decreased efficiency. The educated and entrepreneur class, the elder brothers of society and industry, have the larger measure of responsibility. The unit system of organization substitutes, for the pink-tea contact of the typewriter and the telephone, the strong coffee of the caboose and the ham-and-egg association of the dinner bucket.

Superficial critics of the unit system have deplored the elimination of distinctive titles. They claim that a man loses his identity as an engineer, for example, that he cannot hope to acquire standing in his chosen profession. The answer to this is that great industrial corporations create professions of their own. The whole is greater than any of its parts. A man qualified to be an administrative official of a large corporation is directing an activity greater than any such component as civil engineering, mechanical engineering, electrical engineering, etc. If his ambition is for distinction in any of these honorable branches alone, he should seek general practice and not make the service of any particular corporation his life work. Military rank has not prevented certain engineers and surgeons of the Army and Navy from acquiring distinction in their technical specialities. On the contrary, the prestige of permanent status in an all-including profession creates a presumption most helpful in securing prompt recognition of specialized technique. In the immortal words attributed to the father of the railway profession, George Stephenson, the greatest branch of engineering is the engineering of men.

## OVER-SPECIALIZATION

The increasing difficulty of securing men to fill the higher official positions in large corporations is due mainly to overspecialization. The line of least resistance has proved too tempting. Emerson says that we are all as lazy as we dare to be. A manifestation of unconscious laziness may be the habit, bred by specialization, of side-stepping complete responsibility by passing the question to another specialist. The great problem in organization is to develop, under modern conditions, the old-time feeling of individual responsibility.

A man whose mental tendency is to meet responsibilities squarely must per force acquire knowledge of more than one thing. Such acquisition broadens his concept, increases his confidence, and should delight his superiors. Where highly specialized departments are created, departmental jealousies may normally be expected. Loyalty is measured by devotion to the department rather than to the corporation. Not only is there a negative lack of incentive in learning the work of another department, but there is positive objection to crossing sacred departmental lines. Since owing to the size of the proposition departments are necessary, the problem is to develop the all-round man under such restrictive conditions. One remedy, often difficult of application, is the rotation of selected individuals from one department to another. Another is a sufficiently early elevation of individuals to positions which have dealings with all departments. The latter method, by no means ideal, depends entirely upon the ability and the responsiveness of the individual promoted. In any case, the problem is easier where the number of departments is minimized. Specialization running rampant is often responsible for the creation of unnecessary departments. A striking example is the tendency of corporations to exaggerate the importance of such component functions as accounting, supply and purchase.

Large corporations (including governments, the largest of all), early discover the necessity for a cadet system of training competent officers. This simplifies the problem, since talent can be caught young enough for the broadest development. A cadet system may fall short if post-graduate activities are too highly specialized for too long a period of time. The railways and other industrial corporations are many of them too young, as corporate entities, to have developed as yet a cadet system. As shown by the practical experience of the Harriman Lines, some men old enough to have attained official rank can nevertheless be broadened for the highest positions by a proper system of organization. The amalgamation of the steam engineers with the line of the United States Navy is another notable example. That not all old dogs can be taught new tricks is no reason for denying opportunity to those who can. Every new trick the dog learns becomes an asset of value to his master. Beyond an easily determined point of self-respect it should not be what the dog wants, but what the master needs. The nineteenth century in the name of specialization badly over-specialized. The problem of the twentieth century is to swing back to a balanced specialization. All of us believe in specialization. Where we differ is as to the point where logical specialization ends and over-specialization begins. The corollary of specialization is centralization. The corollary of over-specialization is over-centralization. The more highly specialized the activity, the more remote becomes the point of convergence of complete authority.

Organization as a science demands a check against the amiable failing of human nature to exaggerate the importance of its own specialty. Aesop caught the idea in his fable of the quarrel among the organs of the body as to their relative importance. Each is useless when alone. Each derives its importance from its relation to the others. Perhaps the best practical check against corporate over-specialization is the rotation of functions. The best farmers rotate their crops. Where man is most active and useful, Nature rotates her seasons. Biology teaches that death comes more quickly where rotation is absent. Like all good things, rotation can easily be overdone. The permanent specialist may be justified when he has demonstrated his fitness as an all-round man. He can best learn everything of something when he has first learned something of everything. Epochs in the advance of society are all marked by cosmic tendencies. Modern specialization had its birth in the necessities imposed by the wonderful achievements of the nineteenth century. Invention cleaved its way through the ranks of civilization and scattered complete organizations of local society into groups of specialized activities. Many men mistake the immediate for the ultimate. There was a disposition to regard this condition as permanent. The inventor and the engineer, men of tangible things, outstripped the philosopher and the sociologist, men of intangible things. As society catches its own breath it demands more even running from its leaders.

As specialization produces centralization, so in turn centralization develops bureaucratic administration. The specialist who derived his official existence from expert knowledge carefully acquired may soon lose his sense of proportion. He unconsciously drifts into feeling that anyone in his department must be an expert be cause the head is an expert. Thus we find the chief engineer insisting that technical matters should be handled by his department alone. Investigation may develop that such handling is turned over to a non-technical man, the chief clerk, for final action. The chief engineer feels, unconsciously of course, that even a layman, if so fortunate as to be associated with the head, must absorb both technical knowledge and divine afflatus from such contact. Unquestionably, the best experts are those who can impart a working knowledge to the layman. If the objection to the chief-clerk system is that a half-way condition is stretched into doing duty for what should be a complete proposition. If the matter in hand is so highly technical as to demand an expert, the administrative activity should not be delegated to a layman. If, on the other hand, it has reached the stage of administrative routine, it makes for more comprehensive and harmonious results to have action taken by a duly qualified officer.

Society has so far emerged from feudalism, politically speaking, that a stenographer would no more think of taking the place of a judge on the bench than a lay reader would think of attempting all the functions of a duly ordained clergyman. Organized society, however, as reflected through modern corporations, is so steeped in feudalism, that the stenographer may be habitually signing the name of the corporate officer. It is an echo of the mediaeval period when the feudal lord was considered omnipresent within his dominions even though he might be absent on a crusade to the Holy Land.

When one person signs the name of another the effect produced is not that of either one or the other, but of a fraction of both – an undesirable sociological condition. Collectivism and altruism, as indispensable blessings of modern society, fall short if the individual is not preserved as an indivisible unit. Such violations of principle were less material when society was organized into smaller groups. The advent of the modern corporation necessitates, in administrative life, the same relative checks and balances for the preservation of the identity and responsibility of the individual as have been imposed by constitutional limitations and otherwise in political life. Thus when business was carried on by a family or a partnership it mattered comparatively little if one person signed for another, since the mutual understanding was so thorough and complete, or because each of the persons concerned was a part owner. In the administration of a large corporation, however, the officers and employees are trustees in varying degrees of rank. When an officer is absent, actually or constructively, the person who acts does not represent the absent officer but the corporation. If Richard Roe acts in the absence of John Doe, a corporation officer, the signature should not be 'John Doe, per Richard Roe,' but should be 'Richard Roe for and in the absence of John Doe.' The explanatory phrase 'for and in the absence of' is largely a question of good manners. It explains the seeming presumption of Richard Roe in acting, and the apparent discourtesy or neglect of John Doe to give the matter personal attention. The point of it all is that Richard Roe is acting for the corporation. He has been thrown into administrative gear, more or less automatically as the arrangement for succession in authority is elastic or rigid.

The science of organization insists that chains of authority and lines of succession shall be carefully outlined. The ideal condition would be, after developing competent men, to have the same men continuously doing the same work. This condition of specialization is manifestly unattainable owing to the wear and tear on individuals and to the accidents of service. Specialization in assignment has therefore decided limitations. Wise organizers recognize this fact and provide sufficient officers to give comprehensive action under all conditions of service. Unwise organizers fool themselves into believing that by some hocus pocus a half-baked understudy can perform a complete part.

Under the more primitive conditions of the past there has been less necessity for a knowledge of the science of organization. Supply follows demand, and the practical necessity for this knowledge is attracting the attention of thinking men the world over. Administration as an art is very old. Organization as a science is very new. There are a hundred good administrators for every good organizer. That which often passes for good organization is high-class administration, through splendid personal equations, of what is in fact unscientific organization.

One bar to progress is the fact that nearly every man intrusted with authority over his fellows flatters himself that he is a born organizer. Flattery is never more deceptive than when applied to one's self.

## FALLACIES OF ACCOUNTING

So rapid has been the growth of modern industry, so extensive is the volume of activity, so imperative is the necessity for a check of some kind against extravagance and corruption, that accounting as a function has assumed an importance far beyond its true proportion. Accounts are but a measure of performance, not performance itself. Accounts are but a yardstick. So prone is human nature to mistake incidentals for essentials that through long use the yardstick acquires a fictitious value. Experience, up to the period of obsolescence, ripens the human being and increases his efficiency. The yardstick, however, like most inanimate things, after being once properly tested is none the better for having made ten-thousand measurements. This failure to distinguish between the animate and the inanimate finds extensive expression in the interior organization of modern society.

The accountant attempts to tell us that money has been legally and honestly expended. He is usually powerless to say whether or not the expenditure has been efficient and therefore economical. Anyone can make vouchers match and columns balance if he fudges long enough. It is not every one, however, who can organize and direct the divine forces of nature, divine because they are human. At the outset too often the engineer of men finds himself handicapped by the purveyor of figures. Efficiency too often is measured by book balances and statistical reports rather than by expert inspection of actual conditions and performances.

Class consciousness is as expensive industrially as it is undesirable sociologically. The accountant, being human, exaggerates his own specialty, and gets away with the proposition because the director of men and things may scorn to meet the accountant with the latter's weapons. Organization as a science demands that the two get together, not in combat, but in co-operation. When he wakes up, the technical director has all the advantage. He can learn accounts much more easily than the accountant can acquire technical knowledge. A concrete application of this principal is found on some railways, including the Harriman Lines and the Pennsylvania System. There, the disbursement accounts are kept by geographical operating division under the direction of the responsible operating officer, the division superintendent. The underlying theory is that accounts as part of every-day working tools should be available first hand for prompt and effective measure of performance; that it is manifestly unfair to expect to hold officers responsible for results and at the same time deny them first-hand knowledge of existing conditions. On most railways and in many other large industrial corporations, accounting is regarded as a sacred mystery beyond the ken of the every day operating man. The result of such illogical specialization is reflected in a remote centralization of function. The scorer is too far from the game. Individual batting averages acquire a greater relative value than sacrifice hits which may bring in winning runs.

One of the reasons that banks enjoy the general confidence of the public is because of their highly localized operation. The greatest financial institutions work only through more or less individualized correspondents. Each bank is made a complete, self-contained unit under a president or manager, who controls directly and completely his bookkeepers. If banks had fallen into the fallacy of the industrial world, all the bookkeepers would report to a head bookkeeper in a distant city and all the janitors to an alleged expert chief janitor somewhere else. Much of the local feeling of distrust against the American Telephone and Telegraph Company and its later subsidiary, the Western Union, is traceable to the fact that in few cities is there a recognized head of the company. The work is divided up amongst specialists, who for a time, by increased and intense attention to certain details, are able to show high departmental performance. Complaints of one sort or another may be met with the statement that some other department is responsible. The dissatisfaction of the public sooner or later finds expression in a demand for increased regulation of rates, or public supervision of service through commissions or otherwise. A corporation as an artificial person suffers enough lost motion from lack of inherent red blood without further emphasizing its vulnerability by a conscious or unconscious shifting of responsibility through mistaken notions of the proper division of labor. By all means there must be some division. Where the efficiency doctors disagree is mainly as to the point of complete convergence of activity and authority.

It is a far cry from the old-time watchmaker who wrought every part himself, to the factory operative who knows one machine turning out a very limited portion of the works of the finished watch. Were the making of watches the chief end of man, the highly segregated activity would be ideal. There are so many other things requisite, however, to insure life, liberty and the pursuit of happiness, that true composite efficiency demands, at least, such rotation of function as will prevent the dwarfing of individual development .

Corporations, like society in general, cannot stand still. They must and do advance. The sins of ignorance in one generation find absolution in the more enlightened practices of the next. It is predicted that ere long corporations will so see the light as to reduce accounting to its proper position. Accounting is one of several components of operation, not an independent function in itself. Too often confusion comes from calling the accountant an auditor. The accountant should be a registrar, the auditor a reviewer or inspector. Here is a distinct differentiation of function. Constructive criticism and review have a distinct function. He who criticizes or reviews, be he ever so honest, must be able to suggest practicable improvement, otherwise his criticism degenerates into harmful carping. It follows, therefore, that the inspector must be an expert operator. Audit is one of several components of a broader activity, inspection. The fundamental defect in many modern corporations is in endeavoring to make the accountant an auditor, to check the books before they are made up. This results in one-sided development and more or less unconscious fudging of operation to meet rigid preconceived notions of accounting requirements. Patrons would soon leave in disgust a bank whose teller had his efficiency measured by the bookkeepers farther back from the counter. The teller of necessity relies upon the record of the bookkeeper to protect the bank against the mistakes or designs of the customer. In a small bank one may be both teller and bookkeeper. Later on the work is divided, not because the bookkeeper is considered more honest than the teller, but because there is more work than one man can do and there is a self-suggesting division of labor. The underlying principle is that volume of activity rather than importance of function defines planes of cleavage in the division of labor. Frequently this basic principle is forgotten and class consciousness encourages the belief that segregated activity derives its existence from highly technical knowledge. Organization as a science has a hard task to overcome by proper checks and balances this feeling of 'we are so different' and 'our work is very expert and peculiar.'

The problem mentioned is receiving a practical solution in a variety of ways. The primal instinct of self-preservation in prompting engineers to learn more and more of accounting. Some of the large New York firms of efficiency and production engineers are developing accountants from young engineers. Whether or not the accountant of the future is an engineer, it is certain that the engineer will be an accountant. Where the public accountant leaves off and the muckraker steps in saying that something is wrong, the efficiency or production engineer stands fast and produces improvement. A prerequisite to a knowledge of physical engineering is a grounding in mathematical conceptions far beyond those necessary to cover every phase of financial accounting.

The accountant begins by flattering himself that because entrusted with records of financial transactions, he is more honest than the common run of people who deal with men and things rather than with money. By an easy process of extension this idea is developed into a belief that all the employees connected with the accounting department are perforce of a superior degree of integrity. Apart from the baneful subjective effect of so absurd a fallacy is the objective resultant. Robbed of part of his working tools, denied by inference the fundamental requisite of integrity, the operating man sub-consciously acquires an attitude of defence or of indifference. In either case there is a distinct loss of composite efficiency through failure of the organization to co-ordinate properly all the human elements engaged in the particular activity. There results a condition of having a junior clerk in a distant office question the acts of a highly paid officer on the ground. The presumption should be in favor of the latter, but because efficiency is necessarily relative and intangible, the clerk has a decided advantage position because he measures performance from his little viewpoint with a seemingly tangible report and an apparently effective unit of comparison. This undesirable condition is highly typified in the administration of the United States Government where hundreds of clerks in the accounting bureaus of the Treasury Department at Washington, under a false conception of revenue protection, unconsciously hamper the performance of upright and zealous officers and employees hundreds or thousands of miles away. The Bureau of Insular Affairs in the War Department is in advance of many others in employing in the Philippine Islands numerous traveling auditors. As a broad proposition, the inspector should seek necessary data of audit on the ground rather than have such data seek him in a distant office. It is predicted that the corporation of the future, and government is the largest of all corporations, will develop for its inspection service, including auditing, a corps of high-class men, composites of the inspecting officer of the army, the National bank examiner, and the traveling railroad auditor. At first, probably, such corps will be a set of more or less permanent specialists with the intuitive faculties highly trained. Since history repeats itself in organization as elsewhere, the gradual evolution in industry will be, as shown by the experience of the ages in armies and navies, to insist upon periodical rotation between the staff duties of inspection and the line functions of performance. The mistake made by many corporation officers is in believing that in all such matters the ultimate has been reached. Since all life is evolution, the wise man recognizes the fact that attainment of the ultimate must extinguish existence as surely as the variable of mathematics would be wiped out if its limit could be reached.

Money itself, a measure of value, is but a symbol and a representative, and never performance itself. Because money brings position, power, and influence it is often confused with the result it produces. When in a more primitive state of society a few individuals were exploited at the expense of the many, the glamor of disproportionate individuality often obscured the fallacy of considering money or property as the primal cause of pre-eminence. When such unbalanced individualism yields to more rational collectivism, as reflected through the modern corporate organization of society, money and money accounts very properly lose in relative value.

The present social unrest flows not so much from dissatisfaction with the unequal distribution of wealth as from disappointment at the failure of its possessors to measure up to higher conceptions of stewardship. The people insist upon a regulation of wealth, and particularly upon a regulation of its uses through public service corporations and other indus trial enterprises. The struggle for adjustment now going on in the United States is but a manifestation of a larger cosmic tendency toward equality. The problem in the United States is intensified by reason of the fact that under our theory of government political power is more or less decentralized. The tendency has been toward more and more political and governmental centralization in Washington. All the while financial power is becoming more highly centralized in New York. Much time will be needed for harmonizing these dissimilar conditions. In Europe, the political and the financial capitals are usually identical as seats of centralized power. It is interesting to conjecture the effect upon present conditions had a strong Federalist party been in power during the thirties, forties and fifties, a period of important railway and industrial development. The States Rights party then in power frowned down upon the motion of federal control of railways when their similarity to rivers and canals was mentioned. With so many disproportionate conditions it is little wonder that corporations err on the side of unbalanced organization. Pioneers of thought may point the way, but consummation of scientific ideals in organization becomes fully practicable only when conditions are so acute that the necessity for remedies is self-evident, and the method of solution more or less self-suggesting to the masses of those concerned in the results.

## SUPPLIES AND PURCHASES

Purchasing, as carried on by most modern corporations, is an example of exaggerated specialization of function. Purchasing is merely a component of a larger activity, supply. In turn, supply is a part of operation. A failure to appreciate this component relation often results in distorted and unbalanced administration. A strong personality at the head of a purchasing department may unconsciously hamper the efforts of heads of other departments through a failure to appreciate the proportionate value of supply and purchase to operation. Purchasing was originally segregated not necessarily because it was so different from everything else, but rather on account of the volume of the activity having reached a stage where it justified the undivided attention of one person. Such person, being only human, gradually acquired a habit of mind of considering himself as something apart from those less skilled in the technique of bargaining. Where all heads of departments are closely associated in a restricted area, as in that of a single manufacturing plant, daily personal touch is a wholesome antidote for this 'we are so different' feeling. The trouble begins when several plants are associated under a single management more or less remote. It is then that the acute separation of function is defined by thicker and thicker department walls. What was originally a mathematical plane with out thickness, becomes first a wall and then a fortification.

Tradition says that in 1861 it was intimated to the veteran, General Winfield Scott, that he who had entered the City of Mexico so successfully in 1847, should have no great difficulty in capturing Richmond. General Scott replied in effect that many of the same able officers who helped him to get into the City of Mexico were engaged in keeping him out of the city of Richmond. So it is in a large corporation. The same people who in the days of small things are engaged in helping the head to enter every possible avenue of composite efficiency, are, as the enterprise grows, more or less unconsciously in rebellion to keep their sometime allies from entering the citadel of what, through segregation, has become a sacred cause. It cannot be repeated too often that the solution of the problem lies in the earliest practicable convergence of complete authority covering the entire activity. No exact solution is possible because the focal distance of the individuals concerned is too variable. The most hopeful sign of the times is the willingness of the leaders of industrial operation to discuss the subject. Dogmatic generalizations, induced usually from too few particulars, are giving way to a feeling of doubt as to final conclusions. True science, and organization is a science, ever finds its vindication in calm and dispassionate investigation.

An illuminating example of centralized control and decentralized activity is afforded by the purchasing bureaus of the Harriman Lines. The able director of purchases, Mr. W. V. S. Thorne, in New York, makes blanket contracts, when practicable, for such material and supplies as can be most economically purchased *en bloc* for all the railways constituting the Associated Lines. For example, locomotives, cars, steel rails, car wheels, bridges, etc., etc., will usually fall under this class. Each of the constituent properties has its own purchasing agent who, when acquiring standard articles under the blanket contracts mentioned, becomes an ordering agent. On the other hand the purchasing agent of the Union Pacific Railroad of Omaha can probably drive a better bargain locally for such supplies as ties, timber, shovels, brooms, etc., etc. The point of it all is that the policy of centralization is sufficiently elastic to permit discriminating thought by responsible officers. Too much centralization always dwarfs the initiative of the man on the ground by inferentially denying him the ability to discriminate. In brief, an attempt is made by primary organization to decide a majority of the questions in advance, a hopeless proposition. It is predicted that the supply and purchase administration of the Harriman Lines will be further decentralized, so that perhaps the division superintendent can buy to advantage certain of his supplies in local markets or jobbing centres. Most railways and many industrial corporations reason fallaciously that because some things can best be purchased from a centralized office, that all things should be so purchased. The Harriman Lines' reasoning is that experience must be the guide, that some things must be purchased under one method and some under another. Typical of the other view is the Sante Fe System whose officers complain that the allotted three-score years and ten are too brief a span for the countless transitions of requisitions, and supply correspondence, between the great West and distant Chicago.

Could one man do all the buying and insure prompt action and delivery, the segregation of purchasing would be ideal. Soon, however, the purchasing agent gathers around him a large office force entirely unsympathetic with the particular needs of the users of the material and supplies. The office becomes unwieldy and deals with papers and accounts rather than with men and things. The office employee of limited experience may have a greater voice in the management than the experienced officer charged with the largest outside responsibilities. The purchasing agent boasts that his bright assistant saved the company $a$ dollars by continued correspondence with certain firms. Meantime the company may have lost $xa$ dollars because men were working to poor advantage while awaiting proper tools and material.

Requisitions may be counted a necessary evil to be reduced to the lowest possible terms. Ideal supply would be automatic. Too often a requisition tells a distant officer what it should already known. The largest single item of supply on a railway, fuel for locomotives, is furnished without regular requisition because the necessities are so apparent. A definite amount of fuel is shipped periodically in the absence of requests for variation in quantity. As administration improves and official ideas broaden, more commodities will be included in the list. A start has been made by numerous railways by running monthly supply cars to issue station and track supplies to agents and section foremen. Most of these roads persist in the foolish practice of sending worthless requisitions with these cars, worthless because the responsible officer with the cars should decide on the ground the amount to be issued in each case. An estimate of the probable total requirements can be made with sufficient practical accuracy for stocking the cars for the trip. Apart from the wasted energy in preparing useless papers, is the psychological effect of causing individuals to give greater weight to the requisition, a shadow, than to the article itself, the substance.

Financiers are learning that there is a practical limit to the amount of work which can be effectively performed by a single office. There was a time when very small railways could be combined in a single working system with unquestioned advantage in administration. Long ago such combination passed the peak of efficiency. A decade ago the promoters of the new Rock Island Railway system acquired the Choctaw, Oklahoma and Golf, which had its general offices at Little Rock, Arkansas. About the same time they also absorbed the Burlington, Cedar Rapids and Northern, a distinctively Iowa road with general offices at Cedar Rapids. Each of the roads mentioned, with something over a thousand miles of line, enjoyed a considerable degree of local popularity and, therefore, immunity from drastic legislation. The general officers of these roads had a distinct identity in Arkansas and Oklahoma in one case, and in Iowa in the other. When the citizens of these proud States awoke to the fact that the seats of authority had been removed to far off Chicago, that all purchasing had been centralized in that city, there was a feeling of resentment which necessarily had some bearing in shaping legislation hostile to corporations. To say that ties and timber cut in Arkansas can only be bought to advantage in Chicago is as ridiculous as it is expensive. In sharp contrast to this mistaken policy is the case of the prosperous Louisville and Nashville system, now financially associated with the Atlantic Coast Line. It is an open secret that the Louisville and Nashville controls the Nashville, Chattanooga and St. Louis Railway and the Georgia Railroad; and is a dominant factor in the Atlanta and West Point, which includes the Western Railway of Alabama. Each of the properties mentioned, however, is a distinct local entity with its president and full complement of general officers. It is said that not even are the mechanical appliances standardized as among these different roads. This is perhaps too extreme a condition, but it has at least the value of preventing an undue centralization of supplies and purchases.

The general trend of thought at present is to recognize the sociological element as the most important feature of administration. To offset the local unpopularity of the Southern Pacific in California, some perhaps deserved but much undeserved. a president with large powers has recently been placed in San Francisco. Simultaneously four other presidents were elected for Omaha, Nebraska; Houston, Texas; Tucson, Arizona; and Portland, Oregon. Chairman Lovett has wisely placed upon the shoulders of these five presidents the duty of acquiring that local human touch which becomes more vital as civilization advances. Chairman Lovett and his five presidents now perform with some degree of comfort the, duties which killed that great genius, Edward H. Harriman, who fell a victim to his own juggernaut of centralization.

One of the temptations to which mankind has yielded from the beginning is to seek perpetual motion in administrative, as well as in physical affairs. The hope has been that by some hocus pocus of a constitution, a scheme of government, or a chart of organization, a self-perpetuating entity would be set going to govern internal affairs for an indefinite period. The sociologist sees that systems survive only as they reflect the progress of a people, whether that progress be in government, in administration, or in ability to become self-reliant. A phrase of this general tendency is seen in the segregation of the storekeeping function for large corporations. When irregularities develop, when waste is discovered, when ignorance of materials and their conservation is manifest, the fallacious remedy usually proposed is to place this peculiar activity under the control of a special body of men expert in that one feature. The true function of the specialist and the expert, let it be repeated, is to show the layman how best to perform tasks of a general nature. When a separate department is created such specialization often becomes the lazy man's excuse for sidestepping responsibility. The true solution lies in patient instruction of those who are remiss, in such thorough, broadminded inspection as will insure maximum hearty effort for improvement. Because an artisan is clumsy or ignorant, his superiors should not take away his working tools until they have exhausted every known method of teaching him the trade or art. The Pennsylvania Railroad, whose organization wee laid out by military men a half-century ago, has never yielded to the temptation to create a separate supply department. It has, however, fallen into the mistake of centralizing its purchasing to the extent that a clerk in Philadelphia may discount the judgment of a superintendent in Baltimore or Washington. The Harriman Lines, after various segregations of the supply function, some times under the accounting department and sometimes as a separate branch of the operating department, have recently amalgamated supply under operation by placing all division storekeepers under the respective division superintendents and by including store accounting in the division accounting bureaus. The effect has been to make the superintendent and his various assistants zealous conservers of store supplies, where previously they unconsciously sought to draw the greatest amounts possible from the store because it was in another department for which they had no responsibility. When the bandit really reforms he is an able police chief, a guardian of law and order.

The United States Navy has long had a bureau of supplies and accounts. The members of the pay corps were supposed to be interchangeable as pay officers and storekeepers. This is sound organization and it is to be regretted that a movement is on foot looking to the segregation of supplies from accounts. Both logically and practically the two are closely interwoven. When the volume of business is small the same person can be both pay officer and storekeeper. When warranted by volume the duties can be segregated to advantage, but because the inherent importance of either, but solely because there is more work than one man can do. Off-setting this mistaken agitation is the whole some legislation proposed for amalgamating the pay corps of the Navy with the line. Ultimately, a generation hence, while every seagoing line officer will not be a paymaster, every paymaster will be a seagoing line officer, stripped of that class consciousness which is so fatal to composite efficiency.

Granted the premise that in all organization such ultimate consummation is desired, the conclusion is irresistible that supplies and purchases are but a component of operation whether that operation be the maintenance of a really military navy, the manufacture of steel, or the running of great railroads.

## LINE AND STAFF

Knowledge is power. Knowledge of the principles governing line and staff in organization is often sadly lacking in the training of executive officers. The sins of ignorance are costly. No field of investigation will yield a larger return in efficiency than that of line and staff.

Line functions are those exercised in direct sequence through prescribed and definite channels of authoritative control. The first line officer had no staff because he had time to do both the acting and the thinking parts. As the activity grew in volume, the responsible line head found the necessity for expert advice. Perhaps this came from a lawyer, a surgeon, or an engineer. Whatever the source, there was no suggestion of turning over to the expert adviser the direction of the activity itself. In a less highly organized condition of society the distinction was easily maintained. The lawyer, the surgeon, or the engineer might have many clients. This divided patronage rendered it manifestly impossible for the outsider to become responsible for direction of internal affairs. In the modern corporation it frequently happens that the amount of expert attention demanded will justify engaging the expert to devote his sole attention to the corporation in question. Then the trouble begins. Human nature is such that, unchecked, its ambition leads to meddlesome interference with specific matters beyond its immediate concern. The problem of organization is to impose such checks and balances that each component of the activity will maintain its proper relation to the others.

Staff as contra-distinguished from line originates in the necessity for maximum intellectual attention untrammeled by the demands of administrative routine. Here is a distinct differentiation of function. The officer absorbed in directing large affairs, in getting things done, is of the line. For the time being at least he is too busy to originate better methods or to seek the principles underlying his activities. He is the operator rather than the inventor; the actor rather than the playwright. Science and invention add to the complexities of the art and force the necessity for expert assistance.

The old sailing masters had to be reinforced by engine experts when steam was applied to navigation. Fortunately, the law of the sea demands undivided control in the sailing master, and the marine engineer has always been subordinate to the captain of the ship. Until recently this subordination has been too intense. The marine engineer in a staff corps was out of line for promotion to the captaincy. Perhaps the chief engineer was twice as good a man as the first officer, and perhaps had double the service, but higher than a chief engineer he could not go. Since the splendid progressive amalgamation of the staff steam engineers of the United States Navy into the navigating line, the specialist in engineering finds no hatchway permanently battened between the engine room and the deck. Under the old order of things, there was before a strong man in the engine room a constant temptation to fortify himself behind the technique of his specialty at the possible expense of navigation itself. Now that he is a navigating officer, the direct purpose of the ship, namely navigation, is constantly most prominent. Engine rooms exist to propel ships. Ships do not exist to contain engine rooms, except incidentally.

The recent Titanic disaster has called public attention to the failure to observe the old-time custom of developing all-round men at sea. There were not enough real sailors to man the life boats effectively, and stewards and stokers proved poor substitutes for sailors. This can be traced to the failure on the modern steamship to balance line and staff, to check over-specialization, and to remember that the ship, the whole, is greater than a department, one of its parts. The remedy does not lie necessarily in increasing the number of sailors as such, but rather in rotating stokers and others with sailing duties and rendering them available and more effective in time of need. This means more trouble for responsible heads, more work for officers in educating and training their men. Such increased work is what officers are for. Such constant incentive to endeavor prevents sluggishness and inaptitude for emergencies.

The first staff officer had no authority beyond that of polite inquiry. There was no one whom he could command. Gradually he acquired an office force and assistants. Not satisfied with telling others how to do, he unconsciously began doing things himself. He thus became a line officer burdened with administrative routine precluding proper concentration on that thinking part which the staff officer was himself created to perform. The controversies between line and staff in the Army and Navy of the United States have cost our Government untold millions. Most of the railway and industrial corporations of the United States are wasting some money every day by permitting staff officers to attempt to exercise line functions. The Army and the Navy have found an effectual check by going back to first principles, by amalgamating staff and line, by judicially rotating function, and by substituting periodic details from the line for permanent appointments to the staff.

Such solution is so logical and so practical that it is attracting the attention of the railway and industrial world. As the subject receives the attention that it deserves, the practical application of the principles involved will be prompt and intelligent. So one-sided has been the training of executive officers that most of the so-called captains of industry, narrowed by specialized training, must perforce consume much time in studying subjects previously outside their scrutiny.

Training leaves its marks. A lawyer, called to an executive position, often fails to see the necessity for the direct and ever-present sequence of authority. If all the judges of a city leave town for the week end, little harm may result. So unusual is an application out of regular hours for a writ of injunction or a writ of habeas corpus that the inconvenience of securing a judge would not be serious. Industrial concerns and railways, however, run every day in the week and every month in the year. There must ever be an alert and present incarnation of administrative authority. These administrators are like the firemen and the policemen of a city. There can be no haphazard, indefinite 'take it up next week' method of procedure.

Constitutions of Governments follow scientific differentiation of function. The executive is a line function, continuous in effect and direct in action. The judicial is a staff function, more or less continuous in effect, and presumably operative not directly, but through the executive function. The legislative is a staff function intermittent in action and indirect in the application of its conclusions. Frequently there is a departure from these scientific planes of cleavage and harm results. Just at present the Federal courts are engaged in a futile effort to exercise the line functions of not only regulating but administering numerous great corporations. The fundamental defect is the same as exists in receiverships. When the court at tempts administrative functions, there is no tribunal for judicial review of its own acts. As this principle is understood, receiverships will be supervised by some executive arm of the State, as is done in the case of banks both by the Federal Government and some of the State banking bureaus. Receiverships are seldom denied, for the reason that judges, being human, covet power. Were the receivership ordered by the judge to be conducted by someone else than himself, there would be greater probability of real judicial action on his part. No military commander of modern times has dared exercise the despotic authority that often characterizes a court in conducting a corporation receivership.

The staff function of greatest vital necessity is that of inspection or review. The tendency of inspection is that of extremes. Inspection reports often become perfunctory and colorless. On the other band, they may be hypercritical and demoralizing. True inspection is as open as the day and as welcome as the evening. Tree inspection makes the persons inspected grateful for the inspection. The true inspector is so thorough in his training, so secure in his knowledge, so considerate of his subjects, so forgetful of himself, so devoted to his duty and so worthy of respect, that those whom he inspects pay the unconscious homage of admiration. Such men are rare, but they can be developed. Experience has proven that there are definite limits of time within which an officer can be assigned to staff inspection duty. Some return to the line is essential to retain that human touch with everyday requirements through which alone can the confidence of others be merited.

An important component of inspection is audit. As previously stated, accounting frequently attempts to do duty as auditing. This is another instance of failure to differentiate between line and staff. Accounting is a line function, a part of operation. Auditing is a staff function, a part of comprehensive inspection.

All positions contain their characteristic tendencies and inherent temptations. The line officer, because he is practical and direct, is often impatient of staff suggestion, which he regards as fantastic and theoretical. Too often this prejudice is strengthened by the unfortunate mental attitude of the staff expert. Men who think out of and away from conventional grooves have usually a unique personality. Too often this is coupled with overbearing intolerance for their less gifted brethren. With personal eccentricities that are but manifestations of narrow selfishness, the cause of efficiency has had to struggle against the handicap of the unfortunate personal equations of some of its ablest exponents.

Tactless, intolerant, and inconsiderate treatment of conscientious line officers has discredited many an honest staff expert. The true teacher makes his students love their work and respect him because the work is lovable and because his teachings are sound.

The best antidote for the undesirable condition mentioned is periodic service in the line. It rounds off the square corners and bevels the sharp edges. The staff officer in turn is more valuable when fortified by actual line experience and accomplished results. It is always easier to tell the other fellow how than to do the thing oneself. The most successful man is he who has done both things, who has told and has done, who knows how and who also knows why.

Staff and line functions are often confused because of a loose use of the overworked word 'staff.' It is entirely possible for the same individual to act both in line and staff capacities. Several line officers at the head of distinct departments or groups of activity may collectively constitute the advisory staff of their common superior. Each of the nine heads of the executive departments of the United States Government in Washington is a line officer exercising direct authority over hundreds or thousands of subordinates. Assembled at the White House, the nine become collectively the President's Cabinet, a staff body. The weakness of this governmental organization is the absence of a chief of staff, in effect an assistant president. An attempt is made to supply this defect by having a secretary to the President at $7,500 a year direct and coordinate for the President the activities of nine strong Cabinet officers each rated at $12,000 a year. The President of the United States is too busy a man to bring about complete co-ordination, and much goes by default. In recent months the handling of a delicate situation in Mexico has furnished numerous instances of a glaring lack of co-ordination between the State, Treasury, War and Navy Departments. This was the fault of a defective system rather than of individual shortcomings.

Evolution brings us back to first principles. In the first administration of George Washington, his Secretary of State, Thomas Jefferson, was, in effect, though not in name, prime minister and chief of staff. Foreign affairs were an incident of the State Department. Today the foreign affairs of a mighty nation absorb practically the entire activities of the State Department. It no longer serves as a balance wheel for the other departments. The remedy is to create a Department of Foreign Affairs under a secretary, a member of the Cabinet, and to restore to the State Department many of its original functions. The Secretary of State, in the same building with the President, would be the latter's assistant and chief of staff. The Department of State would, as its name implies, be the department of departments, balancing and co-ordinating the other nine. One of its functions would be that of inspection, including audit and review. It would include a comptroller who would audit the Treasury Department. The anomalous condition of having the Treasury Department audited by its own comptroller would be eliminated. The position of secretary to the President would join the scrap heap of discarded organization.

The greatest boon to modern organization is the chief-of-staff idea, scientific in conception, practical in application, effective in result and as enduring as eternity itself.

### THE GENESIS AND REVELATION OF ORGANIZATION

Organization is a necessity and not an accident. Organization exists in response to some need of the social order. The type of organization adopted, however, is often accidental and frequently unscientific. There are so many more men who know how than there are who know Why, that departures from sound principles should be expected, rather than otherwise.

The first type of organization encountered among all peoples is that of the family, well termed the unit of civilization. This organization is scientifically sound because based up on natural laws. The evolution of this organization is from polygamy to monogamy. At first, the family served all purposes of organization. As new generations came, as populations increased, the distinct limitations of the scope of the family organization necessitated a still larger unit, such as the tribe or the clan. Whenever precedents are lacking any new organization is characterized by rule by the strongest. Thus it happens that despotism alone is able to hold together the more or less heterogeneous elements which have been grouped together to carry out an undertaking.

Gradually, as the component elements crystallize along more or less definite axes of activity, there come demands for protection in the enjoyment of positions attained. In government such demands eventually result in charters of liberty, in guarantees of protection to person and property, in constitutions written and unwritten, and in various other forms of checks and balances. Such organization should be scientific, since it is based upon the practical necessity of checking the natural caprice of those invested with authority and power. Governmental organization, however, is usually more scientific than practically effective. It accomplishes the general purposes in a highly satisfactory manner, but at an enormous and extravagant money cost. The inherent defect is the difficulty in checking the public official effectively, and at the same time leaving him a balance of initiative and, defined responsibility. There is always the sub-conscious fear that the public official will be too powerful.

Government thus differs from other corporations in having its stock holders, the citizens, holding back the duly constituted officers. In most other corporations the proposition is reversed. The stockholder is so fearful that the duly elected officers of the corporation will not produce maximum financial returns that he usually leaves such officers untrammeled and, perhaps, unchecked.

Here are two extremes between which must be fixed a more or less indefinable happy medium. That such medium is being scientifically sought is evidenced, on the one hand, by the growth of commission forms of government, and, on the other, by the increasing interest of stockholders and directors of large corporations in the performance of their officers. The student of organization as a science finds much cause for optimism in contemporaneous developments.

The casualist finds a world of chance in which accident and luck play the leading parts. The scientist, in whatever branch, including organization, finds a world of universal law with every recognized cause producing a corresponding effect. There is no greater evidence of the advancement of mankind than its willingness to discuss subjects of every nature. Previous failures to consider organization as a science may be traced to the same fundamental misconception of individual rights and moral delicacy as has characterized consideration of the science of eugenics. Time is the best regulator of all great questions, because it permits the operation of the fundamental of all laws, that of supply and demand. Organization and eugenics are supplying a demand of a rapidly advancing world for a better grouping of better men and women.

Mankind is prone to mistake the shadow for the substance. Just at present the efficiency of the modern corporation is measuredly decreased by the snap judgment of the financial centers upon too short periods of performance. This condition is reflected in weekly or monthly statements of gross earnings and of net earnings. Efficiency is judged by seeming ability to make a better showing than was made in a corresponding previous period. The result is that subordinate officers are tempted to strive for a paper showing rather than to conduct and conserve along the broadest lines the property entrusted to their charge. For example, the man in the street in New York may judge the efficiency of a western railway by the size of its trainload in a given month or year. Perhaps the apparently wonderful showing has been attained by excessive strain upon the motive power, shortening its life and reducing its ultimate earning capacity. Again, so insistent is the demand for satisfactory balances, periodically struck, that high corporate officers find it necessary arbitrarily to reduce working forces regardless of actual conditions. Vehement and imploring telegrams go from New York to outlying districts demanding reduction of expenses. The local official disbands some of his working forces, lets assembled material lie idle, knowing all the time that the ultimate cost will be greater because of the loss of efficiency in reorganizing his forces and resuming the work.

Apart from the economic loss involved is the sociological unrest engendered by treating men as pawns on a financial checker-board. The offsetting argument of the modern banker is that even though it cost more money later on, it is better to wait until money is more plentiful. The observing citizen is quick to detect the fallacy of this reasoning and quicker to condemn a financial system that demands such departure from real efficiency. A refreshing exception to this general practice is shown by the Chicago & Northwestern Railway which, under the old-fashioned administration of Marvin Hughitt, has actually insisted upon increasing its equipment in dull times because labor and material are then cheaper.

Men are the product of their environment, and the coming captain of industry is the man whose conception of trusteeship will be that of a scientific buffer between the financial power on the one hand and the practical necessity of the property and its employees on the other. The labor unions have been quick to see the weakness and blindness of capital. The tyrannical hold of labor to day is due more to unscientific methods of capital, to absent treatment by large interests from New York, than to the cupidity of labor itself. A concrete case is that unscientific unit of: performance, the train mile, which, leads to many unsound conclusions and expensive outlays in railway operation. So dependable is human nature, so sound is public opinion in the long run, so honest and so able is the corporation officer of today, that the solution of these great questions will come through scientific study of the fundamental principles involved. Evolution will thus preclude the necessity for and prevent revolution.

It sometimes happens that human nature must be hurried to its conclusions. The greatest present need is an antidote for the unwillingness of men to profit by the previous experience of others. It would be amusing, were it not so expensive, to watch the gropings of many corporate officers for methods to test efficiency. Ignorant of fundamental principles, intolerant of outside suggestion, unable to detect the analogy in other undertakings, they repeat the expensive experiments of the past. Nearly every large corporation today is endeavoring to inaugurate some effective system of inspection or review. Nearly every one is falling short, because an attempt is made to have the cheap man check the work of the high-priced man. Nearly every one is disappointing its promoters, because of failure to differentiate between accounting, an operating or line function, and auditing, an inspection or staff function.

It often happens that what unfolds itself as a discovery to one is but a matter of principle long previously enunciated by someone else. Among the ideas that are contemporaneously revealing themselves to searchers after truth is the principle that most modern undertakings are too large to be concentrated in one man, how ever able or zealous, because it is absolutely essential that authority shall converge in some one individual. The false idea has gained sway that such a man alone could act in numerous cases. The application of this idea necessitates minimizing the cases in which the head must himself act. By a process of evolution, the chief-of-staff idea has unfolded itself to relieve such head and, at the same time, provide comprehensive action for a greater number of cases.

Another concept that has forced its attention is that effective means must be provided for a comprehensive review of performance. The railway president cannot be left in definitely to report upon his own performance. Granted this necessity, a fallacious attempt has been made to check the president through inanimate accounts, through reports pre scribed by the Interstate Commerce Commission or other public bodies. It is now dawning upon those who are concerned how inadequate is such a test. A more satisfactory remedy is the outside expert, the disinterested reviewer, who is qualified by training and experience to report upon men and things as well as upon papers and accounts; a man who can draw his conclusions from first-hand information on the ground rather than from second-hand data in the office.

Perhaps the greatest revelation of modern organization is the consciousness, tardy though its arrival, that there is a distinct limitation to the size of undertakings, that volume may be the determining condition. The operating activities of many corporations have outgrown detailed direction from a central source. The self-suggesting remedy is a decentralization of detailed activity and a retention of centralized control. In many cases such efforts at decentralization are still very crude. It is hard to teach old dogs new tricks. Here again time and intelligent effort will supply the adjustment which the conditions demand.

Modern organization reveals to the student a far more pleasing picture than that beheld by the prophet of old. The religion of Fear, with its bottomless pit and lake of brimstone, has been replaced by a religion of Love with its heights of hope and its valleys of peace. Modern requirements have brought men together in large masses. They have organized together for one purpose or another. Political and economic efficiency have long been their cherished desires. As weaknesses developed in this organization they have sought improvement. Sometimes the attempt was wise, sometimes foolish, often ineffectual, but nearly always sincere. Whenever the effort ran counter to the general welfare or to the normal advancement of mankind, the organization quickly showed the defect. Out of it all, as modern organization sweeps into the newer day of composite efficiency, comes the delightful realization that its beacon light is scientific and enlightened altruism.

# Military History and the Science of Business Administration[1]

## Edward D. Jones

### THE UTILITY OF THE STUDY OF HISTORY

The art of administration is as old as the human race. Even the leading wolf of a pack is an administrator. Organization is older than history, for the earliest documents, such as the code of Hammurabi, show the evidences of many generations of systematized social life. The real pioneers are the unknown promoters of the stone age, and the system-makers of the bronze age. Long ago almost every conceivable experiment in organization was first made. The records of history tell us of large units and small ones, of great and slight differentiation of functions, of extreme division and extreme concentration of authority, of mild and severe sanctions, of appeal to system and appeal to passion, of trust in numbers and trust in leadership. Of the vast variety of units of organization through which human intelligence has worked, and through which human purposes have been achieved, or thwarted, the greater part has passed away; and the names of them, even, have been forgotten.

In politics, the evolution has passed through the horde, the patri-archal family, the clan, and the classical city state. Nations have tried despotisms, oligarchies and theocracies, absolute and constitutional monarchies, and republics. In military matters the phalanx gave way to the legion and cohort, and these, in turn, to the division, brigade, battalion, regiment, and company. Throughout history, the survival of the fittest, as between nations, has been fought out, in part, on the basis of the ability to use organized and co-operative methods of action. What a wealth of experience has been gained – and lost! How many times, in the long journey of history, have underlying administrative principles been, with enthusiasm, discovered, and rediscovered!!

And yet we seem to have accumulated but a small reserve stock of knowledge on this important subject. We are still eagerly searching for

[1] [*Engineering Magazine*, vol. 44, 1912, pp. 1–6, 185–90, 321–6.]

the most elementary principles of administration. With countless generations of experience, in the conduct of affairs, behind us, the individual business executive of today is feverishly trying to broaden and intensify his personal experience – to live fast and hard – so that, in the short span of his life, he may discover *de novo*, for himself, the principles and policies required in the government of the complicated economic organizations of the present day.

Since a knowledge of the principles of administration is now of so great importance, we should add to the agencies now being established, for the study of current performance, a provision for the systematic review of the history of administration. An analogy exists between the present needs of the American business executive, into whose hands in a generation a great increase in power has come, and the needs of the German army officers before the development of that splendid system which made Germany the leading military power of the world. A hint may, therefore, be gained from their experience. The Prussian General Staff and War College were organized to gather all engineering, topographic, and other technical knowledge, which could be made of use in war. But, especially, there was entrusted to them the function of reviewing military history in a scientifically thorough manner, to obtain from it the maxims and principles which possess validity for future operations. In the hands of general historians, history is worth less for military guidance; but to Scharnhorst, von Clausewitz, von der Goltz, von Moltke, and the other students of the General Staff, is due the credit of having so sifted their facts, and so brought them to bear, in the criticism of principles, that they have made them a firm foundation for the scientific conduct of war. Nor have they confined their attention to military affairs alone; the entire history of administration has been laid under tribute. The suggestion we would offer is that a similar study of administrative history should now be made in the interest of the business executive.

This study, to be fruitful, must be strictly scientific in its character. Many men of affairs are much prejudiced against the invasion of business by science and theory. They conceive of these things as something new and untried, and something opposed to experience. A certain excuse for this view exists in the fact that the scientific method has, thus far since its discovery, been applied most prominently to facts which ordinary experience does not furnish, but which are attainable only through the somewhat rigid and refined methods of the laboratory. Many persons have concluded from this that the method cannot be applied to the facts of ordinary experience.

Again, the results of science which have come forth from the laboratories, in the form of theories, have often presented themselves in the guise of something new and not previously heard of, and something requiring the most suspicious treatment before being admitted to any part in practical affairs. And so again, a conflict between new and old, between 'theory' and 'practice,' has seemed to exist.

He would be a rash man, in this day of grace, who would deny that laboratory science has gloriously triumphed, and made contributions of incalculable worth to the advancement of the human race. This triumph is a demonstration of the efficiency of the scientific method. It certainly establishes a presumption that its application to bodies of fact which arise outside the laboratory will, also, be attended by valuable results. It may be safely affirmed that the way by which a maximum utilization of experience can be attained is through the application of the scientific method. Only in the delicate scales of science can the complicated conditions of practical affairs be accurately weighed, and the various factors contributing to success or failure be disentangled and separately weighed. Through its careful method of study alone, can we be sure that the part which accident and favor have played has been reasonably allowed for. This much the application of science to the recording and measuring of current performance is now demonstrating. The riches of past experience still constitute a great unutilized opportunity for science to render service.

The fundamental bases upon which the scientific method rests are two. The first is that all parts of truth are in harmony with all other parts. If there is not a rational order in the world, the mind of man is incapable of understanding the universe in which it is placed. The second basis is that any truth possesses equal validity for every normally constituted mind. On these two bases the scientific method proceeds. This method is not different in kind from the methods of ordinary observation and thinking; it rather differs from these in degree. Briefly characterized, it is an orderly, persistent, and thorough use of the mind. More fully stated, the scientific method is the analysis of problems into their elements; an extensive and thoroughly adequate collection of data; an exact and truthful classification of facts on the basis of their nature; such an arrangement and grouping of them as will best reveal agreements, differences, and concomitant variations between them; and the making of inferences, or the discovery of new facts, by means of induction, deduction, and analogy. The new truths, or inductions, are then subject to criticism and test in every possible way. The scientific method calls for the eradication of prejudice which may interfere with the just estimate of any facts; and it requires open-mindedness, or willingness to receive new facts at any time, and to make such revisions in conclusions as may be required.

This method is universal in its applicability. It can be set at work upon the organizations of which we find records in history, as well as upon the fossil remains of organisms in the earth's strata. It can work upon data which are the product of the most haphazard, partial, or impassioned of experiences, as it can upon the exactly controlled processes of a laboratory experiment. The results obtained will, of course, depend upon the quality of the materials furnished to it, and upon the degree to which the material can be controlled to compel it to reveal its true nature fully and clearly.

When, now, we turn to the practical consideration of the study of the history of administration, various objections interpose themselves. For one thing, there is very little history of private business administration available. Many men prominent in industry and commerce, in the past, have left us no records. Some of them, no doubt, made their way by tact, or overmastering personal energy, in spite of defective administration; some have preferred darkness because their deeds were evil. Many excellent administrators have never formulated their ideas far enough, dressing away the incidents of time and place, to enable them to observe that there were permanent principles underlying their actions. Competition has often spread a mantle of secrecy over the essential facts.

Some of these forces, which have repressed economic facts from the record of history, may be seen at work in America today. A generation of great leaders, which developed with the progress of the country's industry, and has come up from the day of small things to an exercise of power rivaling that of the rulers of kingdoms, is now passing off the stage of action. With rare exceptions, these men vanish away mute, leaving no autobiographies. Examine a British book list and you will find that every month some diplomat, or officer of state, or traveler, or colonial governor has, in the evening of life, set down what ever may be of permanent value in his experience, and published his reminiscences. In no country of the world have greater things been done, during the last generation, than in America; but our doers of them are inarticulate. Conscious enough that the tangible things they have wrought will quickly crumble, they yet fail to round out the purpose of life, and distill a final essence of principles and policies which might possess lasting utility. Their estates are scarcely distributed before the question, 'How did they achieve their success?' is given up forever.

In this dilemma we may turn to the history of political and military institutions, and find ample materials for the study of administration. These lines of activity have swept together millions of people into single organizations, and have made the leaders the cynosures of innumerable eyes. If Crassus, at one time the richest man in Rome, is little more than a name to us, we know of his contemporary, Caesar, the private life, the motives and methods, the hesitations and resolves. If there is but an odd book or two of colorless record of Mayer Bauer, the Napoleon of Finance of the latter half of the eighteenth century, and the founder of the house of Rothschild, we have of the Emperor Napoleon an enormous literature, contributed to not only by the great men who either aided or opposed him, but by his valet and the palace ladies-in-waiting. Thus there has been insured, in certain departments of administration, at least, searching publicity, and an abundant record of all that has been done.

But another difficulty will doubtless be urged, namely, that industry is neither war nor politics, so that the study of the administrative methods used in those fields will not yield results which can be applied to the conduct of industry. The usages of common speech indicate, however, that we constantly observe the similarity between the forces and conditions in these fields of activity. We commonly speak of 'captains of industry,' of the 'strategy' of great business, and of 'tactics' and 'campaigns,' and 'line' and 'staff.' Argument from analogy is one of the valid forms of reasoning. It is the method of homologous series, which rests upon the assumption that what is true of one set of circumstances, is likely to be true, in some degree, of similar sets of circumstances. It fastens upon a resemblance between two sets of relations, by which each case is made to reveal more fully the nature of the other.

As a means of gaining insight, analogy has been used since the dawn of wisdom. In the Bible we find the deepest spiritual truths suggested by analogies from nature, and from the simple relations of the household and the crafts. In the parable of the sower, we review the various types of human nature. By means of the porter, commanded to watch lest his lord, returning suddenly, find him sleeping, and by the man trying to serve two masters, we learn of surprise tests, and indefinite responsibility. In the case of the house divided against itself we see the evil of faction, and of departmental rivalries. In the piece of new cloth sewed onto an old garment, and the new wine put into old skins, we learn the law of harmonious coordination of agencies.

The strictness of an analogy depends upon the similarity of the subject matters involved. If we compare organizations for war and politics with those for industry, we shall find the conditions vital to administrative success markedly similar. There is the same human nature, with its equipment of physical and mental faculties. The same protection is required against careless ness, laziness, jealousy, fear, and selfishness; the same reliance can be placed upon generosity, intelligence, energy, and loyalty. There are always the unchangeable factors of time, space, and the properties of matter, and force, presenting themselves in different degrees of importance. Some of the factors change in their nature, though gradually; knowledge increases, and the state of the arts progresses; so also do the customs of society, and the moral standards which must be observed. For these changes allowance can be made, and should be made with the greatest care.

The peculiar value of analogy is that by it certain cases, in which relations are clear and conspicuous, are used to familiarize the mind with the nature of the relation, so that, when similar phenomena, differently grouped, are studied, we are able to detect the relationship, even though it be subtle and partly hidden in its new form. We know that when once a figure in a picture-puzzle has been pointed out it seems so prominent that we wonder how we could have previously overlooked it. One hears a note in a chord distinctly, when it has been previously sounded separately. So the analogy aids us by familiarizing us with the idea of the relationship for which we seek. When we know intimately the characteristic signs of a thing, we are able to detect its presence or absence readily.

The greatest body of valuable data on any particular subject is likely to be found where circumstances have made the corresponding element of performance unusually important, or where a force has triumphed over unusual opposition, or where a man of unusual capacity has obtained the authority and resources to do things. We should seek for the circumstances which have specially emphasized or stressed the thing that we would study. This suggests the value, to the student of administration, of giving himself free range over the entire field of administration, not confining himself to industrial administration alone; for only by wide comparisons will he be able to select the type of cases which most clearly reveals to him the workings of the force he desires to study. He will, for example, turn to military operations to observe how leadership has been exercised when responsibilities are terrifying, and the greatest resource of soul is required to make decisions. Or in diplomacy, he will find circumstances which emphasize harmony and balance of character, and respect for custom. If one desires to study preliminary preparation, the subject will be quickly opened by studying Nansen's remarkable preparation for his journey in the Fram; if one desires to study economy of time he may advantageously begin with a city fire department. A knowledge of the military manual of arms would be a suggestive preliminary to motion study, and an examination of the national mints would suggest methods of preventing waste.

In the study of the extreme case, the thing sought is presented distinctly and emphatically to the attention. And this is a great advantage, for all perceptions tend to fuse in the mind into a general impression, unless forcibly prevented by the expenditure of the energy necessary to effect their analysis and separate consideration. The person who cuts himself off from subjects analogous to his own loses something of the force of the contrasts and similarities of the facts with which he deals. To refuse the comprehensive and flexible service of analogy is to rob oneself of much of the resource by which the probability, or improbability, of all forms of conclusions is established.

## MILITARY HISTORY

Military history divides itself broadly into great periods, in each of which certain definite ideals and enthusiasms have moved the minds of men, seeking embodiment in appropriate military units and authorities, and finding expression in characteristic movements of strategy and tactics. Let us briefly glance at the leading characteristics of some of these periods, with a view to suggesting analogies which have interest from their bearing upon the administration of industrial enterprises.

### Roman Arms

The Roman military unit was the legion of from 4,000 to 6,000 men, divided into ten cohorts. The strength of Roman arms lay in three things. The first of these was a careful selection of men from among such citizens as were practised in arms. The second dependence was upon discipline. Warlike youths were accustomed to the use of arms as a recreation, so that it was said that their sports were battles without blood shed, and their battles bloody sports. The third point was the prompt adoption of all improvements suggested by the experience of foreign wars. The Roman legion was practically never defeated, so long as these three principles remained in force. The secret of its strength was the spirit of the men who, in their perfect discipline, expressed their glory in Rome, and their confidence in themselves.

The most brilliant achievements of this military instrument were attained by Caesar, who aroused the devotion of his troops to the highest point, by making common cause with them in the pursuit of valor. As

Plutarch says, 'He showed them that he did not heap up wealth from the wars for his own luxury, or the gratifying of his private pleasures, but that all he received was but a public fund, laid by for the reward and encouragement of valor.'

Defeat came to Roman arms only when numerous wars had made it necessary to sweep together heterogeneous classes, which did not feel the old confidence in each other, and to introduce barbarians who did not feel enthusiasm for Roman triumphs. Rome fell, furthermore, because it became a house divided against itself. The civil wars made it no longer Rome for which the troops fought, but the triumph of a faction. The leaders of factions being disinclined to disband their armies, the civilian troops disappeared, and in their place came bands of paid professional fighters.

### The Byzantine Empire
After the decline of Rome, the center of the world's military progress was, for seven or eight centuries, transferred to the Greek empire. Constantinople ruled elements of a much less homogeneous nature than Rome, in her prime, had depended upon. There was less loyalty to the central rule there, and far less liberty under it.

The decisive military fact of the East was, however, that Byzantium had to contend against overwhelming numerical superiority in its enemies. South of it, from the Indies to the Atlantic, was the Saracen empire, burning with the zeal of a new religion. To the east were the Seljuk Turks, while to the north were the Bulgarians, and the Slavonian and Hunic tribes.

Against such odds it was useless simply to match than for man. The military leaders of the empire were full of military spirit, and took keen delight in war as a game; but they were the descendants of Ulysses, and they made of war a game of finesse, of cleverness, in short, a war of wits. By their spying and bribes, by stirring up treason in the enemy's camp, by surprises, simulated retreats, and ambush, they illustrated the saying of Bacon that stratagem is a weaker kind of policy, used by those who are not strong enough to win by fairer methods.

The Byzantine empire, weakened by the destruction of its patriotic middle classes, and robbed of the protection of buffer states through its own folly, was, at last, finished by the marauding expedition called the Fourth Crusade; and it broke in to fragments.

### Middle Ages
When the Roman empire became a shadow, and the Church was the one remaining bond of western Christendom, political rule in Europe was

scattered into the hands of numerous feudal lords. Military operations were carried on then by small bands of aristocratic mounted men in armor, who followed the banners of their overlords through fealty. The Roman troops were originally infantry, but the mounted plundering hordes of eastern Germans and Hungarians had already, in later Roman times, forced some of the legions to mount, in order to gain in speed. For western Europe, the call to horse was given by the terrifying raids of the Vikings. Armor was necessary because of the introduction, of the long bow mid cross-bow, the pike, the two-handed sword, and the axe.

In armor and in fortification of towns the defensive gained, during the Middle Ages, a temporary advantage over the offensive, with consequent disintegration into small military units. Armor and fortifications. were, however, but negative measures. So that when the Viking raids became more frequent and extended, and were followed by permanent settlements, it became necessary to increase the power of the offensive by combination into larger units. Loyalty to local lords gave way, therefore, to loyalty to the king. The royal armies which, at first, were small shabby bands of mercenaries, received additions of superior quality from the nobility. This movement toward concentration was hastened and completed by the introduction of firearms, which took away the superiority of the aristocratic professional fighter, and enabled the fortifications of castles and cities to be speedily battered down.

### Frederick The Great

The crowning example of a royal army, used as the personal weapon of a Sovereign who united in his hands absolute political rule and the powers of a commander-in-chief, is the army of Frederick the Great. The way was prepared for this great Prussian genius by a thrifty father who built up an army and a treasury for him. As an administrator, the father stands in much the same relation to him that a Benjamin Franklin, expounding maxims of thrift, would bear to a dashing organizer like E. H. Harriman. Frederick was an intensely active, highly capable, strong-willed and self-reliant commander. He concentrated all power in his own hands, reducing his ministers to clerical work, and his generals to the duties of personal lieutenants. Below him the Prussian administration was a thing of stiff and mechanical obedience, lacking in initiative and individuality. Several of Frederick's military losses were due to the fact that he gave his generals such minute orders, and was so severe in case of disregard of instructions, that they did not dare to use their own judgment, when unforeseen conditions presented themselves. He personally foresaw and provided for everything; and he inspected frequently and thoroughly. His discipline was severe; his organization good; his calculation accurate, and limited to what was possible. His movements, which were skillfully disguised, were rapid. So superior was Frederick to his opponents in strategy that they were obliged for safety to keep their troops in so concentrated a form that there was not sufficient space for effective manoeuvers. He was more capable in marching and manoeuver than in battle; more capable in battle than in siege.

His great defect as an administrator lay in the fact that he dwarfed the growth of those below him, and so educated no talented corps to bear the political and military burdens of the State, when he should be obliged to lay them down. He apparently could do things only through himself. Having a supreme contempt for the capacities of most mortals, he had no mind to make experiments which might have changed his opinions. Although he knew, for many years, that his successor was to be a man without ability, he handed down to him a system which required a Frederick. We may say that he brilliantly administered a system which was badly organized.

After his death, the prestige of his name and deeds was so great that it was considered blasphemy to suggest that any change could improve the Prussian army. Its methods could, therefore, suffer no alteration, except a refinement of punctilios, such as drill and uniforms. This army which had gloriously finished the seven years war, in 1763, against the united force of nearly the whole of the Continent, was utterly routed by hesitating and divided leadership, when it met Napoleon at Jena, in 1806, twenty years after Frederick's death.

*Napoleon*
Napoleon and Frederick resemble one another, in many ways, as administrators. The aims of the two men were, however, entirely different. While Frederick was devoted wholly to the advancement of Prussia, identifying himself completely with his people, Napoleon desired power as a means of personal aggrandizement, and was at bottom selfish and vain.

As military leaders the great difference between the two men lies in the fact that while Frederick's army was a small professional one of recruits hired wherever they could be secured, Napoleon had the leadership of civilian armies enormously larger than any ever before put in the field. The French Revolution awakened the passions of the common people of France so that, when the monarchs of Europe combined in an attempt to force royalty back upon them, they flocked in great numbers to the national standards. These men were animated by a terrible intensity of spirit and purpose, and willingly met deprivations in the field. When, later, conscription took the place of volunteering, and a war of defense of a republic changed into one of offense for an empire, Napoleon knew how to arouse in the breasts of his men the love of glory as a main-spring of action.

The leading military principles of Napoleon were to seize the initiative by concentrating one's forces from marching into fighting order as quickly as possible, and, having massed the troops as compactly as effective action will permit, to attack swiftly.

This attack must be made upon a portion only of the enemy's army, and the weight of one's whole force must be crowded in, so that at the point of action a decided superiority is attained. This theory of action he often explained to his generals. Moreau, in conversation with Napoleon in 1799, remarked that it was always the greater numbers that won. To which Napoleon replied: 'You are right. When, with inferior forces, I had a large army before me, I concentrated mine rapidly, and fell like lightning upon one of the enemy's wings and routed it. Then I took advantage of the confusion which this maneuver never failed to produce in the opposing army to attack it on another point, but always with my whole force. Thus I beat it in detail, and the victory which was the result was always, as you see, the triumph of the larger over the lesser.'

In one way Napoleon possessed a defect similar to that of Frederick. He provided no adequate staff to relieve himself of details. During his early years he made up for this lack by remarkable physical activity, but when still in early middle age his energies began to decline. He allowed himself ease and luxury, and showed an increasing dislike for the hardships of the field at a time when his enterprises were growing rapidly in size, and were passing into a serious stage. The lack of staff was net from inability to create the necessary administrative machinery, and insure its efficient working, for he maintained a spy system which rivaled that of Cardinal Richelieu. It is more likely that his intense desire to stand alone, in order to receive all the credit for what was done, was the secret of his action.

This brings us to the chief defect of his character. Although undoubtedly the greatest military genius that ever lived, he over-reached himself. This is shown in a single enterprise like the Russian campaign; but it is shown in the life as a whole. He could probably have accomplished the anomaly, with the mercurial French, of founding a personal dynasty upon the French Revolution which beheaded royalty and announced the rights of man; but when he attempted to remake the map of Europe he reckoned beyond his power. He realized that the armies of the Republic had been animated by a passion for liberty, equality and fraternity, but he could not understand that his aggressions upon other countries deprived his armies of this moral force and implanted it in his enemies; and that no skill in strategy and tactics could long withstand it. He would not permit a group of great administrators and military loaders to share his honors, and form around him a cabinet, which might have protected him against himself. And so he plunged forward, unadvised, and talking of his star and destiny, to his Waterloo.

*Modern Conditions*
The new features appearing in modern war are, the vast increase in the size of armies, and the deadly power of firearms. In preliminary mobilization the chief advantage to be gained is speed. To this end, and because the conditions of mobilization can be largely foreseen and controlled, the solution which is applied is detailed preliminary planning. Duties are carefully assigned to separate individuals, in such a manner as to effect the utmost speed, through a smooth co-ordination of movements, without overloading any one person.

The first great master of modern preliminary planning of mobilization was Von Moltke. His description of the plans for the advance, before the Franco-Prussian war of 1870–71, is as follows:

The means of mobilizing the North German army had been reviewed year by year, in view of any changes in the military or political situation, by the Staff, in conjunction with the ministry of war. Every branch of the administration throughout the country had been kept informed of all it ought to know of these matters. The orders for marching, and travelling by rail or boat, were worked out for each division of the army, together with the most minute directions as to their different starting points, the day and hour of departure, the duration of the journey, the refreshment stations and place of destination. At the meeting-point cantonments were assigned to each corps and division, stores and magazines were established, and thus, when war was declared, it needed only the royal signature to set the entire apparatus in motion with undisturbed precision. There was nothing to be changed in the directions originally given; it sufficed to carry out the plans pre-arranged and prepared.

In strategy, which includes the general movements of a campaign, preliminary planning is of course impossible. The distances separating the several divisions of a great army, the time which would be required to make voluminous reports to headquarters, and to receive back detailed instructions, and the innumerable local conditions which can not be adequately grasped by one at a distance, make it impossible that highly centralized control should exist.

Here the flexibility of the German army system is shown. In contrast to the rigid plan of mobilization imposed by central authority, when the campaign is once under way, and changing and uncertain conditions have to be dealt with, the headquarters becomes responsible only for the general features of the plan of operations.

Authority immediately passes down the line to army commanders, and regimental and company officers, lodging as close as possible to the time, place, and agencies of specific action. The army then becomes, not a mechanism under the thumb of a single leader, but an organism with great liberty of action, and corresponding responsibility, resting upon the parts.

It is reputed that Von Moltke once said that nothing should be ordered which it was conceivable could be carried out by the proper officers without orders. Certain it is that the orders from headquarters in the Austrian and Franco-Prussian wars were very few in number, and composed of but a few sentences each. Passing from higher to lower units, orders from the leaders of separate armies, corps orders, and division orders, were, of course, progressively firmer and more detailed.

In the modern tactics of engagements, a similar rule as to the location of authority is followed. While each army headquarters retains sufficient control to insure harmony of plan, details of execution are intrusted largely to the officers on the field, and in direct command of the minor divisions of troops. The old ramrod drill movements of troops on the field of battle are no longer possible. Discipline is now interpreted broadly that each individual shall apply sound principles in every emergency, remaining as continuously in touch with authority as this will permit. The fear of minor mistakes is as nothing, with modern military administrators, in comparison with the fear of crushing out the spirit and energy of troops and lower officers by unduly suppressing initiative.

All this manifestly calls for a superior class of executives of all ranks, adequately prepared for their duties. To provide such officers, Germany has perfected her War College and General Staff with every educational and scientific agency which human ingenuity can devise. To these institutions the flower of the regimental officers is drawn for training, and to assist in the solution of the problems upon which the Staff works. From these institutions they soon return to the regiments. A constant transfusion of talent is taking place between the regimental line and the

General Staff. Thus is insured to the commander-in-chief a body of capable officers familiar with each element of service, and trained to intelligent co-ordination of efforts. When shall the great affairs of a country's industry be administered with equal enlightenment with this business of war and bloodshed?

## ADMINISTRATIVE PRINCIPLES CONCRETELY DEFINED

In comparing the administration of military and business affairs, I do not wish to create the impression that business should be run exactly as an army is commanded; much less to imply that a defense for anything harsh and brutal in business can be found in considering it as a kind of warfare. When Sherman once made a celebrated remark about what war was, he referred only to the immediate results, and not to the ultimate purpose. It may be said that the sufferings of a just war lead to the joys of a nobler peace, as the drudgery of industry leads to economic well being. The nature of these activities is to purchase a desired good through suffering.

No doubt the harshness of the immediate purpose of one tinges its methods in a way wholly unjustified in the other. In one the tests of efficiency of the executive are few and irregular, inexact, and darkly confused by uncertain knowledge; but they are of enormous importance, so that an early failure seldom permits a retrieval. Industry enjoys the ad vantage of many-times recurring, easily measured tests, so capable of classification that a gradual growth in responsibility is possible as individual capacity is proved. In the one case, costs are almost ignored; in the other, they are a large part of the essence of victory. In one the issues are striking, and naturally stir the soul of man; while in the other, in sight of interpretation is needed to perceive that, under a prosaic exterior, the results are of the nature of life itself.

The purpose of comparing the two with respect to administrative procedure is to make each illuminate the real nature of the other, for each simply clothes in concrete forms the workings of general principles which are based upon the ways of human nature and the material world.

*Decision*
War presents to us cases where the word of a commander-in-chief will mean the death of thousands of men in a few hours. So clearly does this show the harrowing anxiety which must rest upon the mind of the military leader, that we can see, through this emphasized case, that it is doubt and anxiety which are the great enemies to be conquered by the executive who would assume responsibility. Napoleon said at St. Helena:

'People rarely have an idea of the strength of soul it requires to deliver, after full reflection on its results, one of those great battles on which depends the fate of an army, or a country, or the possession of a throne. And,' he added, 'few generals are diligent in seeking battle, although without it no decisive results can be gained.'

Great leaders have always shown facility in passing over the deadline which separates deliberation from action. Frederick the Great, in the earliest work assigned to him, in his twenty-third year, showed great power of making up his mind clearly and definitely. Wellington, in the most anxious weeks of his life at Brussels, showed a decision following so instantly upon perception, that his mind was unembarrassed and perfectly at ease. Caesar is recorded to have hesitated at the point of decision only once, and then but for a few hours on the banks of the Rubicon; and this may have been to test his generals.

The executive must have the power to concentrate attention, to think things through to conclusion, and to master and exterminate doubt. Then, by act of will, he must decide; and show that his shoulders are broad enough to bear the responsibility. The first requisite in the executive, therefore, is the power of decision.

*Initiative*
Decision insured, the next question is the proper time for it. There is much to be found in the literature of war in favor of taking the initiative, and forcing the opposition to a course of action which it might not otherwise have freely chosen. As we have seen Napoleon's plan was to concentrate, and strike, before the enemy was prepared. Jomini, who first formulated Napoleon's practice into a system, says: 'If the art of war consists in throwing the masses upon the decisive points, to do this it will be necessary to take the initiative. The attacking party knows what he is doing, and what he desires to do; and he leads his masses to the point whore he desires to strike. He who awaits the attack is everywhere anticipated; the enemy fall with large force upon fractions of his force; he neither knows where his adversary proposes to attack him, nor in what manner to repel him.'

The party which takes the initiative can make specific preliminary preparation for what is next to happen; while the party which is on the defensive cannot do so. The initiative brings one to the decisive point under the moral headway of an affirmative state of mind, and with the consciousness of being committed The cultivation of the initiative stimulates activity. As the late Professor James might have said, by acting as if one possessed courage, courage is produced.

It was the historian Livy who first observed what many a military writer has since repeated: 'People's apprehensions are greater in proportion as things are unknown.' The initiative lessens apprehension and makes the decision easy in two ways – it gives us other occupation than foreboding and it reveals in the true state of things a situation better than that imagined. Active initiative develops the habit of decision; and the results of it yield us the greatest variety of experience, not only of others, but of ourselves as well.

One of the chief advantages of the policy of taking the initiative is that it permits the utilization of the strategic moment. The first operation which raised Napoleon to fame involved the strategic moment. He was besieging Mantua, and the Austrians, sending a relieving army south from the Tyrol, made the mistake of dividing it, sending a column on either side of Lake Garda. The lightning is not quicker than was Napoleon to seize the advantage offered him. He abandoned the siege of Mantua, and attacked first one and then the other of the separated armies, before they could unite, driving them with great loss back into the Tyrol. He who takes the initiative has, in a measure, the choice of the place, the time, and many of the circumstances of action.

*Preliminary Planning*
Preliminary planning is a form of taking the initiative; it is distinguishable from it only by the length of time involved, and by the degree of probability that what is done will eventually apply. It co-ordinates itself perfectly with the policy of taking the initiative, for, as we have seen, only that can be specifically anticipated, and prepared for, which one himself initiates.

As the current power of an organization, as of an individual, has a limit, preliminary preparation is a means of increasing force; for by it energy, or the results of energy, may be stored up ready for concentrated delivery, at the desired moment. It makes action more decisive by giving a sort of strength different from that of initiative; for it provides what cannot be prepared later, together with what can as well be prepared in advance.

The most scientific preparation now made for any form of human activity is probably that made for war by the German War Academy and the General Staff. The Academy admits young officers, on efficiency tests, and completes their military training. It covers not only the subject of war, in all its branches, but science and modern languages. Formal studies are supplemented by constant field exercises in collecting information, and in the solution of practical problems, and by exercise with 'war games.'

The Staff is recruited from the best men who pass through the Academy. Its functions are to gather information about all countries, to make topographical surveys, to test new arms, rations, and equipments, to standardize camp and supply methods, to compile the official military history, to plan mobilization, and, generally, to serve as the inventing, organizing, and inspecting authority of the army.

The results of German wars show whether these agencies are efficient or not. In the case of the Austrian war of 1866, in fourteen days from the declaration of hostilities, Prussia was in possession of Hanover, Hesse Cassel, and Saxony. In nineteen days the battle of Koniggratz which decided the war, was fought. It was all over in seven weeks. Likewise in the war of 1870–71, although France confidently expected to invade Germany, she found herself in a few days fighting an invasion. The armies of France were promptly separated, and all the decisive work was over again in seven weeks.

These institutions are the embodiment of two comparatively simple, but exceedingly fundamental, principles of efficiency. The first is vocational training for all persons placed in important positions; the second is the compilation of all useful knowledge which can be better gained in advance, by experts, through study, than later, by general executives, through action. These two institutions so successful in making Germany the leading military nation of the world, could be duplicated by us, in America, as industrial institutions, for a tithe of the waste they would save, and would exercise the most beneficent effects upon the general welfare.

*Subordination of Detail*
Military history has passed through the stage in which the affairs of a standard-sized army can be con trolled in matters of detail, as well as in matters of general plan, by any one person, even though he be an all-around genius. Frederick's kingdom was of such small size that he could keep his fingers upon every thing, even the daily culinary arrangements of the royal household. Napoleon with matchless celerity in work, confessed that he fully controlled his affairs only in the short period of his prime. In war the day of piling up tasks in such an indiscriminate manner at headquarters that only a heaven-sent genius can insure success, passed when the Germans began the application of the principles of administration to military matters.

It is clear that for the lodging of any administrative function, and the resting of the corresponding responsibility, there must be a certain ideal point in the administrative hierarchy of any organization. This point is where the problem of keeping in touch with the specific details of the agencies of the action controlled, is approximately equal in difficulty to the problem of keeping in touch with the general plan of which that action is a part. To move a function from this point towards headquarters is to lose touch with specific conditions; to move it closer to the agencies of performance is to lose touch with the general plan.

As organizations grow, one function after another should take its departure from headquarters and pass down the line of administration, drawn to lower levels, by the necessity of keeping in touch with local conditions. The definition of what constitutes detail for an officer, in a growing organization, expands. Headquarters gradually change from a directing into a co-ordinating agency.

From the point of view of a superior officer, this sifting of every thing to its proper level is the problem of the subordination of detail. The man of capacity often errs by working with energy rather than intelligence; not seeing that efficiency does not mean alone to do a great deal, and do it well, but also to be constantly engaged upon tasks of one's caliber. If an organization is not large enough to keep a man of talent at his maximum work, the permanent solution is not to allow the individual to add lower functions, and shade out the subordinate executives, but to use this surplus talent for attacking the most important difficulties which restrain growth, so that with the increase in the size of the organization there will come abundance of the proper kind of work. It is undoubtedly a fact that most organizations are in a state of being strangled by undue concentration of work at headquarters, while the subordinate ranks are soldiering. The proper place for deliberation, and even leisure, is where the far reaching decisions are being made.

From the point of view of the minor official, the proper division of administrative functions means dignifying him in the eyes of those over whom he is set. Stimulus comes from the opportunity to do a task large enough to arouse the interest; and efficiency from the freedom to bring one's personality to bear in a manner harmonious with its nature. Well scattered responsibility sobers and settles a force of executives, and develops and seasons their talents; for individual character is not developed by imagining responsibility, but by actually carrying it.

In conclusion, it is good policy to push decentralization and discriminating deputizing, somewhat ahead of the needs of the immediate situation, with a view to the advance preparation of those agencies which growth will require. The progress of an organization is largely due to the ambitious upward pressure of the ranks below. Judicious liberty will increase this pressure, and form a prime means of insuring the future.

*Discipline*
The preceding discussion may suggest the fear that freedom of individual action will destroy discipline. The object of discipline is concert of action. The essence of it is the development, in a body of men, of such confidence on the part of each individual that every other person will play his part, that expenditure of energy to make sure of this is saved, and the full force of each is free to be expended in doing his own work.

The amount of freedom which is compatible with discipline depends not only upon preliminary practice, and action made second-nature, as in the drill of the parade ground, but it depends upon the quality of the human material involved. Upon this depends what will appeal, and so what means must be used to make harmony of action doubly secure.

On its lowest plane, discipline insures a step-by-step compliance with a series of acts, which are means to an unexplained end. On its highest plane, it is such enthusiasm for the end, that the full use of the powers of each individual, in choosing the wisest steps to attain it, may be depended upon. The great point is that these different planes tend to be mutually exclusive; so that it is of the greatest moment to choose that form of discipline which best agrees with the nature of the circumstances, and of the end in view.

*Concentration to Secure Success*
An analogy is suggested between Napoleon's practice of concentrating the masses of his troops to attain superiority at the point of contact with the enemy, and similar policies in industrial affairs. This rule of at tacking the opposition piecemeal, with one's full force, is described by Mr. F. W. Taylor in his 'Shop Management.' He says (p. 144) 'It is of the utmost importance that the first combined application of time study, slide rules, instruction cards, functional foremanship, and a premium for a large daily task should prove a success, both for the work men and for the company, and for this reason a simple class of work should be chosen for a start. The entire efforts of the new management should be centered on one point, and continued there until unqualified success has been attained.... Thus,' continued Napoleon, 'I beat it in detail, and the victory which was the result was always, as you see, the triumph of the larger over the lesser.'

Nor must the effect of success upon the spirit of resolve in the individual, and upon the morale of a group, be forgotten. To induce a body of human beings to exert their powers, in combined action, with some degree of completeness, the aims must be worthy, they must be joint aims, in which all share, the relation between the work of each and the realization of the aims must be clear, and there must be faith that success will be achieved.

It may be said that the more precarious the prospects of an organization are, the more essential to it is a series of successes, even though they be very small ones. The position of a captain of industry, who has but a slight hold upon the public through advertising, and who must deal with an unstable body of stock holders, is somewhat similar to the position of Wellington in Spain, who dared not run any avoidable risks, for fear a defeat would cost him the support of the government at home.

# Internal Organization of a Going Corporation[1]

## Lewis H. Haney

### ORGANIZATION IN GENERAL; AND THE ACCOUNTING AND ECONOMIC POINTS OF VIEW

The corporation is easily the central figure in the world of business organization in the United States. Whether viewed as the culmination of association among individual business men, or as the initial unit of the material out of which combinations are built, it is without question the most important primary form of business organization; and there is little need for a more detailed discussion of unincorporated organizations. It is most important, however, to know the structure and the life history of the business corporation. With this end in view, we will first examine the internal organization of a going corporation. Taking the corporation for granted, we will inquire into its organs and their functions. How are they arranged and coordinated and directed? What, in short, are the anatomy and the physiology of a business corporation regarded as an operating organization? We may then pass more intelligently to a consideration of the formative stage of corporate existence, covering the periods of promotion and underwriting.

In looking at the corporation as an operating business unit, business men take two points of view which we will call the accounting and the economic points of view. The former generally means an individual way of looking at the business; for it concerns a relation between the business unit and its proprietors. In a word, it is the function of accounts to show the condition of a business organization regarded as a source of income to its owners. In a way analogous to that in which economists are wont to distinguish the wealth of a nation from its annual income, accountants set forth the condition of a business unit under two heads, the balance (as shown in a 'balance sheet') and the income (shown in an 'income account').

The balance sheet is a sort of periodic inventory which shows the standing of the business at any given time. On the one hand are summed

---

[1] [Chapter 17 of *Business Organization and Combination*, New York: Macmillan, 1913, pp. 259–81.]

up the 'assets'; on the other the 'liabilities.' The assets show what the proprietors have put into the business as it exists at any given time and what others owe the business, and includes such items as plant and equipment, materials, cash, and accounts receivable. The liabilities show what the business owes to the proprietors and others, embracing such accounts as stock, bonds, accounts and bills payable, and profits. The income account is designed to show the net return from the business to the owners on what they have put into it, the two main heads, of course, being revenue and expenditures. Thus it shows the results of operations over a period of time, a month or a year. The operating expenses and others are deducted from the receipts from all sources to ascertain the net revenue, out of which dividends may be paid or a surplus be accumulated.

We, however, are not here concerned with accounts. We are to take the economic point of view, which regards the business as a productive unit, or means of organizing and directing the factors of production; and it follows that attention will be devoted to the productive cooperation of land, labor, capital, and entrepreneurial ability, rather than to the relation among them as set forth in accounts.

In the chapters describing the evolution of business organization, attention was centered chiefly on the ownership of the units, and the formal external aspects were emphasized. Now, it behooves us to take a glance within and see the organization from the internal operating point of view. We have seen that the operation of a business unit is affected by the character of ownership and the external form of organization, but chiefly, of course, it is dependent upon the kind of work that is done. The operating organization of a bank differs from that of a factory, and both are unlike that of a railway. Factories, in turn, are variously organized according as they produce steel or cloth or ice. All, however, are engaged in production, and have the same general problem. All must combine land, labor, and capital, under the direction of an entrepreneur; all take in some 'raw' materials, and, by applying labor power with capital, must operate to turn out a finished good or service; all must sell the product, collect the income, and account to the owners for expenditures and receipts. In each case these various processes must be more or less subdivided, and at the same time they must be so interrelated and coordinated that they will work together for the good of the business unit. There will be certain classes of interests which must be effectively subordinated and directed; and the internal aspects of the organization of ownership and administration are found on the one hand, while the organization of the technical processes of operation (manufacturing, transportation, mining, etc.) lie on the other.

Just as there are general principles of anatomy and physiology which can be studied by dissecting cats or corpses, so certain general forms and principles of business organization exist, and in a brief sketch like the following these general features alone can be taken up. They will concern (1) the division of the work into departments (differentiation), and (2) the central direction of these departments to secure cooperation (integration).

## CLASSES OF INTERESTS

Several classes of interests are to be distinguished in any discussion of the internal organization of a business unit, and notably so in case of a large corporation. In single-entrepreneur and partnership organization the situation is relatively simple, for ordinarily those who are the owners are at the same time the ones who direct and manage the business, – although a salaried manager is not uncommonly employed. Then there are laborers, of course; and, when capital is borrowed, the creditors who hold the owner's notes may in practice have some voice in his affairs. In such a case, however, they can hardly have the long-time, organized influence often exerted by corporation bondholders.

The typical corporation is a much more highly differentiated organization. First come the stockholders, who are nominally the owners and the ultimate source of authority. They, however, exercise their authority through an elected board of directors, composed of men who are supposed to represent them. Very commonly there is also a body of bondholders; and, as bonds are in practice regarded merely as one means of raising capital and as being a part of the corporation's capitalization, and as they generally run for long periods of time, without any thought of their being really retired, the bondholders not infrequently play a considerable part in the direction of the corporation. In rare instances they are represented on the board of directors.[2] The directors choose an executive head, which may be either a president or an executive committee, or both. Associated with the executive are a secretary and a treasurer. The executive chooses a general manager, and under the manager are placed superintendents of departments. Foremen under the superintendents supervise the labor force. The whole organization has been likened to an hourglass, in one section of which lie the owning interests pouring authority through the executive head to the manager who supervises the manufacturing and commercial operations.

[2]  E.g. American Rope and Twine Co., and Wabash R.

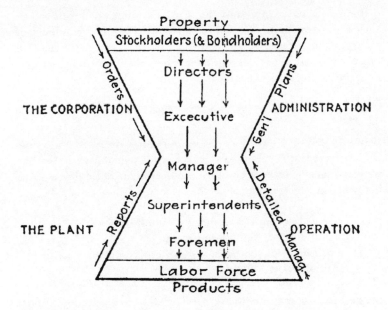

Clearly the human exertions or services comprised within this scheme
may be divided into four great groups: (1) investment risk (or owner's
responsibility); (2) administration, including direction and executive
service; (3) management; and (4) labor.[3] The ownership and administration, under our existing social order, fill the top cup of the hourglass;
the management and labor force lie in the lower. We may logically
discuss the internal operating organization of a corporation under the two
general heads thus indicated.

### ORGANIZATION OF OWNERSHIP AND ADMINISTRATION

The organization of the ownership and administration of a business is
generally the corporate organization, and where this is the case, the
corporation may be regarded as a sort of political machine for enabling
the stockholders to govern their property. Within the sphere of the
corporation so regarded, we find authority concentrated and directed
much as in a political unit, the body of stockholders being roughly
comparable to the voters in a democracy, the directors to a parliament
the executive head to a prime minister, and the other executive officials
to his cabinet.

---

[3] Executive work and management may be regarded as kinds of labor.

It is to be observed in advance that it will be difficult to discuss organization pure and simple without encroaching on the subject of management; but the point of view is to be that of one concerned with organization, and where management is brought in it will be to throw light on the functions of the organs.

## STOCKHOLDERS

Being the nominal owners of the corporation's property, the stockholders are the ultimate source of authority, subject only to the law, the property rights of creditors, and the personal rights of employees. As a body they generally have the following rights: –

(1) To amend the certificate of incorporation and by-laws;
(2) To elect directors of the corporation;
(3) To pass upon the mortgaging or sale of its permanent assets;
(4) To dissolve the corporation.

In another chapter the certificate was likened to a constitution and the by-laws to a body of statutes. It is fitting, then, that the owners of the 'little republic' should have the franchise in amending these instruments. Generally a two-thirds majority is required to change the 'charter.' Of course, the stockholders act subject to the general corporation law and public policy; and in practice it seems that their power over by-laws may be somewhat reduced. Thus, the charter of the United States Steel Corporation says: 'Subject always to by-laws, made by the stockholders, the board of directors may make by-laws, and from time to time, may alter, amend, or repeal any by-laws;' and that corporation's by-laws themselves vest in the board full power to make new by-laws or change the existing ones.

The two most important powers are the second and third of the above list. The election of directors need not be discussed here. As we shall see, all direct control over the corporation is nominally in their hands. It is not a universal rule that the stockholders consent must be given to validate any disposition of permanent assets, for the courts of some States take the position that all administrative power is turned over to the directors. However, the form is generally gone through, even in such States. The incorporation certificate of the Steel Corporation provides that a two-thirds majority of the shareholders must sanction any mortgage or pledge of the corporation's real property or of the stocks of constituent companies.

As individuals, stockholders generally have these additional rights: –

(1) To representative general meetings, embracing the right: -
   (a) To receive notice,
   (b) To attend,
   (c) To participate,
   (d) To be represented by proxy.
(2) To an inspection of the books when consistent with the corporation's interest.
(3) To a share in dividends.
(4) To a share in additional stock issues.
(5) To a share in assets when the corporation is dissolved.

The first of these rights is nearly self-explanatory. What shall constitute due notice, however, is a serious question. The trend of development in this right has been to insist that notice shall be given at a certain time in advance of the meeting, and that it shall contain a statement of the subjects to be taken up. The proxy right has been much abused, being used to secure a majority by getting the proxies of scattered small holders, and so to run corporations in an undemocratic way. It seems essential, however, that the distant holders of small amounts of stock should have the power to send their representatives. The length of life of a proxy is sometimes wisely limited by law. The stockholders have no unlimited right to inspect the books of their corporation. Thus the certificate of the Steel Corporation says:

> The board of directors from time to time shall determine whether and to what extent, and at what times and places, and under what conditions and regulations the accounts and books of the corporation, or any of them, shall be open to the inspection of the stockholders; and no stockholder shall have any right to inspect any account or book or document of the corporation except as conferred by statute or authorized by the board of directors, or by the resolution of the stockholders.

At common law, however, this right exists when sought at proper times and places and for proper purposes. When sought for speculative purposes, or for giving information to a competitor, or for mere curiosity, it does not exist. 'If every shareholder could inspect for such purposes, at his own will, the business of most corporations would be greatly impeded.'[4] The statutes of several States specifically authorize the inspection of books by stockholders, generally at 'reasonable' times. In such cases it seems that no reason need be given by any *bona fide* stockholder.

As to sharing in dividends, that right exists only if the directors declare any. Generally the power to declare dividends is conferred upon directors, in which case the stockholders cannot compel the declaration of a dividend nor determine its amount. Of course, dividends are shared according to the kind and amount of stock held.

By the right to share in new issues is meant the right to subscribe for shares issued subsequently to those held by the stock holders. This privilege has been upheld by the courts on the ground that the new issue affects the value of the existing stock holder's equity and dilutes his voting power.

### BONDHOLDERS

To an increasing extent, nowadays, corporations of all sorts raise funds by issuing their notes in uniform series; and generally, in America, such notes are secured by a mortgage on some tangible property. These notes are called 'bonds.' Of course the bondholder is primarily a creditor rather than a proprietor; but, when he holds a mortgage, he has a claim which may become ownership in case the interest is not paid currently or the principal is not paid at maturity. It may be said, then, that the bondholders have a sort of contingent ownership. From this it results that if interest payments to them are defaulted they may throw the property into the hands of a receiver to be operated in their interest; and in case the corporation becomes bankrupt, as holders of the first claim against it, they have a strategic position in bidding for its assets and reorganizing it. In a word, bondholders may be thought of as 'proprietors who have relinquished the privilege of actively directing the business in which they are interested in exchange for a first claim upon the earnings during operation, and upon the assets in case of dissolution.'[5]

More than this, the courts will not allow the owners to act in such a way that the security for the bonds is wrongfully impaired. For example, corporate mortgages often provide that real estate covered by bonds cannot be sold without the bond holders' assent. In general, new

---

[4] See to *Cyc.* 958. N. J. Eq. 392, 398; Matter of Steinway, 159 N. Y. 250 (1899).

[5] Robinson, *Modern Business Organization and Management* (Chicago, 1911), p. 86.

issues of bonds having a claim prior to an outstanding issue cannot be made without the consent of the holders of the latter. And, under several conditions, the bondholders may legally interfere in the management of the corporation: when stockholders fraudulently divert income to their own use, the bondholders may demand an accounting; where low rates are prescribed by a commission so as to violate the State or Federal constitution, the bondholders may have their enforcement enjoined; and any encroachment on the security for the mortgage which is not in the ordinary course of the corporation's business may be prevented.

In practice, considerable attention is paid to the wishes of bondholders. They may be consulted as to proposed action, and may even be given a definite representation. In case of reorganization, the bondholders act through committees. Some of their number will constitute themselves a committee and appeal to the others to deposit all bonds with them. They thus become trustees with full power to act, and, by presenting a united front, prevent hasty action contrary to their best interests. Ordinarily the security pledged by the corporation is deeded to a trustee, and he takes such action as may be necessary to protect that security.

Of course, the stockholders' share in the assets of a dissolved corporation would be subject to the prior claims of creditors, bondholders, and higher grades of stock, if any such exist.

The liabilities of stockholders may be very briefly stated. All stockholders are individually liable to creditors for any part of the par value of their shares that may remain unpaid. Only a few States by statute add to this limited personal liability.[6] In the second place, stockholders are liable for any dividends which are not earned, but instead are paid out of capital. It follows from their power to pass upon what is done with permanent assets that stockholders should be held accountable for any wasting of such assets. It is obvious that to pay out as current income what must economically be kept intact as a capital asset is a fraud upon creditors and a prostitution of the corporation.

In Indiana, New York, North Dakota, Pennsylvania, South Dakota, and Tennessee employees may recover for wages directly from the individual stockholders when they cannot collect from the corporation but in some of these States this rule applies only to manufacturing, mining, and other industrial corporation.

---

[6] See below, p. 294.

## DIRECTORS

In this country it is usually provided by law that the affairs of business corporations shall be conducted by directors; and, in the absence of express provision in the corporation regulations to the contrary, directors are always elected by the stockholders. Boards of directors vary in size, seldom consisting of less than three or more than twenty-four members. In general terms it may be said that the powers of directors are those possessed by the corporation itself: what the corporation may do, that its directors may do it. In some respects they are like the agent of the corporation; but the relation between the two is even closer than that between principal and agent, for, in dealing with third parties, the directors are equal to the corporation. They as it were, have full powers of attorney; and between the stockholders' meetings, their power is nearly unlimited.

Such limitations as affect the powers of directors may be summed as follows: (1) Their powers are limited to the regular business of the corporation. Thus, they have no power to increase the capital stock nor do any other act which would change the fundamental constitution of the corporation, without the consent of the stockholders. The directors have no primary powers to make by-laws or to dissolve the corporation. (2) Directors are subject to the general control of the stockholders, and 'have no right to violate a resolution of the shareholders prescribing the policy to be pursued by the company,[7] providing that resolution is in accord with the constitution of the corporation. (3) Also, special powers, such as that of levying an assessment, may be conferred by statute upon the stockholders, and these powers the directors cannot exercise.

The main points concerning directors which are found in the by-laws of the United States Steel Corporation will be of interest here. In this corporation there are twenty-four directors who are elected for three years, with the terms of eight expiring each year. They are required to hold only one share of stock in the corporation. The compensation is ten cents per mile traveled in attending directors' meetings, and $20 per day in attendance. Regular meetings are to be held each month without notice, and special meetings may be held at the call of the president or of one third of the members, with two days' notice by mail or one day's notice by telegram. A majority forms a quorum, but an affirmative two-fifths vote of all members is necessary to pass any resolution. The

---

[7] Machen, *Modern Law of Corporations*, p. 1192.

directors may elect and remove officers, create and select from their members executive and finance committees, provide for the inspection of the books, fix the working capital, declare dividends out of net profits, use the same in purchasing and retiring shares of the corporation's stock, and make or amend by-laws.

More specifically, a corporation's board of directors generally exercises, or may exercise, the following powers or functions:—

(1) Connect the stockholders with the operation of the corporation.
(2) Determine the general business policy, including dividends.
(3) Appoint and remove officers.
(4) Fill vacancies in itself.

Under the first function comes the calling of stockholders' meetings and the making of such reports as may be required by law or by the corporation's constitution. Although in practice sadly modified, it is undoubtedly the sound doctrine that the prime function of directors is to administer the corporation's business in the interests of its owners, the shareholders.

The second head is most important. Here fall the powers of determining the organization of the business into departments, and the interrelation among those departments; of deciding the general business policy as to buying and selling, especially buying; and of declaring dividends. As stated in discussing stock holders' powers, the authority to declare dividends is usually vested in the board. Here, naturally, enough, lies an opportunity for manipulation and abuse of power which is not seldom taken advantage of.

In all the foregoing statements, it must be remembered that we are dealing with powers which according to law may be exercised, but which often are not possessed in practice. In practice, it appears to be growing more and more common in our large corporations for the directors to turn most of the direction over to executive officers or special committees. Often the directors know little or nothing about the business, being chosen for their financial connections. Not infrequently, economy of operation suffers as a result.

Under the head of directors' personal liability, the following points may be made:

(1) Directors are liable for injury to the corporation which is caused by their neglect or wrongdoing.
(2) Directors are liable for issuing stock as fully paid which in fact is not paid up.

(3) Directors are liable for declaring dividends out of capital.
(4) Directors are liable for disobedience of statutes.

So long, however, as the members of the board stay within the bounds of lawful action and commit no fraudulent or neglectful act, they incur no personal liability.

## THE EXECUTIVE

As we follow the sands of authority down the upper cup of the hourglass, the one containing the organization for ownership and general administration, we next come to the executive; and here we begin to see the transition to the organization for operating management, for the executive's position is characterized by its location between the corporation and the plant, between the owners and the operation, between the entrepreneur's direction and the labor of managers, clerks, and workmen. his services are such that he is best classed with the administrative group. The chief executive is elected by the stockholders or directors and generally is required to be a director, which means the ownership of some stock.

In the organization of the smaller corporations, the chief executive is the president. The president represents the board of directors, and, subject possibly to an executive committee of directors, he has general supervision of the business. Ordinarily his functions are to preside at the meetings of stockholders and directors, to sign important documents such as stock certificates, bonds, and contracts, and to make an annual report to the stockholders. He is generally made an ex-officio member of committees. His position is indicated by a provision in the by-laws of a leading corporation that 'he shall do and perform such other duties as from time to time may be assigned to him by the Board of Directors.'

The larger companies have an executive committee as the seat of chief executive power, and when this is the case the chairman of the executive committee, may be said to be the chief executive. This committee is composed of directors; and it includes the president, who generally, though not always, is the chairman. During the intervals between directors' meetings, the executive committee exercises all the powers of the board; while between the committee's sessions those powers pass to its chairman. The reason for this development in corporate organization is the fact that the huge and complex affairs of the largest business units cannot be adequately comprehended by one mind. This is indicated in a by-law of the Steel Corporation which reads: 'So far as practical each of the six elected members of the Executive Committee shall be a person having, or, having had, personal experience in the conduct of one or the other of the branches of manufacturing or mining, or of transportation in which the company is interested.'

When the corporation is of considerable size, the work of administration is generally subdivided into departments, and a vice president is given supervision over each. There may be several vice presidents, one for legal affairs, one for operating affairs, one for financial affairs, and others. In very large companies, a special finance committee may exist.

Other executive officers are the secretary and the treasurer, each of whom does the work ordinarily handled by such offices.

All these executive officers are personally liable for damages caused by their neglect or wrongdoing in office, their duty, of course, being faithfully to serve the corporation. It is not always easy, however, to decide what constitutes wrongdoing or neglect. Two acts which one might not think of are generally made the basis of personal liability by statute: (1) failure to keep stock and transfer books open during business hours; (2) making loans to other officers or stockholders.

## ORGANIZATION FOR OPERATION AND MANAGEMENT

Authority passes on through the executive to those who manage the labor force and capital engaged in the technical processes of production. Indeed, nothing said in the preceding section should be construed to deny that, under the general direction of the board, the executive determines many important matters of operating policy and supervises the cooperation of the operating departments. The inverted cone containing the administrative organization has ownership as its base; the cone below is based on the cooperation of labor, land, and capital in production. In the one, the form of organization varies with the character of ownership; in the other, it is dependent upon the work that is being done. The chief problem of organization in the former field is that of securing concentration of administration: how can a large body of investors cooperate so as to function as an entrepreneur, is the question. In the latter field, which we are about to enter, the problem lies in securing first an efficient division of labor, and second an efficient management of the parts. In this field, organization consists in sub-dividing the management of a business into parts small enough for an individual to handle, and in so devising the subdivision that the parts can cooperate efficiently. Accordingly, we will first turn to the division of the operating plant into departments.

If the reader is a student of economics he will recall what is meant by 'division of labor' and the stock statements of its advantages. Simply stated, the idea is that, by dividing great processes into stages or sub-process both labor and capital can be more economically employed. A place can be made for the full utilization of each special ability in some special subdivision. Time is not lost in passing from one process to another, nor is capital allowed to be idle the while: all the processes go on all the time. Moreover, greater skill, the skill of the specialist, is acquired. In fact, division of labor is specialization of function, and that is just what the aspect of organization which we now approach stands for. The division of plant operations into departments is adopted in order to adjust organization to the different kinds of work that exist in the nature of things, and the more complicated the work is, if on a large enough scale, the greater the number of departments that are naturally called for. Speaking of department divisions one writer says:–

The number of these will depend upon the number of processes into which the manufacture of a given product can be naturally or economically divided. There are two lines of division in every factory. In the first place, there is the separation into departments; and, in the second place, with the increasing volume of business there is the further division of each department into sections. It is this that gives to the factory its unique position as a type of organization. As an illustration of this general truth, we may refer to the manufacture of machine-made shoes. In order to be able to use machinery, the shoes must pass through many stages of manufacture for the reason that each machine must repeat its own work. Each step requires special machinery, special workmen, and special super vision, so that each department is made by the grouping of machinery and workmen around each definite process. This becomes fundamental to the economy of every manufacturing establishment. As a rule, the number of processes will be determined by the degree to which machinery can be used, and the site of each department will depend upon the amount of business which the factory is doing…. Everything is graded and subordinated from the work of the manager down to that of the least employee.[8]

The object in all such arrangement of business organization into departments and their adjustment to the work to be done, is, of course,

[8]    Sparling, *Business Organization* (N. Y., 1906), p. III.

economy in operation. This is brought about in two ways: (a) by increasing motivation through increased definiteness of responsibility, (b) by decreasing friction through simplified processes.

When it was said above that operating departments are called for by the nature of things, it should not have been inferred that the formation of departments can be left to take care of itself, for so closely interwoven are the different processes that it is often a nice question to know where to divide them, or even whether they should be divided at all. Take the case of the accounting, credit, collection, and legal processes, for example. Again, consider some process which is subsidiary to two other processes; with which shall it be affiliated? This is the case with the purchasing department, and it is hard to say whether it belongs with the manufacturing or the commercial process. Or, some processes may concern the business as a whole in a general way, as do those of the accounting and legal departments; whereas others are specialized and may be pigeonholed along with related but distinct processes, as is the case with the tool room, the blacksmith shop, and the drafting room in a factory, or the train dispatching care of locomotives, and care of roadbed of a railway. And the problem of keeping the departments in cooperation and harmonious adjustment is always present. In the field of biology, we study living organisms and seek to understand their differentiation as well as their integration and central nervous systems; in technical machine production, economists have long talked of 'division of labor' and of management; but, in the field of business organization relatively little scientific attention has been given to differentiation or division of labor, and to integration or composition of labor. Meanwhile, business men have worked out various schemes appropriate to their particular businesses, and some general principles have begun to emerge. At least we can make a chart like that which accompanies, which will give a fair idea of a typical manufacturing organization.

Perhaps the first point noticed in the operating organization is the division of operation into two great groups of processes, the manufacturing (or mining or transportation, as the case may be) and the commercial or business groups. This is entirely logical, although overlapping makes it difficult to carry out at points; for the one suborganization embraces the technical physical processes of receiving and working up raw material and storing and shipping the finished goods, while the other is concerned with the technical economic processes of receiving orders, selling, and collecting for finished goods. The latter is the business operating organization, standing between the physical processes of manufacture and the demands of consumers. Accordingly, a 'superintendent' is put in charge of the one suborganization and a 'business manager' is set over the other.  It would be a more logical terminology, perhaps, to call one 'superintendent of manufacturing' and the other 'superintendent of business.'

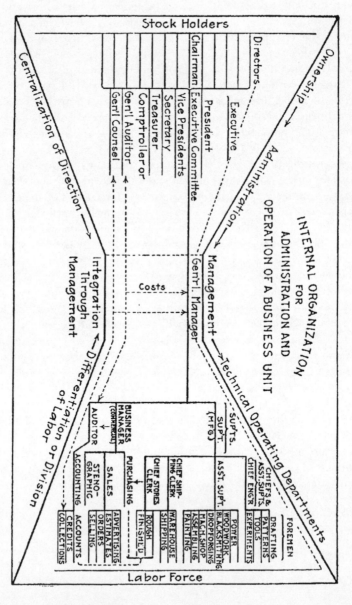

One difficulty lies in the location of the purchasing department, an important subdivision for buying all materials and supplies needed by the whole operating organization. Some business men have put it with the manufacturing suborganization on the ground that it starts manufacturing processes by supplying the raw materials, and that in purchasing the raw materials an intimate knowledge of the technical processes of manufacture is desirable; but it seems to be the better practice to put it with the commercial suborganization, inasmuch as it is concerned with the buying, and naturally cooperates with the work of estimating and selling.

The accounting department also offers a peculiar problem. Formerly it was the practice to have the work of accounting parceled out among the several operating departments, each keeping its own record of receipts and disbursements; but the tendency now is to make a separate accounting department, and to place it farther toward the top of the operating organization. It is important to have the accounts of all processes brought together, and to keep them without bias in favor of any department. An independent auditor may well be associated with the executive. To go into the details of the work of the various departments would take us too far out of the field of organization and into the subject of management. At any rate, the diagram is for the most part self-explanatory.[9]

One great problem in operating organization remains for discussion and that is the issue between 'line' organization and 'staff' organization,[10] and its particular manifestation in the conflict over the relative merits of 'departmental' and 'divisional' organization. Line organization is concerned with the transmission and perpetuation of authority. These ends it achieves by maintaining a series of officers one directly over the other, all exerting a similar kind of authority and differing only in the amount of power possessed. As in the fighting force of an army there are generals, colonels, captains, and lieutenants, so in a corporation's plant there may be a general manager, superintendents, foremen, and so on. The subordinate decides all questions in his small field, and when the question is too big it goes to his

---

[9]  The reader who desires a detailed statement of the functions of the several departments may find it in Sparling, *Business Organization*, Chaps. V and VI, and in Robinson, *Modern Business Organization*, pp. 125–68. See Duncan, J. C., *The Economic Side of Works Management*, and *The Principles of Industrial Management*.

[10]  See Emerson, H., *Efficiency as a Basis for Operation* (N. Y., 1912), Chaps. III and IV.

superior. Staff organization, on the other band, stands for expertness in function, seeking to gain its ends by specialization and departmental subdivisions. Instead of a hierarchical series of all-embracing authorities, it establishes groups of parallel specialists, – specialists by function. Staff officers serve not any one locality or part, primarily, but the whole organization, – to the extent of their special functions. As a matter of fact, these two plans are complementary and not antagonistic; but the old idea of line organization has become so dominant that a great need at present is the introduction into business organization of more of the staff idea, that is, the introduction of experts who have specialized in buying, or selling, or managing employees, or supervising tools, etc., to render services to the whole organization in so far as their several functions are concerned.

One special phase of the line vs. staff problem is found in the issue between the 'departmental' and the 'divisional,' or territorial-unit, plans of organization. This issue has been notably prominent in the railway business, but also arises in the organization of large manufac-turing and mercantile corporations. Briefly, the issue is this: Shall all the operations of a division or territorial unit be put in charge of a single local manager, or shall the operations of separate departments be kept separate within the division, or territorial unit, and remain in charge of central departmental superintendents? Under the former, or divisional plan, a railway's operating organization would run somewhat like the first chart, in which it will be observed the division superin-tendent has entire charge of all operating departments within the area of his division.

Under the departmental system, however, the local officers report not to the local division manager but directly to the central department heads. Such organization is illustrated in the second chart.

The arguments *pro* and *con* are interesting, and it will be noticed that they all center around the ideas of breadth, elasticity, and local autonomy as opposed to those of specialization, uniformity, and centralization.

ADVANTAGES OF DIVISIONAL
ORGANIZATION

1. It is elastic in that each division is freer to adjust itself to local conditions.
2. It favors prompt action in that the officer in charge is local.
3. It brings effective responsibility, the superintendent being responsible for all operating conditions in his division as a unit.
4. It produces broadly trained officers.

ADVANTAGES OF DEPARTMENTAL
ORGANIZATION

1. Uniformity: System coöperation is achieved by having local experts report direct to a few department superintendents.
2. Specialization: The best experts in each department are in charge.

DISADVANTAGES OF DIVISIONAL
ORGANIZATION

1. Harmony of operations as a whole, or system coöperation, is difficult on account of different superintendents and separate boards of local experts. Lack of uniformity.
2. Responsibility of local experts is divided: they are responsible partly to the superintendent and partly to the heads of their departments.
3. Limitations of the capacity of a non-specialized individual.

DISADVANTAGES OF DEPARTMENTAL ORGANIZATION

1. Lack of harmony within the division.
2. Slowness in emergency. The division superintendent must report to the general manager for instructions, and local experts are responsible to different departmental heads.
3. Responsibility not so effective, because, (a) authority is more remote, (b) it is not so well informed on local conditions, and (c) there is difficulty in separating the departments in practice.

## DIVISION OPERATING ORGANIZATION

General Manager

— Chief Engineer (Standards) — Division Engr's
- Signal Inspectors
- Road Masters
- Bridge Foremen } TRACK FORCES

— General Supt. — Division Sup'ts.
- Dispatchers — Station Agents
- Train Masters
- Yard Masters } CREWS, SWITCHMEN, ETC.

— Supt. of Motive Power (Standards) — Master Mechanics
- Road Foreman of Engines
- Master Carpenters
- Shops & Roundhouse } SHOP FORCES

## OPERATING DEPARTMENTAL ORGANIZATION

General Manager

— Chief Engineer — Division Engineers
- Bridge Foremen
- Road Masters
- Signal Inspectors } TRACK FORCES

— General Supt. — Division Sup'ts.
- Train Masters
- Yard Masters
- Dispatchers
- Station Agents } TRAIN CREWS SWITCH MEN, ETC.

— Supt. of Motive Power — Master Mechanics
- Road Foreman of Engines
- Master Carpenter Etc.
- Shop & Roundhouse Foremen } SHOP FORCES

In terms of line and staff, it is clear that 'divisional' organization subordinates the staff to the line while 'departmental' organization subordinates the line to the staff. In the one case the staff (departmental) lines are drawn together near the bottom and the division or plant superintendent reports to his managerial superiors after the fashion of a fighting military organization. In the other case, on the contrary, the staff lines run parallel nearly to the top of the operating organization.

In the railway practice of the United States, the divisional system is decidedly predominant. Of course, with a small road with only one division there is little choice between the rival systems.

If the foregoing pages suffice to give a rough sketch of the operating organization of a typical business unit, we may end the discussion with a word about the work of the general manager. Management is to be sharply distinguished from direction; for the manager is an employee receiving general instructions from the owners through the executive, whereas directive authority is exercised by the owners or their duly authorized and elected representatives. The line between the executive and the manager is not so clear: the functions of the two officials shade into one another and the chief difference is that the one has its principal affinities with the owning group and the corporate administration, while the other is aligned more closely with the operating group and the technical and business processes of the plant. The manager is a supervisor he stands at the head of the departments of the business, and on him are focused the reports of the departmental superintendents. Within the limits of power set by his lack of authenticity to make decisions on broad questions of policy or matters fundamentally affecting the business, he manages or supervises the technical and commercial operation of the plant. Through him the operations of business are made to work in harmony, and the differentiated parts are integrated into a whole.

Under the supervision of the general manager comes a more or less complicated series of superintendents and foremen, shading finally, and almost imperceptibly, into the labor force.

The whole story of the reason for internal business organization may be compressed into outline form as follows: –

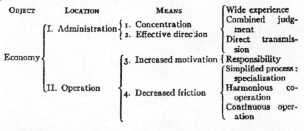

International College
Information Resource Center
2655 Northbrooke Drive
Naples, Florida USA 34119
www.internationalcollege.edu